Ecological Economics and Sustainable
Development, Selected Essays of
Herman Daly

ADVANCES IN ECOLOGICAL ECONOMICS

Series Editor: Jeroen C.J.M. van den Bergh, *ICREA Professor, Universitat Autònoma de Barcelona, Spain and Professor of Environmental and Resource Economics, Vrije Universiteit, Amsterdam, The Netherlands*

Founding Editor: Robert Costanza, *Director, University of Maryland Institute for Ecological Economics and Professor, Center for Environmental and Estuarine Studies and Zoology Department, USA*

This important series makes a significant contribution to the development of the principles and practices of ecological economics, a field which has expanded dramatically in recent years. The series provides an invaluable forum for the publication of high quality work and shows how ecological economic analysis can make a contribution to understanding and resolving important problems.

The main emphasis of the series is on the development and application of new original ideas in ecological economics. International in its approach, it includes some of the best theoretical and empirical work in the field with contributions to fundamental principles, rigorous evaluations of existing concepts, historical surveys and future visions. It seeks to address some of the most important theoretical questions and gives policy solutions for the ecological problems confronting the global village as we move into the twenty-first century.

Titles in the series include:
Economic Growth, Material Flows and the Environment
New Applications of Structural Decomposition Analysis and Physical
Input–Output Tables
Rutger Hoekstra

Joint Production and Responsibility in Ecological Economics
On the Foundations of Environmental Policy
Stefan Baumgärtner, Malte Faber and Johannes Schiller

Frontiers in Ecological Economic Theory and Application
Edited by Jon D. Erickson and John M. Gowdy

Socioecological Transitions and Global Change
Trajectories of Social Metabolism and Land Use
Edited by Marina Fischer-Kowalski and Helmut Haberl

Conflict, Cooperation and Institutions in International Water Management
An Economic Analysis
Ines Dombrowsky

Ecological Economics and Sustainable Development,
Selected Essays of Herman Daly
Herman E. Daly

Ecological Economics and Sustainable Development, Selected Essays of Herman Daly

Herman E. Daly

Professor, School of Public Policy, University of Maryland, USA

ADVANCES IN ECOLOGICAL ECONOMICS

Edward Elgar
Cheltenham, UK • Northampton, MA, USA

Published by
Edward Elgar Publishing Limited
The Lypiatts
15 Lansdown Road
Cheltenham
Glos GL50 2JA
UK

Edward Elgar Publishing, Inc.
William Pratt House
9 Dewey Court
Northampton
Massachusetts 01060
USA

A catalogue record for this book
is available from the British Library

Library of Congress Cataloguing in Publication Data

Daly, Herman E.
    [Selections, 2007]
    Ecological economics and sustainable development, selected essays of Herman Daly/Herman E. Daly.
      p. cm. — (Advances in ecological economics)
    Includes bibliographical references and index.
      1. Environmental economics. 2. Sustainable development. I. Title.
  HC79.E5D3242   2007
  338.9'27—dc22
                        2007001391

Printed on elemental chlorine free (ECF)
recycled paper containing 30% Post-Consumer Waste

ISBN   978 1 84720 101 0 (cased)
        978 1 84720 988 7 (paperback)

Printed and bound in the USA

Contents

Figures and boxes

FIGURES

BOXES

Acknowledgments

The author and publisher wish to thank the copyright holders who have kindly given their permission for the use of copyright material:

Chapter 1. "Limits to Growth", *Encyclopedia of Population*, Paul Demeny and Geoffrey McNicoll, eds, Macmillan Co., 2003, pp. 602–3.

Chapter 2. "Economics in a Full World", *Scientific American*, September 2005.

Chapter 3. "The Challenge of Ecological Economics: Historical Context and Some Specific Issues", Heineken Prize Lecture, Amsterdam, September 30, 1996.

Chapter 4. Invited Address, World Bank, April 30, 2002, Washington, DC. Previously published in Marco Keiner, ed., *The Future of Sustainability*, Springer, Dordrecht, The Netherlands, 2006.

Chapter 5. Previously published as "The Illth of Nations: When Growth Becomes Uneconomic", in *Managing Sustainability World Bank-Style* (An Evaluation of the World Development Report 2003), Heinrich Boell Foundation, Washington, DC, August 2002.

Chapter 6. Invited Speech/Debate, World Bank, Washington, DC, March 2, 2004.

Chapter 7. "Consumption and Welfare: Two Views of Value Added", *Review of Social Economy*, Vol. LIII, No. 4 (Winter 1995), pp. 451–73.

Chapter 8. "Ecological Economics: The Concept of Scale and Its Relation to Allocation, Distribution, and Uneconomic Growth", Keynote address, Canadian Society for Ecological Economics, October 16–19, 2003, Jasper, Alberta, Canada.

Chapter 9. "Sustaining Our Commonwealth of Nature and Knowledge", originally presented in Forum on Social Wealth, University of

Massachusetts, Amherst, September 29, 2005. Published in *International Journal of Ecodynamics*, Vol. 1, No. 3, 2006, pp. 1–9.

Chapter 10. "The Steady-State Economy and Peak Oil", presented at Peak Oil Conference, George Washington University, Washington, DC, May 9, 2006, sponsored by the Program in Conservation Biology and Sustainable Development, University of Maryland.

Chapter 11. "How Long Can Neoclassical Economists Ignore the Contributions of Georgescu-Roegen?", in Kozo Mayumi and John Gowdy, eds, *Bioeconomics and Sustainability: Essays in Honor of Nicholas Georgescu-Roegen*, Edward Elgar, Cheltenham, UK, 1999, pp. 13–24.

Chapter 12. Testimony before Senate Democratic Policy Committee, March 5, 2004, Washington, DC.

Chapter 13. Invited Statement to Russian Duma, Committee on Natural Resources, SubCommittee on Land and Ecology, December 18, 1998.

Chapter 14. Invited paper, "Economics and Involuntary Displacement", National Academy of Sciences Workshop, September 23, 2004, Washington, DC, organized by Michael M. Cernea.

Chapter 15. Invited paper for OPEC conference, "OPEC and the Global Energy Balance: Towards a Sustainable Energy Future", September 2001, Vienna, Austria.

Chapter 16. *BioScience*, Vol. 54, No. 10 (October 2004), pp. 956–7, review of Paul and Anne Ehrlich, *One With Nineveh* (Politics, Consumption, and the Human Future).

Chapter 17. *Ecological Economics*, November 1997, review of Roy Beck, *The Case Against Immigration* (The Moral, Economic, Social, and Environmental Reasons for Reducing US Immigration Back to Traditional Levels).

Chapter 18. *American Prospect*, April 24, 2000, review of Peter Huber, *Hard Green: Saving the Environment from the Environmentalists* (A Conservative Manifesto).

Chapter 19. "The Return of Lauderdale's Paradox", *Ecological Economics*, Vol. 25, 1998, pp. 21–3.

Chapter 20. "When Smart People Make Dumb Mistakes", *Ecological, Economics*, Vol. 34, No. 1 (July 2000), pp. 1–3.

Chapter 21. "Globalization versus Internationalization, and Four Reasons Why Internationalization is Better", address at Southwestern University, Georgetown, Texas, February 21, 2002.

Chapter 22. "Population, Migration, and Globalization", *Ecological Economics*, special issue on immigration, Vol. 59, 2006, pp. 187–90.

Chapter 23. "Policy, Possibility, and Purpose", *Worldviews* (September 2002).

Chapter 24. "Feynman's Unanswered Question", *Philosophy & Public Policy Quarterly*, Vol. 26, No. 1/2 (Winter/Spring 2006).

Chapter 25. "Roefie Hueting's Perpendicular 'Demand Curve' and the Issue of Objective Value", *Economic Growth and Valuation of the Environment: A Debate*, edited by Ekko C. van Ierland, Jan van der Straaten, and Herman R.J. Vollebergh, Edward Elgar, Cheltenham, UK, 2001.

Introduction

This book is a collection of articles, speeches, testimonies, and reviews written over the past decade on themes related to ecological economics and sustainable development. The 25 articles have been grouped into seven categories, each with its own short introduction. First is an overall presentation setting forth a basic vision and a few big ideas—limits, throughput, entropy, steady state, recent history of economic thought and the place of ecological economics in it, and so on. Second are some lectures to the World Bank. Third are articles and speeches (lectures) on conceptual issues of sustainability and ecological economics proper, and its relation to neoclassical economics. Fourth are congressional testimonies on related policy issues, and short opinion pieces. Fifth are a few book reviews and critiques of specific economic arguments that have played important roles in policy debate. Sixth are discussions of globalization and its nullifying effect on the ecological economic policies of nations. Seventh are essays on the philosophical presuppositions of policy—including of course the policies recommended in earlier sections of this book—and how those presuppositions are being undermined by what Alfred North Whitehead called "the lurking inconsistency." Finally there is a brief summary of main conclusions regarding the shortcomings of standard economics and improvements suggested by ecological economics.

Articles written by one person, even if over a period of time and for different occasions, usually have a certain underlying unity imposed by their origin in a single mind. Indeed, the unity may reach the unfortunate extreme of mere repetition! In putting together a collection of articles the author-editor's problem is to highlight the underlying unity and suppress the excessive repetition. At the same time one must not force spurious unity on to real diversity, nor eliminate repetition of basic ideas when it helps to relate different issues into a unified context. Furthermore, if I found it necessary to repeat an idea or argument in various contexts, that just might be a reflection of the objective importance of that idea, and suppression of repetition would obscure that fact. Also, the din over which one has to shout to be heard in today's public forum requires saying things more than once. I have tried to balance these considerations. Those diligent readers who read straight through from cover to cover will find more repetition than they need; in compensation, those who skip around will benefit from

1

the extra context provided by some of the repetitions. My apologies to the diligent. May virtue be its own reward.

Anyone who has been writing on controversial issues of economics and ecology for nearly 40 years will have collected a number of critics. While an Introduction is not the place to offer detailed replies to one's critics, it would not be amiss to acknowledge them with some appreciative reflections.

Critics are of two kinds, supportive and dismissive. Supportive critics accept one's basic position, but suggest clarifications, better arguments or the pruning of weak arguments, and the elimination of irrelevancies. Supportive critics are good friends. God bless them! Dismissive critics want to disprove or discredit one's position. Of course if they are right they provide a valuable service to the world, even if they are harder for an author to love than the supportive critic.

My dismissive critics seem, in turn, also to fall into two categories. First are those who say that I am simply wrong, should totally recant, and henceforth shut up (these are often my fellow economists). Second are those who assert that what I say is absolutely true, but also absolutely trivial, because no sane person ever claimed otherwise (these critics are frequently scientists). I take some solace in the fact that both sets of critics cannot be right. I would like to just cancel them out and go on my way, but I cannot because even though it is impossible for both to be right, the possibility remains that one of them is right. So both have to be considered.

Let us consider the second critic first, since I think that form of criticism is more just. I have been asserting that continued growth of the economy in its physical dimensions is limited by the fact that the economy is a subsystem of the ecosystem, and the containing ecosystem is finite, non-growing, and materially closed. Although open to a flow of solar energy, that flow is itself finite and non-growing, and its collection requires space and materials, which are scarce. Furthermore, both materials and energy used by the economy are entropically degraded by that use. Low-entropy resources are extracted from the containing ecosystem, degraded in the economic subsystem by transformations that we misleadingly call "production" and "consumption," and then the degraded matter-energy is returned to the ecosystem as waste, some of which is reconstituted by slow biogeochemical processes as new resources, and some of which accumulates as permanent waste. The economy lives off the environment in the same way that an animal does—by ingesting low entropy and expelling high entropy—by depletion and pollution. Clearly there are physical limits to growth of the economic subsystem. Perhaps welfare and happiness, which are experiences not things, can increase forever if based on qualitative improvements (development) rather than quantitative increase (growth) in the throughput of matter-energy. The problem is growth, not development.

Now my scientific critic tells me that all this is trivially true—a simple restatement of the first and second laws of thermodynamics. Yes, but the important thing is that it really is true. If it is obviously and trivially true, as I agree that it is, then so much the better, because this is not an originality contest. What is not trivial are the economic and political implications of these well-known scientific laws and facts about the world. Has my scientific critic ever noticed that all nations are hell-bent to foster the growth of their economies, and that growth is the summum bonum of economists and politicians? Bringing the laws of economics into conformity with biophysical laws, no matter how trivially true the latter, is no trivial task! Perhaps the scientist has a trivially simple policy solution for ensuring this consistency. If so, let him offer it.

My first type of critic says that I am simply wrong. Perhaps so. There are two ways in which an argument can be wrong: in its premises, or in the logic of its reasoning from those premises. In which way does my argument fail? Which of the premises (taken as trivially true by the scientists!) are wrong? Or where is the logical false step in reasoning? Is it logically false that the growth of a subsystem is constrained by the non-growth and finitude of the total system of which it is a part? Or is future growth, unlike past growth, assumed to be purely qualitative improvement with no quantitative increase of matter-energy throughput? As mentioned before, everyone accepts qualitative improvement. Certainly I do, and this appeal by my critic would provide no basis for refuting me. If this were my critic's objection, then we could easily reach policy consensus by agreeing to institute limits to growth of throughput, thereby forcing progress on to the path of development. This would force technology to evolve in the direction of more efficient digestion of the throughput rather than in the direction of an ever-bigger digestive tract through which to run more matter-energy.

As my persistence in publishing this collection indicates, I have so far not been convinced by either type of dismissive critic. Yet I confess that I, and ecological economists in general, have not made much of an impression on them either. I am not sure why this is the case, but I am reminded of the early American economist Daniel Raymond who in his 1820 treatise, *Thoughts on Political Economy*, explained to his readers why he had omitted any consideration of the then current ideas of Thomas Robert Malthus:

Although his [Malthus's] theory is founded upon the principles of nature, and although it is impossible to discover any flaws in his reasoning, yet the mind instinctively revolts at the conclusions to which he conducts it, and we are disposed to reject the theory, even though we could give no good reason.

The disposition of the economist's mind to instinctively revolt at any remotely "Malthusian" proposition, without needing to give good reason, has not changed since 1820. Mr. Raymond's basic approach remains very much in vogue—only his disarming honesty has fallen out of fashion.

PART 1

Basic Concepts and Ideas

Basic concepts and point of view are the focus in these three introductory articles. The first, "Limits to Growth" was written for the *Encyclopedia of Population*, and the second, "Economics in a Full World" was part of a *Scientific American* special edition (September 2005) on sustainable development. I put them first because the editors under whose guidance they were written made sure they were relatively free of jargon, and were intelligible to a reader coming to this subject for the first time. The editors of *Scientific American* are especially activist in this regard. They give you a word limit, you then submit a draft. The first editor asks for many further explanations, clarifications, examples, and so on, and you end up at twice the word limit. Then the "expansion editor" passes it on to a "contraction editor" who starts cutting back to the original word limit. This annoying process is only made tolerable by the fact that the editors are very good. Perhaps I should list them as co-authors! They also inserted in the middle of my article a one-page "counterpoint" by another author (Partha Dasgupta) with different views. I think that was an excellent idea and suggested to *Scientific American* that they make it a more frequent practice. Other articles in the special issue would have also benefited from a "counterpoint" page, but mine was the only one so favored. I mention this as evidence of the fact that pro-growth is overwhelmingly the default position, and that the burden of proof in public discussion falls entirely on growth critics. Growth critics always face demands to "present the other side," while growth proponents never do. My reply is that I am presenting "the other side," the side you never get in economics textbooks.

The 1972 book *Limits to Growth* by Donella Meadows et al. provoked considerable debate at the time. It was based on a systems dynamics computer model elaborated by a team at MIT. I became friends with Donella and Dennis Meadows before publication of *Limits to Growth*, and have continued to value their work, even though I am not a computer modeler. Many considered the conclusions of the complex systems dynamics model to be "counterintuitive." I have always thought that the main conclusions were completely intuitive. Only the calculations of timing and sequence of limits were sufficiently complex to overwhelm intuition, and it is certainly important to have a model as a calculating device. I mention this because it raises a general methodological difficulty. If one develops a complex model, and draws from it only intuitive conclusions, then critics will say that you have wasted your time and used a cannon to shoot a rabbit. So modelers are perhaps too eager to look for counterintuitive conclusions.

Yet intuition should not easily be dismissed in favor of a counterintuitive result from a "black box" model so complex that one cannot really grasp the totality of causal interactions that led to the result. Maybe one should keep working both on the model and on one's intuition, until they match. The late Donella Meadows was especially good at this, and her wise presence is missed.

The third inclusion is a speech I gave on receiving the Heineken Prize in Environmental Science in 1996, financed by the Heineken Brewing Company, and judged by the Royal Netherlands Academy of Arts and Sciences. This made me twice the beneficiary of the Heineken Brewing Company, since the building in which I have an office at the University of Maryland, Van Munching Hall, is named for the regional Heineken Beer distributor who generously endowed it. So, dear reader, please drink Heinekens!

A speech on the occasion of an award is an opportunity not only to say thank you, but also to try to relate one's work to a larger context. It is a wonderful and magnanimous thing to give prizes and awards. It is a great encouragement to the recipient and his co-workers, especially if they are accustomed to being ignored. As argued earlier, critics can be very valuable—but supporters are essential. And surely the generous souls who give awards also benefit from being forced to carefully review the work of others—an activity much neglected in today's academic atmosphere of publish or perish. One manifestation of the "full-world economy" is that publications have grown much more than the number of readers. Most articles published in academic journals are never cited. And I suspect that many that are cited were never read! The occasion of an award carries with it the obligation to say something about the area in which one has chosen to work, and why one thinks it is important enough for someone else to read.

1.   Limits to growth[1]

For demographers limits to growth is an old subject, at least as it relates to population growth. Since the 1972 publication of the book *Limits to Growth* the term has come to refer to both population and economic growth—that is to growth in population and to growth in per capita resource use, the product of which gives the total resource use growth rate. This total resource use is a flow from nature's sources (mines, wells, forests, fisheries, grasslands), through the transformations of production and consumption within the economy, and back as wastes to nature's sinks (atmosphere, oceans, your neighbor's back yard). Just as an animal lives from its metabolic flow, beginning with food from the environment, and ending with the return of wastes to its environment, so the economy lives from its metabolic flow, or "throughput" as it is called (by combination of the terms input and output). The throughput, like the metabolic flow, is entropic and irreversible. That is not to say that most waste materials are not recycled by biogeochemical processes powered by the sun. It is only to point out that such recycling is external to the animal or economy whose life depends on these natural services provided by its environment.

In physical terms human bodies are dissipative structures, which is to say that their natural tendency is to decay, rot, die, and fall apart. The same is true for artifacts that we accumulate as wealth. A car, a house, or a shirt is a dissipative structure that requires a throughput to maintain and replace itself. For demographers it is easy to think in terms of two populations of dissipative structures, one consisting of human bodies, the other of artifacts, basically extensions of human bodies. Each population, if it is to remain in a steady state, has both short-term maintenance requirements, and long-term reproduction requirements that are both supplied by the entropic throughput from and back to nature. If these two steady-state populations are so large that the throughput necessary to maintain them requires inputs from nature's sources and outputs to nature's sinks at rates beyond nature's replenishing and absorptive capacities, then the throughput flow becomes ecologically unsustainable, and so do the two populations.

The limits to growth, in today's usage, refers to the limits of the ecosystem to absorb wastes and replenish raw materials in order to sustain the economy (the two populations of dissipative structures). The economy is a subsystem of the larger ecosystem, and the latter is finite, non-growing, and materially closed. Although the ecosystem is open with respect to solar energy, that solar flow too is non-growing. Therefore in a biophysical sense there are clearly limits to growth of the subsystem. The difficulty is that these limits are not experienced as an absolute crash into an unyielding brick wall. They are rather like the limits imposed by a budget when you can borrow against the future, or put off maintenance and replacement costs. Although limits to growth are ultimately physical and biological in their origin, we feel their effects economically long before we experience any absolute physical crash. The challenge of limits to growth is to express these limits in economic terms, and institutionalize them in our decision-making. We not only need to know what scale of economy and throughput will terminally disrupt the ecosystem, we need to know when the extra ecosystem disruptions required by a growing throughput begin to cost us more in terms of sacrificed ecosystem services than they benefit us in terms of extra production. In other words we must think in terms of the optimum scale of the economic subsystem (the two populations) relative to the total ecosystem. Beyond this optimal point further growth becomes uneconomic.

The term "uneconomic growth" will not be found in the index of any textbook in macroeconomics. All growth (as measured by GDP) is considered economic growth. The term "uneconomic growth" does not compute in standard economics. Yet the concept of optimum is central to economics, and nothing could be clearer than that growth beyond the optimum must be uneconomic—in the strict sense that it increases costs by more than benefits, thus making us poorer, not richer. Politically it would be extremely inconvenient to discover that we have exceeded the optimal scale and that growth was now uneconomic. How could we fight poverty without growth? We might have to share! How can we trust the demographic transition to automatically limit births as wealth increases, if growth no longer makes us richer? We might have to purposefully limit births! How can we clean up the environment without growth to make us richer so that we can afford the costs of cleaning up? We might have to pay those costs out of a lower income! A world without growth has become politically unthinkable. Is it any wonder that there is an enormous effort devoted to debunking or minimizing the notion of limits to growth? It is true of course that GDP growth can be made less material intensive. By the same token we could also make people less material intensive (smaller) in order to allow for a larger population. But these are limited adjustments, and appeal to them only serves to highlight the extent to which growth is the dominant value around which our society is organized. None of these considerations alters the reasoning in support of the reality of limits. Currently it seems that we are witnessing the conflict between a physical impossibility (continual growth) and a political impossibility (limiting growth). But in the long run the physically impossible is more impossible than the merely politically impossible. One hopes that growth will not prove politically impossible to limit, once we come to accept that growth can be uneconomic. But we may have to suffer a bit before that becomes clear.

NOTE

1. *Encyclopedia of Population*, Paul Demeny and Geoffrey McNicoll, eds, Macmillan Co., 2003, pp. 602–3.

REFERENCES

Meadows, Donella H. et al. (1972), *The Limits to Growth*, New York: Universe Books.
Meadows, Donella H. (1992), *Beyond the Limits* (Confronting Global Collapse, Envisioning a Sustainable Future), Post Mills, VT: Chelsea Green.
Daly, Herman E. (1996), *Beyond Growth* (The Economics of Sustainable Development), Boston, MA: Beacon Press.

2. Economics in a full world[1]

The global economy is now so large that society can no longer safely pretend it operates within a limitless ecosystem. Developing an economy that can be sustained within the finite biosphere requires new ways of thinking.

Growth is widely thought to be the panacea for all the major economic ills of the modern world. Poverty? Just grow the economy (that is, increase the production of goods and services and spur consumer spending) and watch wealth trickle down. Don't try to redistribute wealth from rich to poor, because that slows growth. Unemployment? Increase demand for goods and services by lowering interest rates on loans and stimulating investment, which leads to more jobs as well as growth. Overpopulation? Just push economic growth and rely on the resulting demographic transition to reduce birth rates, as it did in the industrial nations during the 20th century. Environmental degradation? Trust in the environmental Kuznets curve, an empirical relation purporting to show that with ongoing growth in gross domestic product (GDP), pollution at first increases but then reaches a maximum and declines.

Relying on growth in this way might be fine if the global economy existed in a void, but it does not. Rather the economy is a subsystem of the finite biosphere that supports it. When the economy's expansion encroaches too much on its surrounding ecosystem, we will begin to sacrifice natural capital (such as fish, minerals and fossil fuels) that is worth more than the man-made capital (such as roads, factories and appliances) added by the growth. We will then have what I call uneconomic growth, producing "bads" faster than goods—making us poorer, not richer. Once we pass the optimal scale, growth becomes stupid in the short run and impossible to maintain in the long run. Evidence suggests that the US may already have entered the uneconomic growth phase. (See Box 2.5.)

Recognizing and avoiding uneconomic growth are not easy. One problem is that some people benefit from uneconomic growth and thus have no incentive for change. In addition, our national accounts do not register the costs of growth for all to see.

Humankind must make the transition to a sustainable economy—one that takes heed of the inherent biophysical limits of the global ecosystem so that it can continue to operate long into the future. If we do not make that transition, we may be cursed not just with uneconomic growth but with an ecological catastrophe that would sharply lower living standards.

THE FINITE BIOSPHERE

Most contemporary economists do not agree that the US economy and others are heading into uneconomic growth. They largely ignore the issue of sustainability and trust that because we have come so far with growth, we can keep on going ad infinitum. Yet concern for sustainability has a long history, dating back to 1848 and John Stuart Mill's famous chapter "Of the Stationary State," a situation that Mill, unlike other classical economists, welcomed. The modern-day approach stems from work in the 1960s and 1970s by Kenneth Boulding, Ernst Schumacher and Nicholas Georgescu-Roegen. This tradition is carried on by those known as ecological economists, such as myself, and to some extent by the subdivisions of mainstream economics called resource and environmental economics. Overall, however, mainstream (also known as neoclassical) economists consider sustainability to be a fad and are overwhelmingly committed to growth.

But the facts are plain and uncontestable: the biosphere is finite, nongrowing, closed (except for the constant input of solar energy), and constrained by the laws of thermodynamics. Any subsystem, such as the economy, must at some point cease growing and adapt itself to a dynamic equilibrium, something like a steady state. Birth rates must equal death rates, and production rates of commodities must equal depreciation rates.

In my lifetime (68 years) the human population has tripled, and the number of human artifacts, or things people have produced, has on average increased by much more. "Ecological footprint" studies show that the total energy and materials needed to maintain and replace our artifacts has also vastly increased. As the world becomes full of us and our stuff, it becomes empty of what was here before. To deal with this new pattern of scarcity, scientists need to develop a "full world" economics to replace our traditional "empty world" economics.

In the study of microeconomics, the branch of economics that involves the careful measuring and balancing of costs and benefits of particular activities, individuals and businesses get a clear signal of when to stop expanding an activity. When any activity expands, it eventually displaces some other enterprise and that displacement is counted as a cost. People stop at the point where the marginal cost equals the marginal benefit. That is, it is not worth spending another dollar on ice cream when it gives us less satisfaction than a dollar's worth of something else. Conventional macroeconomics, the study of the economy as a whole, has no analogous "when to stop" rule.

Because establishing and maintaining a sustainable economy entails an enormous change of mind and heart by economists, politicians and voters, one might well be tempted to declare that such a project would be politically impossible. But the alternative to a sustainable economy, an ever

---

BOX 2.1   CROSSROADS FOR THE ECONOMY

THE PROBLEM:

The economic status quo cannot be maintained long into the future. If radical changes are not made, we face loss of well-being and possible ecological catastrophe.

THE PLAN:

- The economy must be transformed so that it can be sustained over the long run. It must follow three precepts:

1. Limit use of all resources to rates that ultimately result in levels of waste that can be absorbed by the ecosystem.
2. Exploit renewable resources at rates that do not exceed the ability of the ecosystem to regenerate the resources.
3. Deplete nonrenewable resources at rates that, as far as possible, do not exceed the rate of development of renewable substitutes.

---

growing economy, is biophysically impossible. In choosing between tackling a political impossibility and a biophysical impossibility, I would judge the latter to be the more impossible and take my chances with the former (see Box 2.1).

WHAT SHOULD BE SUSTAINED?

So far I have described the "sustainable economy" only in general terms, as one that can be maintained indefinitely into the future in the face of biophysical limits. To implement such an economy, we must specify just what is to be sustained from year to year. Economists have discussed five candidate quantities: GDP, "utility," throughput, natural capital and total capital (the sum of natural and man-made capital).

Some people think that a sustainable economy should sustain the rate of growth of GDP. According to this view, the sustainable economy is equivalent to the growth economy, and the question of whether sustained growth is biophysically possible is begged. The political purpose of this stance is to use the buzzword "sustainable" for its soothing rhetorical effect without meaning anything by it.

Even trying to define sustainability in terms of constant GDP is prob-lematic because GDP conflates qualitative improvement (development) with quantitative increase (growth). The sustainable economy must at some point stop growing, but it need not stop developing. There is no reason to limit the qualitative improvement in design of products, which can increase GDP without increasing the amount of resources used. The main idea behind sustainability is to shift the path of progress from growth, which is not sustainable, toward development, which presumably is.

The next candidate quantity to be sustained, utility, refers to the level of "satisfaction of wants," or level of well-being of the population. Neoclassical economic theorists have favored defining sustainability as the maintenance (or increase) of utility over generations. But that definition is useless in practice. Utility is an experience, not a thing. It has no unit of measure and cannot be bequeathed from one generation to the next. Nor does it impinge on the environment.

Natural resources, in contrast, are things. They make a difference to the environment, and can be measured and bequeathed. In particular, people can measure their throughput, or the rate at which the economy uses them, taking them from low-entropy sources in the ecosystem, transforming them into useful products, and ultimately dumping them back into the environ-ment as high-entropy wastes. Sustainability can be defined in terms of throughput by determining the environment's capacity for supplying each raw resource and for absorbing the end waste products.

To economists, resources are a form of capital, or wealth, that ranges from stocks of raw materials to finished products and factories. Two broad types of capital exist—natural and man-made. Most neoclassical econo-mists believe that man-made capital is a good substitute for natural capital and therefore advocate maintaining the sum of the two, an approach called weak sustainability.

Most ecological economists, myself included, believe that natural and man-made capital are more often complements than substitutes and that natural capital should be maintained on its own, because it has become the limiting factor. That goal is called strong sustainability (see Box 2.2).

Furthermore the relation of substitution is reversible. If man-made capital is such a good substitute for natural capital then why did we convert so much natural capital into man-made capital in the first place? Clearly they are complementary. For example, the annual fish catch is now limited by the natural capital of fish populations in the sea and no longer by the man-made capital of fishing boats. Weak sustainability would suggest that the lack of fish can be dealt with by building more fishing boats, or fish farms. Strong sustainability recognizes that more fishing boats are useless

---

BOX 2.2   NATURAL CAPITAL AS LIMITING FACTOR

MAN-MADE CAPITAL cannot substitute for natural capital. Once, fish catches were limited by the number of fishing boats (man-made capital) at sea. Few fishing boats were exploiting large populations of fish. Today the limit is the number of fish in the ocean—many fishing boats are competing to catch the few remaining fish. Building more boats will not increase catches. To ensure long-term economic health, nations must sustain the levels of natural capital (such as fish), not just total wealth. Indeed without the complementary natural capital of fish populations, the man-made capital of fishing boats will lose most of their value. The same could be said of forests and sawmills, aquifers and irrigation systems, petroleum deposits and drilling rigs, etc.

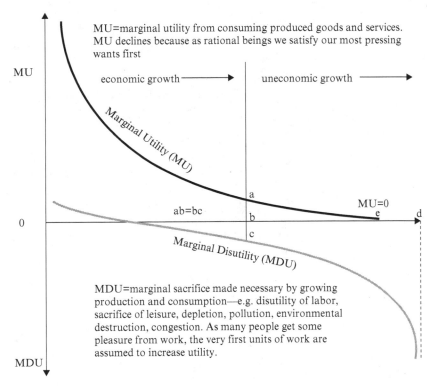

MU=marginal utility from consuming produced goods and services. MU declines because as rational beings we satisfy our most pressing wants first

MU

economic growth ⟶   uneconomic growth ⟶

Marginal Utility (MU)

a
ab=bc   MU=0
b   e
0   d
c

Marginal Disutility (MDU)

MDU=marginal sacrifice made necessary by growing production and consumption—e.g. disutility of labor, sacrifice of leisure, depletion, pollution, environmental destruction, congestion. As many people get some pleasure from work, the very first units of work are assumed to increase utility.

MDU

Figure 2.1   When growth is bad

BOX 2.3 WHEN TO STOP

UNECONOMIC GROWTH OCCURS when increases in production come at an expense of resources and well-being that is worth more than the commodities made. It arises from an undesirable balance of quantities known as utility and disutility. Utility is the level of satisfaction of the population's needs and wants; roughly speaking, it is the population's level of well-being. Disutility refers to the sacrifices made necessary by increasing production and consumption. Such sacrifices can include use of labor, loss of leisure, depletion of resources, exposure to pollution, and congestion.

One way to conceptualize the balance of utility and disutility is to plot what is called marginal utility (upper quadrant) and marginal disutility (lower quadrant). (See Figure 2.1.) Marginal utility is the quantity of needs that are satisfied by going from consuming a certain amount of goods and services to consuming one unit more. It declines as consumption increases because we satisfy our most pressing needs first. Marginal disutility is the amount of a sacrifice needed to achieve each additional unit of consumption. Marginal disutility increases with consumption because people presumably make the easiest sacrifices first. The optimal scale of consumption is the point at which marginal utility and marginal disutility are equal. At that point, a society enjoys maximum net utility. Increasing consumption beyond that point causes society to lose more in the form of increased disutility than it gains from the added utility. Growth becomes uneconomic.

Eventually a population having uneconomic growth reaches the futility limit, the point at which it is not adding any utility with its increased consumption. The futility limit may already be near for rich countries. In addition, a society may be felled by an ecological catastrophe, resulting in a huge increase of disutility (the vertical dive of the MDU curve). This devastation could happen either before or after the futility limit is reached. The diagram represents our knowledge of the situation at one point in time. Future technology might shift the lines so that the various features shown move to the right, allowing further growth in consumption before disutility comes to dominate.

It is not safe to assume, however, that new technology will always loosen limits. For example, discovery of the ozone hole and global warming, both consequences of new technologies, changed the graph as we knew it, shifting the marginal disutility line downward (more negative), moving the economic limit to the left and constraining expansion.

if there are too few fish in the ocean and insists that catches must be limited to ensure maintenance of adequate fish populations for tomorrow's fishers. It also recognizes that fish farms require the use of other forms of complementary natural capital.

The policy most in accord with maintaining natural capital is the cap-and-trade system: a limit is placed on the total amount of throughput allowed, in conformity with the capacity of the environment to regenerate resources or to absorb pollution. The right to deplete sources such as mines and fisheries or to pollute sinks such as the atmosphere is no longer a free good but a scarce asset that can be bought and sold on a free market, once its initial ownership is decided. Cap-and-trade systems that have been implemented include the Environmental Protection Agency's scheme for trading sulfur dioxide emission permits to limit acid rain, and New Zealand's reduction of overfishing by individual transferable fish-catch quotas.

The cap-and-trade system is an example of the distinct roles of free markets and government policy. Economic theory has traditionally dealt mainly with allocation (the apportionment of scarce resources among competing uses). It has not dealt with the issue of scale (the physical size of the economy relative to the ecosystem), nor much in recent times with distribution (the apportionment of resources and goods among different people). Properly functioning markets allocate resources efficiently, but they cannot determine a sustainable scale or a just distribution; those can be achieved only by government policy.

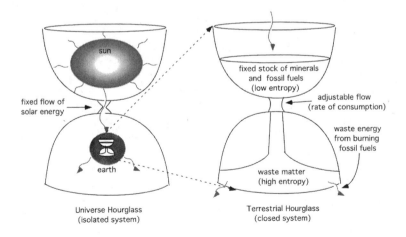

Figure 2.2   Entropy hourglasses (based on Georgescu-Roegen)

BOX 2.4   THERMODYNAMIC BASIS OF THE ECONOMY

HUMANKIND'S CONSUMPTION of resources is somewhat akin to sand flowing through an hourglass that cannot be flipped over. (See Figure 2.2.) We have a virtually unlimited supply of energy from the sun (left), but we cannot control the rate of its input. In contrast, we have a finite supply of terrestrial fossil fuels and minerals (right), but we can increase or decrease our consumption rate. If we use those resources at a high rate, we in essence borrow from the supply rightly belonging to future generations and accumulate more wastes in the environment. Such activity is not sustainable in the long run.

Some economists express these facts in terms of physical laws. They argue that this lack of sustainability is predicted by the first two laws of thermodynamics, namely that energy is conserved (finite) and that systems naturally go from order to disorder (from low to high entropy). Humans survive and make things by sucking useful (low-entropy) resources—fossil fuels and concentrated minerals—from the environment and ultimately converting them into useless (high-entropy) wastes. The mass of wastes continuously increases (second law) until at some point all the fuel and minerals are converted to useless detritus.

ADJUSTMENTS NEEDED

The transition to a sustainable economy would require many adjustments to economic policy. Some such changes are already apparent. The US Social Security system, for example, faces difficulties because the demographic transition to a nongrowing population is leading to a smaller number of working-age people and a larger number of retirees. Adjustment requires higher taxes, an older retirement age or reduced pensions. Despite assertions to the contrary, the system is hardly in crisis. But one or more of those adjustments are surely needed for the system to maintain itself.

Product Lifetimes

A sustainable economy requires a "demographic transition" not only of people but of goods—production rates should equal depreciation rates.

The rates can be equal, however, at either high or low levels, and lower rates are better both for the sake of greater durability of goods and for attaining sustainability. Longer-lived, more durable products can be replaced more slowly, thus requiring lower rates of resource use. The transition is analogous to a feature of ecological succession. Young, growing ecosystems have a tendency to maximize growth efficiency measured by production per unit of existing biomass. In mature ecosystems the emphasis shifts to maximizing maintenance efficiency, measured by how much existing biomass is maintained per unit of new production— the inverse of production efficiency. Our economic thinking and institutions must make a similar adjustment if sustainability is to be achieved. One adaptation in this direction is the service contract for leased commodities, ranging from photocopiers to carpets; in this scenario, the vendor owns, maintains, reclaims and recycles the product at the end of its useful life.

GDP Growth

Because of qualitative improvements and enhanced efficiency, GDP could still grow even with constant throughput—some think by a great deal (see Box 2.5). Environmentalists would be happy because throughput would not be growing; economists would be happy because GDP would be growing. This form of "growth," actually development as defined earlier, should be pushed as far as it will go, but there are several limits to the process. Sectors of the economy generally thought to be more qualitative, such as information technology, turn out on closer inspection to have a substantial physical base. Also, to be useful to the poor, expansion must consist of goods the poor need—clothing, shelter and food on the plate, not 10,000 recipes on the Internet. Even the wealthy spend most of their income on cars, houses and trips rather than on intangibles.

The Financial Sector

In a sustainable economy, the lack of growth would most likely cause interest rates to fall. The financial sector would probably shrink, because low interest and growth rates could not support the enormous superstructure of financial transactions—based largely on debt and expectations of future economic growth—that now sits uneasily atop the physical economy. In a sustainable economy, investment would be mainly for replacement and qualitative improvement, instead of for speculation on quantitative expansion, and would occur less often.

BOX 2.5   MEASURING WELL-BEING

To judge from how gross domestic product (GDP) is discussed in the media, one would think that everything good flows from it. Yet GDP is not a measure of well-being or even of income. Rather it is a measure of overall economic activity. It is defined as the annual market value of final goods and services purchased in a nation, plus all exports net of imports. "Final" means that intermediate goods and services, those that are inputs to further production, are excluded.

GDP does not subtract either depreciation of man-made capital (such as roads and factories) or depletion of natural capital (such as fish stocks and fossil fuels). GDP also counts so-called defensive expenditures in the plus column. These expenditures are made to protect ourselves from the unwanted consequences of the production and consumption of goods by others—for example, the expense of cleaning up pollution. Defensive expenditures are like intermediate costs of production, and therefore they should not be included as a part of GDP. Some economists argue for their inclusion because they appear to improve both the economy and the environment. We can all get rich cleaning up one another's pollution!

To go from GDP to a measure of sustainable well-being requires many more positive and negative adjustments. These adjustments include uncounted household services (such as those performed for free by spouses); increased international debt; loss of well-being resulting from increasing concentration of income (the well-being induced by an extra dollar for the poor is greater than that for the rich); long-term environmental damage such as ozone layer depletion or loss of wetlands and estuaries; and water, air, and noise pollution. When all these adjustments are made, the result is the index of sustainable economic welfare (ISEW), as developed by Clifford W. Cobb and John B. Cobb, Jr., and related measures. These indices have been used by ecological economists but are largely ignored by others in the field.

For the US, it appears that, beginning in the 1980s, the negative factors in the ISEW have been increasing faster than the positive ones. Similar results have been found for the U.K., Austria, Germany and Sweden. In other words, for some countries in recent years, the costs of growth are rising faster than the benefits.

As important as empirical measurement is, it is worth remembering that when one jumps out of an airplane, a parachute is more beneficial than an altimeter. First principles make it abundantly clear that we need an economic parachute. Casual empiricism makes it clear that we need it sooner rather than later. More precise information, though not to be disdained, is not necessary, and waiting for it may prove very costly.

Trade

Free trade would not be feasible in a world having both sustainable and unsustainable economies, because the former would necessarily count many costs to the environment and future that would be ignored in the growth economies. Unsustainable economies could then underprice their sustainable rivals, not by being more efficient but simply because they had not paid the cost of sustainability. Regulated trade under rules that compensated for these differences could exist, as could free trade among nations that were equally committed to sustainability.

Taxes

What kind of tax system would best fit with a sustainable economy? A government concerned with using natural resources more efficiently would alter what it taxes. Instead of taxing the income earned by workers and businesses (the value added), it would tax the throughput flow (that to which value is added), preferably at the point where resources are taken from the biosphere, the point of "severance" from the ground. Many states have severance taxes. Such a tax induces more efficient resource use in both production and consumption and is relatively easy to monitor and collect. Taxing what we want less of (resource depletion and pollution) and ceasing to tax what we want more of (income) would seem reasonable.

The regressivity of such a consumption tax (the poor would pay a higher percentage of their income than the wealthy would) could be offset by spending the proceeds progressively (that is, focused on aiding the poor), by instituting a tax on luxury items or by retaining a tax on high incomes.

Employment

Can a sustainable economy maintain full employment? A tough question, and the answer is probably not. In fairness, however, one must also ask if full employment is achievable in a growth economy driven by free trade, offshoring practices, easy immigration of cheap labor and adoption of labor-saving technologies? In a sustainable economy, maintenance and repair become more important. Being more labor-intensive than new production and relatively protected from offshoring, these services may provide more employment.

Yet a more radical rethinking of how people earn income may be required. If automation and offshoring of jobs results in more of the total product accruing to capital (that is, the businesses and business owners profit from the product), and consequently less to the workers, then the principle of distributing income through jobs becomes less tenable. A practical substitute may be to have wider participation in the ownership of businesses, so that individuals earn some income through their share of the business instead of only through full-time employment.

Happiness

One of the driving forces of unsustainable growth has been the axiom of insatiability—people will always be happier consuming more. But research by experimental economists and psychologists is leading to rejection of that axiom. Mounting evidence, such as work in the mid-1990s by Richard A. Easterlin, now at the University of Southern California, suggests that growth does not always increase happiness (or utility or well-being). Instead the correlation between absolute income and happiness extends only up to some threshold of "sufficiency"; beyond that point only relative position influences self-evaluated happiness.

Growth cannot increase everyone's relative income. People whose relative income increased as a result of further growth would be offset by others whose relative income fell. And if everyone's income increased proportionally, no one's relative income would rise and no one would feel happier. Growth becomes like an arms race in which the two sides cancel each other's gains.

The wealthy countries have most likely reached the "futility limit," at which point further growth does not increase happiness (see Figure 2.1). This does not mean that the consumer society has died—just that increasing consumption beyond the sufficiency threshold, whether fueled by aggressive advertising or innate acquisitiveness, is simply not making people happier, in their own estimation.

A fortuitous corollary is that for societies that have reached sufficiency, sustainability may cost little in terms of forgone happiness. The "political impossibility" of a sustainable economy may be less impossible than it seemed.

If we do not make the adjustments needed to achieve a sustainable economy, the world will become ever more polluted and ever emptier of fish, fossil fuels and other natural resources. For a while, such losses may continue to be masked by the faulty GDP-based accounting that measures consumption of resources as income. But the disaster will be felt eventually. Avoiding this calamity will be difficult. The sooner we start, the better.

NOTE

1. Text from *Scientific American*, September 2005, diagrams altered.

REFERENCES

Cobb, Clifford W. and John B. Cobb, Jr. (1994), *The Green National Product: A Proposed Index of Sustainable Economic Welfare*, Lanham, MD: University Press of America.
Daly, Herman E. and Joshua Farley (2004), *Ecological Economics: Principles and Applications*, Washington, DC: Island Press.
Easterlin, Richard (1995),"Will Raising the Incomes of All Increase the Happiness of All?", *Journal of Economic Behavior and Organization*, **27**, 35–47.

3. The challenge of ecological economics: historical context and some specific issues[1]

I. HISTORICAL CONTEXT

Over the past century and a half, three major criticisms have been raised against the economic orthodoxy of the time. Malthus criticized economists for abstracting from population growth as a cause of impoverishment; Marx criticized economists for abstracting from class struggle and inequality; Keynes criticized economists for abstracting from uncertainty and from the very possibility of a level of aggregate demand insufficient to provide full unemployment. Modern economists have earnestly tried to repair the defects pointed out by these major critics. Overpopulation, class inequality, and involuntary unemployment have each received much attention from several generations of economists. In each case, however, their solution has been the same—to advocate more economic growth.

To the Malthusians and neo-Malthusians, economists reply,

> rich countries have lower birth rates than poor countries, therefore we will automatically solve the population problem by more economic growth in poor countries. It helps poor countries to grow if rich countries are also growing and providing bigger export markets and accumulating more capital to invest in the poor countries. Malthus was wrong to claim that wealth can only grow arithmetically while population grows geometrically. Both populations of people and populations of goods can grow geometrically. The whole economy can and must grow exponentially.

To the Marxists and neo-Marxists, economists reply,

> we will take care of poverty by more growth—if the poor are getting better off in absolute terms, that is enough, don't be envious of the relative position of the rich. Inequality does not justify class warfare and in fact helps provide incentives which are good for growth, and ultimately for the poor. A rising tide lifts all boats, garbage scows as well as luxury liners. Focus on aggregate growth— distribution, like population, will take care of itself.

To, and along with the Keynesians and post-Keynesians, economists say,

> we will increase aggregate demand and provide full employment by stimulating investment. Investment means growth, and therefore even more productive capacity to keep fully employed tomorrow. But that just means we need still more growth, and that is good because growth makes us richer and assuages our anxieties and uncertainties about the future, leading us to consume and invest still more, further boosting confidence, aggregate demand and employment. Economic growth is a self-reinforcing spiral without limit. It is our destiny, as well as the solution to our problems.

In the face of this formidable historical consensus favoring growth as the general panacea, now come the ecological economists to challenge and criticize today's standard economists for "growthmania"—for abstracting from environmental and social limits to growth. Growth, yesterday's panacea, is rapidly becoming today's pandemic. Economists are so devoted to growth in GNP that they prejudge the whole growth question by calling GNP growth "*economic* growth"—thus ruling out from the beginning the very possibility that growth in GNP might be "uneconomic"—might at the margin cost more in terms of environmental and social sacrifices than it is worth in terms of production benefits. Such growth would make us poorer rather than richer, in an inclusive sense, and should be called "*uneconomic* growth." For now I only call attention to the theoretical possibility of "uneconomic growth." Later I will briefly consider empirical evidence that the US and a few other northern countries have already entered the phase where growth has become uneconomic.

But if growth is uneconomic, if it makes us poorer rather than richer, then how in the world do we deal with poverty? The answer is clear, if unpalatable to many: by redistribution, by population control, and by increases in natural resource productivity. The first two are considered politically impossible. The third is endorsed by all until it is realized that we have bought increasing productivity and incomes for labor and capital by using resources lavishly, by sacrificing resource productivity and the interests of resource owners (landlords). This has seemed a small price to pay for reducing class conflict between labor and capital and buying industrial peace. Nobody loves a landlord. But now it has become evident that, however unworthy of his rents the landlord may be, the social cost of today's low resource prices is being shifted to future generations, and to the other species whose habitats we are taking over.

In addition to making every *technical* effort to increase resource productivity, reducing poverty will also require facing up to the *moral* issues of income redistribution and population limitation. Growthmania is the attempt to grow our way around these moral problems by means of technical psuedo-solutions. But if we simply cannot grow that much for ecological reasons, then we must find new solutions to the problems raised by Malthus, Marx, and Keynes. The challenge of ecological economics is therefore enormous. It is by no means confined to just reducing depletion and pollution—it requires a rethinking of the major problems of the past century and a half—problems that were temporarily solved by economic growth, but are now being made worse by uneconomic growth!

As the economic subsystem grows physically it must become larger relative to the nongrowing ecosystem of which it is a part. The nearer the subsystem approaches the total system in scale, the more it must become like the total system in its basic characteristics—finitude, nongrowth, material closure, and reliance on the flow of sunlight as its main energy source. The path of progress for the economy must shift from quantitative growth to qualitative development. It must enter a phase of sustainable development—qualitative improvement without quantitative expansion—a steady-state economy, or to use John Stuart Mill's classical term, a "stationary state of population and capital." The classical economists other than Mill all recognized the ultimate necessity of the stationary state, but dreaded it. Mill, however, welcomed it:

> It is scarcely necessary to remark that a stationary condition of capital and population implies no stationary state of human improvement. There would be as much scope as ever for all kinds of mental culture, and moral and social progress; as much room for improving the art of living and much more likelihood of its being improved, when minds cease to be engrossed by the art of getting on.

To meet the challenge of ecological economics we must first abandon the illusions of growthmania and start from Mill's vision as the foundation. Next, we must face a number of more specific issues, to which I now turn.

II.   SOME SPECIFIC ISSUES IN THE CHALLENGE

1.   Recognizing a changed pattern of scarcity. The world was relatively empty of us and our furniture, now it is relatively full. But we have not yet switched our thinking from empty-world economics to full-world economics. Manmade capital has become relatively plentiful, and remaining natural capital is becoming more and more scarce. This changed pattern of scarcity would not be very important if manmade and natural capital were good substitutes, and since standard economists seem to believe in easy substitution they do not worry about the changed pattern of scarcity even when they recognize

it. Of course, if manmade capital were a good substitute for natural capital then natural capital should also be a good substitute for manmade capital. One then wonders why we went to the trouble to accumulate manmade capital in the first place if we were originally endowed with such a good substitute! The answer is that manmade and natural capital are complements, not substitutes (except over a very small margin). When factors are complements then the one in short supply is limiting.

Economic logic tells us to focus on the limiting factor—to economize on it in the short run and to invest in its increase in the long run. Economic logic has not changed, but the identity of the limiting factor has—it was manmade capital, now it is increasingly natural capital. The fish catch is no longer limited by the number of fishing boats (manmade capital), but by the remaining populations of fish in the sea (natural capital). Cut timber is no longer limited by saw mills, but by standing forests. Energy from petroleum is no longer limited by pumping and drilling capacity, but by remaining geological deposits— indeed it is limited more stringently by capacity of the atmosphere to absorb the CO_2 from combustion, but that too is a service of natural capital. Irrigated agriculture is limited not by pipes, pumps, and sprinklers, but by the amount of fresh water in aquifers and rivers; and so on. In sum, full-world economics must focus on natural capital—but we are still following the dictates of empty-world economics to grow, to convert more natural capital into manmade capital. Ecological economists are trying to correct this error.

2. Stop counting natural capital consumption as income. Income is the maximum amount that a community can consume over some time period, and still be in a position to produce and consume the same amount in the next period. In other words, income is maximal sustainable consumption, the maximum consumption that will still leave productive capacity intact at the end of the period. How, then, can there be a problem of sustainability if the standard definition of income explicitly incorporates sustainability? The difficulty is that the condition of maintaining productive capacity intact has in the empty world been applied only to manmade capital. Natural capital has not been maintained intact by any depreciation or depletion set-asides. The unsustainable depreciation and depletion of natural capital has therefore been counted as income, as if it were sustainable consumption. This error is pervasive. It is committed in the System of National Accounts (macroeconomics); in Balance of Payments Accounts (international economics); and in Project Evaluation (microeconomics). Ecological economists are trying to correct these errors.

3. Recognize three economic problems (allocation, distribution, and scale—not just one (allocation)). Efficient allocation of resources among alternative uses is the most discussed economic problem. The decentralized market system of pricing solves this problem very well under certain conditions. It does not solve the problem of providing the "certain conditions" that markets require (perfect information, competition, no externalities), discussed below in (5). But in addition to providing its own institutional base, there are two other economic problems that the market cannot solve—the problem of a just distribution of ownership of natural and manmade capital, and the problem of a sustainable scale of the macroeconomy relative to the ecosystem— that is, a sustainable scale of manmade capital relative to the complementary natural capital that remains. In fact, the individualistic market solution to the problem of efficient allocation *presupposes* prior political and social solutions to the problems of just distribution and sustainable scale. In general, for each independent policy goal we need a separate policy instrument (Jan Tinbergen). To kill three birds we have to be very lucky to do it with less than three stones. For allocation we have the market. For distribution we have separate income and welfare policy. For scale we have at present no clear goal aiming at sustainability, nor any institutions for serving that goal. We are trying to kill three birds with two stones.

4. Discounting, intergenerational distribution, and scale. In some ways the scale question overlaps with the issue of just distribution in its intergenerational aspect—an unsustainable scale of the present macroeconomy is unjust with respect to future generations since it will leave them with an unsustained and therefore diminished macroeconomy. The attempt of standard economics to solve the intergenerational distribution problem by discounting is illegitimate. The discount rate (interest rate) is a price, and like all prices it is determined subject to a given distribution of income and a given scale of the macroeconomy. Different distributions of the ownership of the resource base over generations, and a different scale of the macroeconomy, will result in different prices, including different interest rates. Since the interest rate is determined by the scale and intergenerational distribution of ownership of the resource base, it cannot be used as the criterion for determining either scale or intergenerational distribution via discounting. To do so would be circular reasoning. Ecological economists are trying to straighten out proper relations among allocation, distribution, and scale—and how these relate to discounting.

5. Improving market allocation by internalizing environmental and social costs—while recognizing the conflict with globalization. The goal of

cost internalization is shared by all economists in principle. Probably ecological economists take it more seriously, however, and are more willing to defend it in the face of conflict with other principles, especially in the conflict with globalization (free trade combined with free capital mobility). In today's world it is the nation that internalizes environmental and social costs into prices. If a cost-internalizing nation establishes relations of free trade and free capital mobility with cost-externalizing nations, then it will lose out in the competition. Its own producers will move to the cost-externalizing countries since capital is mobile, and still sell without penalty in the market they just left, since trade is free. Many ecological economists therefore argue for a new kind of protectionism—not protection of an inefficient national industry, but protection of an efficient national policy of cost internalization.

Free trade and free capital mobility lead to a standards-lowering competition—a kind of Gresham's Law in which bad cost accounting drives out good cost accounting—cost externalization drives out cost internalization. Ricardo's nineteenth century comparative advantage argument that guaranteed mutual benefit from free trade was explicitly premised on internationally immobile capital. In the twentieth century world of free capital mobility it is no longer applicable. Free traders must either advocate capital immobility to keep the world safe for comparative advantage, or else abandon the comparative advantage argument and recur to arguments based on absolute advantage. Certainly one can argue that world output will increase under free trade based on absolute advantage, but it no longer is the case that each nation must gain. Some may lose, and it would be necessary to face the issue of compensation for countries that lose. The gains from counting all costs at the national level are considered more important by ecological economists than the gains from international trade based on absolute advantage. Standard economists seem unable to give up the comparative advantage argument even when its main premise no longer holds, and also seem willing to give up the gains of national cost internalization in favor of "globalization"—an unexamined ideal that they mistakenly identify with nineteenth-century free trade.

6. Facing uneconomic growth as an empirical fact. Some countries, the USA for one, seem already to have entered the era of *uneconomic* growth, of growth in GNP that results in extra environmental and social costs that are greater than the extra production benefits. Economists tell us that GNP was never designed to be an index of welfare—only of economic activity. That is certainly true. However, it is also true that economists believe that GNP is sufficiently well correlated with welfare to serve as a practical guide for policy. But this belief fails a simple test.

One can construct an index designed to measure economic welfare and then see how well it correlates with GNP. This has been done for the US, and the finding was that since about 1980 the positive correlation disappeared and has actually become negative. Measuring welfare is very difficult, but given the conservative assumptions of this particular study, it seems safe to say that the usual assumption of a good positive correlation between GNP and welfare has no empirical support in recent years in the US. Policies designed to increase GNP make little sense if there is zero or negative correlation between GNP and welfare! The data are consistent with the hypothesis that we have entered the era of uneconomic growth. The challenge of ecological economics is to recognize this and to shift the path of progress from quantitative growth to qualitative improvement—to move from an economics of bigger to an economics of better.

NOTE

1. Heineken Prize Lecture, Amsterdam, September 30, 1996.

PART 2

Issues with the World Bank

For six years (1988–94), I worked for the World Bank trying to help some excellent colleagues introduce more environmental criteria into World Bank policy and project evaluation. It seems to me that whatever progress we might have made has by now been undone. I hope my negative view of the World Bank turns out to be overly pessimistic, but for now I count it a big disappointment. Reasons for this disappointment find expression in this section and the one on globalization. Nevertheless, in recent years my former colleagues have been kind enough to invite me back on two occasions for lectures and debates on sustainable development. I reprint here a speech on sustainable development, a critical review of the 2003 *World Development Report* that was on the subject of sustainable development, as well as my remarks at a debate with Paul Portney (then President of Resources for the Future) sponsored by the World Bank in March 2004. The "movie versions" of the first and last of these events is available on the World Bank web site, as of this writing, by Googling "B-SPAN, Herman Daly." The question and answer periods at the end will be more interesting than the repeated presentations.

I am often asked if I think the World Bank does more harm than good and should be abolished. I am really not well enough informed to draw such a large balance, but it is sad to see the efforts of so many good people at the Bank add up to so little. At least some of the blame for so many failures should be traced back to the prestigious academic economics departments in which most Bank staff are trained to "think like an economist." World Bank staff may be diverse in the sense of representing many nationalities, but they all studied in a handful of universities learning basically the same neoclassical economic theory. The failures of the practicing church may be due to the bad theology dispensed in seminaries. The economic seminaries seem immune to feedback from the world, and the practicing church keeps peddling its crackpot dogma of salvation by growth.

4. Sustainable development: definitions, principles, policies[1]

INTRODUCTION

I begin by considering two competing definitions of sustainability (utility-based versus throughput-based), and offer reasons for rejecting the former and accepting the latter. Next I consider the concept of development as currently understood (GDP growth led by global economic integration), and why it conflicts with sustainability, as well as with the premises of comparative advantage. Then I turn to the more general necessity of introducing the concept of throughput into economic theory, noting the awkward consequences to both micro and macro economics of having ignored the concept. Finally I consider some policy implications for sustainable development that come from a more adequate economic theory. These policies (ecological tax reform and/or cap and trade limits on throughput) are based on the principle of frugality first, rather than efficiency first.

I. DEFINITIONS

Sustainability is one of those troublesome abstract nouns like justice, truth, and beauty. Rather than discuss justice in the abstract it is often more productive to say something like: "I think Jones should go to jail for five years for setting fire to Smith's house." We can argue that proposition with a good idea of what we are talking about, and without defining the essence of justice in the abstract. In like manner instead of discussing "sustainability" in the abstract we should make it an adjective—we then must at least name something that is sustainable. Even better is the transitive verb "to sustain." Grammar then obliges us to name both what is being sustained and what is doing the sustaining. This is not difficult. It is the economy that is being sustained, and the biosphere that is doing the sustaining. The biosphere is the total natural system of biogeochemical cycles powered by the sun. The economy is the subsystem dominated by transformations of matter and energy to serve human purposes. The problem is that the scale and

36

quality of these transformations interferes significantly with the biosphere, reducing its capacity to sustain the economy.

Exactly what is it that is supposed to be *sustained* in "sustainable" development? Two broad answers have been given.

First, *utility* should be sustained, say the neoclassical economists; that is, the utility of future generations is to be non-declining. The future should be at least as well off as the present in terms of its utility or happiness as experienced by itself. Utility here refers to average per capita utility of members of a generation.

Second, physical *throughput* should be sustained say ecological economists; that is, the entropic physical flow from nature's sources through the economy and back to nature's sinks, is to be non-declining. More exactly, the capacity of the ecosystem to sustain those flows is not to be run down. Natural capital[2] is to be kept intact. The future will be at least as well off as the present in terms of its access to biophysical resources and services supplied by the ecosystem. Throughput here refers to total throughput flow for the community over some time period (i.e., the product of per capita throughput and population).

These are two totally different concepts of sustainability. Utility is a basic concept in standard economics. Throughput is not, in spite of the efforts of Kenneth Boulding and Nicholas Georgescu-Roegen to introduce it. So it is not surprising that the utility definition has been dominant.

Nevertheless, I adopt the throughput definition and reject the utility definition, for two reasons. First, utility is non-measurable. Second, and more importantly, even if utility were measurable it is still not something that we can bequeath to the future. Utility is an experience, not a thing. We cannot bequeath utility or happiness to future generations. We can leave them things, and to a lesser degree knowledge.[3] Whether future generations make themselves happy or miserable with these gifts is simply not under our control. To define sustainability as a non-declining intergenerational bequest of something that can neither be measured nor bequeathed strikes me as a nonstarter.[4] I hasten to add that I do not think economic theory can get along without the concept of utility. I just think that throughput is a better concept by which to define sustainability.

The throughput approach defines sustainability in terms of something much more measurable and transferable across generations—the capacity to generate an entropic throughput from and back to nature.[5] Moreover this throughput is the metabolic flow by which we live and produce. The economy in its physical dimensions is made up of things—populations of human bodies, livestock, machines, buildings, and artifacts. All these things are what physicists call "dissipative structures" that are maintained against the forces of entropy by a throughput from the environment. An animal can only maintain its life and organizational structure by means of a metabolic flow through a digestive tract that connects to the environment at both ends. So too with all dissipative structures and their aggregate, the human economy.

Economists are very fond of the circular flow vision of the economy, inspired by the circulation of blood discovered by William Harvey (1628), emphasized by the Physiocrats, and reproduced in the first chapter of every economics textbook. Somehow the digestive tract has been less inspirational to economists than the circulatory system. An animal with a circulatory system, but no digestive tract, could it exist, would be a perpetual motion machine. Biologists do not believe in perpetual motion. Economists seem determined to keep an open mind on the subject.

Bringing the concept of throughput into the foundations of economic theory does not reduce economics to physics, but it does force the recognition of the constraints of physical law on economics. Among other things, it forces the recognition that "sustainable" cannot mean "forever."[6] Sustainability is a way of asserting the value of longevity and intergenerational justice, while recognizing mortality and finitude. Sustainable development is not a religion, although some seem to treat it as such. Since large parts of the throughput are nonrenewable resources the expected lifetime of our economy is much shorter than that of the solar system. Sustainability in the sense of longevity requires increasing reliance on the renewable part of the throughput, and a willingness to share the nonrenewable part over many generations.[7] Of course longevity is no good unless life is enjoyable, so we must give the utility definition its due in providing a necessary baseline condition. That said, in what follows I adopt the throughput definition of sustainability, and will have nothing more to say about the utility definition.

Having defined "sustainable" let us now tackle "*development.*" Development might more fruitfully be defined as more utility per unit of throughput, and growth defined as more throughput. But since current economic theory lacks the concept of throughput, we tend to define development simply as growth in GDP, a value index that conflates the effects of changes in throughput and utility.[8] The hope that the growth increment will go largely to the poor, or at least trickle down, is frequently expressed as a further condition of development. Yet any serious policy of redistribution of GDP from rich to poor is rejected as "class warfare" that is likely to slow GDP growth. Furthermore, any recomposition of GDP from private goods toward public goods (available to all, including the poor) is usually rejected as government interference in the free market—even though it is well known that the free market will not produce public goods. We are assured that a rising tide lifts all boats, that the benefits of growth will eventually trickle down to the poor. The key to development is still aggregate growth, and the key to aggregate growth is currently thought to be global economic integration—free trade and free capital mobility. Export-led development is considered the only option. Import substitution, the orthodoxy of the 1960s, is no longer mentioned, except to be immediately dismissed as "discredited."

Will this theory or ideology of "development as global growth" be successful? I doubt it, for two reasons, one having to do with environmental sustainability, the other with social equity.

1. Ecological limits are rapidly converting "economic growth" into "uneconomic growth"—that is, throughput growth that increases costs by more than it increases benefits, thus making us poorer not richer. The macroeconomy is not the Whole—it is Part of a larger Whole, namely the ecosystem. As the macroeconomy grows in its physical dimensions (throughput), it does not grow into the infinite Void. It grows into and encroaches upon the finite ecosystem, thereby incurring an opportunity cost of pre-empted natural capital and services. These opportunity costs (depletion, pollution, sacrificed ecosystem services) can be, and often are, worth more than the extra production benefits of the throughput growth that caused them. We cannot be absolutely sure because we measure only the benefits, not the costs.[9] We do measure the regrettable defensive expenditures made necessary by the costs, but even those are *added* to GDP rather than subtracted.

2. Even if growth entailed no environmental costs, part of what we mean by poverty and welfare is a function of relative rather than absolute income; that is, of social conditions of distributive inequality. Growth cannot possibly increase everyone's *relative* income. Insofar as poverty or welfare is a function of relative income, then growth becomes powerless to affect it.[10] This consideration is more relevant when the growth margin is devoted more to relative wants (as in rich countries) than when devoted more to absolute wants (as in poor countries). But if the policy for combating poverty is *global* growth then the futility and waste of growth dedicated to satisfying the relative wants of the rich cannot be ignored.

Am I saying that wealth has nothing to do with welfare, and that we should embrace poverty? Not at all! More wealth is surely better than less, up to a point. The issue is, does growth increase net wealth? How do we know that throughput growth, or even GDP growth, is not at the margin increasing *illth*[11] faster than *wealth*, making us poorer, not richer? Illth accumulates as pollution at the output end of the throughput, and as depletion at the input end. Ignoring throughput in economic theory leads to treating depletion and pollution as "surprising" external costs, if recognized at all.

Building the throughput into economic theory as a basic concept allows us to see that illth is necessarily generated along with wealth. When a growing throughput generates illth faster than wealth then its growth has become uneconomic. Since macroeconomics lacks the concept of throughput it is to be expected that the concept of "uneconomic growth" will not make sense to macroeconomists.

While growth in rich countries might be uneconomic, growth in poor countries where GDP consists largely of food, clothing, and shelter, is still very likely to be economic. Food, clothing, and shelter are absolute needs, not self-canceling relative wants for which growth yields no welfare. There is much truth in this, even though poor countries too are quite capable of deluding themselves by counting natural capital consumption (depleting mines, wells, forests, fisheries, and topsoil) as if it were Hicksian income.[12] One might legitimately argue for limiting growth in wealthy countries (where it is becoming uneconomic) in order to concentrate resources on growth in poor countries (where it is still economic).

The current policy of the IMF, WTO and WB, however, is decidedly *not* for the rich to decrease their *uneconomic* growth to make room for the poor to increase their *economic* growth. The concept of uneconomic growth remains unrecognized. Rather the vision of globalization requires the rich to grow rapidly in order to provide markets in which the poor can sell their exports. It is thought that the only option poor countries have is to export to the rich, and to do that they have to accept foreign investment from corporations who know how to produce the high-quality stuff that the rich want. The resulting necessity of repaying these foreign loans reinforces the need to orient the economy toward exporting, and exposes the borrowing countries to the uncertainties of volatile international capital flows, exchange rate fluctuations, and unrepayable debts, as well as to the rigors of competing with powerful world-class firms.

The whole global economy must grow for this policy to work, because unless the rich countries grow rapidly they will not have the surplus to invest in poor countries, nor the extra income with which to buy the exports of the poor countries.

The inability of macroeconomists to conceive of uneconomic growth is very strange, given that microeconomics is about little else than finding the optimal extent of each micro activity. An optimum, by definition, is a point beyond which further growth is uneconomic. The cardinal rule of micro-economic optimization is to grow only to the point at which marginal cost equals marginal benefit. That has been aptly called the "when to stop" rule—when to stop growing, that is. Macroeconomics has no "when to stop" rule. GDP is supposed to grow forever.[13] The reason is that the growth of the macroeconomy is not thought to encroach on anything and thereby incur any growth-limiting opportunity cost. By contrast the micro-economic parts grow into the rest of the macroeconomy by competing away resources from other microeconomic activities thereby incurring an opportunity cost. The macroeconomy, however, is thought to grow into the infinite Void, never encroaching on or displacing anything of value. The point to be emphasized is that the macroeconomy too is a Part of a larger finite Whole, namely the ecosystem. The optimal scale of the macroeconomy relative to its containing ecosystem is the critical issue to which macroeconomics has been blind. This blindness to the costs of growth in scale is largely a consequence of ignoring throughput, and has led to the problem of ecological unsustainability.

II. GROWTH BY GLOBAL INTEGRATION: COMPARATIVE AND ABSOLUTE ADVANTAGE AND RELATED CONFUSIONS

Under the current ideology of export-led growth the last thing poor countries are supposed to do is to produce anything for themselves. Any talk of import substitution is nowadays met by trotting out the abused and misunderstood doctrine of comparative advantage. The logic of comparative advantage is unassailable, given its premises. Unfortunately one of its premises (as emphasized by Ricardo) is capital immobility between nations. When capital is mobile, as indeed it is, we enter the world of absolute advantage, where, to be sure, there are still global gains from specialization and trade. However, there is no longer any guarantee that *each* country will necessarily benefit from free trade as under comparative advantage. One way out of this difficulty would be to greatly restrict international capital mobility thereby making the world safe for comparative advantage.[14] The other way out would be to introduce international redistribution of the global gains from trade resulting from absolute advantage. Theoretically the gains from absolute advantage specialization would be even greater than under comparative advantage because we would have removed a constraint to the capitalists' profit maximization, namely the international immobility of capital. But absolute advantage has the political disadvantage that there is no longer any guarantee that free trade will mutually benefit all nations. Which solution does the IMF advocate—comparative advantage vouchsafed by capital immobility, or absolute advantage with redistribution of gains to compensate losers? Neither. They prefer to pretend that there is no contradiction, and call for both comparative advantage-based free trade, and free international capital mobility—as if free capital mobility were a logical extension of comparative advantage-based free trade instead of a negation of its premise. This is incoherent.

In an economically integrated world, one with free trade and free capital mobility, and increasingly free, or at least uncontrolled, migration, it is difficult to separate growth for poor countries from growth for rich countries, since national boundaries become economically meaningless. Only by adopting a more nation-based approach to development can we say that growth should continue in some countries but not in others. But the globalizing trio, the IMF, WTO, and WB cannot say this. They can only advocate continual global growth in GDP. The concept of uneconomic growth just does not compute in their vision of the world. Nor does their cosmopolitan ideology recognize the nation as a fundamental unit of community and policy, even though their founding charter defines the IMF and World Bank as a federation of nations.

III.   IGNORING THROUGHPUT IN MACROECONOMICS: GDP AND VALUE ADDED

As noted, throughput and scale of the macroeconomy relative to the ecosystem are not familiar concepts in economics. Therefore let us return for a while to the familiar territory of GDP and value added, and approach the concept of throughput by this familiar path. Economists define GDP as the sum of all value added by labor and capital in the process of production.[15] Exactly what it is that value is being added to is a question to which little attention is given. Before considering it let us look at value added itself.

Value added is simultaneously created and distributed in the very process of production. Therefore, economists argue that there is no GDP "pie" to be independently distributed according to ethical principles. As Kenneth Boulding put it, instead of a pie, there are only a lot of little "tarts" consisting of the value added by different people or different countries, and mindlessly aggregated by statisticians into an abstract "pie" that doesn't really exist as an undivided totality. If one wants to redistribute this imaginary "pie" one should appeal to the generosity of those who baked larger tarts to share with those who baked smaller tarts, not to some invidious notion of equal participation in a fictitious common inheritance.

I have considerable sympathy with this view, as far as it goes. But it leaves out something very important.

In our one-eyed focus on value added we economists have neglected the correlative category, "that to which value is added," namely the throughput. "Value added" by labor and capital has to be added *to something*, and the quality and quantity of that something is important. There is a real and important sense in which the original contribution of nature is indeed a "pie," a pre-existing, systemic totality that we all share as an inheritance. It is not an aggregation of little tarts that we each baked ourselves. Rather it is the seed, soil, sunlight, and rain from which the wheat and apples grew that we converted into tarts by our labor and capital. The claim for equal access to nature's bequest is not the invidious coveting of what our neighbor produced by her own labor and abstinence. The focus of our demands for income to redistribute to the poor, therefore, should be on the value of the contribution of nature, the original value of the throughput to which further value is added by labor and capital—or, if you like, the value of low entropy added by natural processes to neutral, random, elemental stuff.

IV. IGNORING THROUGHPUT IN MICROECONOMICS: THE PRODUCTION FUNCTION

But there is also a flaw in our very understanding of production as a physical process. Neoclassical production functions are at least consistent with the national accountant's definition of GDP as the sum of value added by labor and capital, because they usually depict output as a function of only two inputs, labor and capital. In other words, value added by labor and capital in production is added to nothing, not even valueless neutral stuff. But value cannot be added to nothing. Neither can it be added to ashes, dust, rust, and the dissipated heat energy in the oceans and atmosphere. The lower the entropy of the input the more capable it is of receiving the imprint of value added by labor and capital. High entropy resists the addition of value. Since human action cannot produce low entropy in net terms we are entirely dependent on nature for this ultimate resource by which we live and produce.[16] Any theory of production that ignores this fundamental dependence on throughput is bound to be seriously misleading.

As an example of how students are systematically misled on this issue I cite a textbook[17] used in the microeconomic theory course at my institution. On p. 146 the student is introduced to the concept of production as the conversion of inputs into outputs via a production function. The inputs or factors are listed as capital (K), labor (L), and materials (M)—the inclusion of materials is an unusual and promising feature. We turn the page to p. 147 where we now find the production function written symbolically as $q = f(K, L)$. M has disappeared, never to be seen again in the rest of the book. Yet the output referred to in the text's "real world example" of the production process is "wrapped candy bars." Where in the production function are the candy and wrapping paper as inputs?[18] Production functions are often usefully described as technical recipes. But unlike real recipes in real cookbooks we are seldom given a list of ingredients!

And even when neoclassicals do include resources as a generic ingredient it is simply "R" raised to an exponent and multiplied by L and K, also each raised to an exponent. Such a multiplicative form means that, for a given output, R can approach zero if only K and L increase sufficiently. Presumably we could produce a 100-pound cake with only a pound of sugar, flour, eggs, and so on, if only we had enough cooks stirring hard in big pans and baking in a big enough oven!

The problem is that the production process is not accurately described by the mathematics of multiplication. Nothing in the production process is analogous to multiplication.[19] What is going on is *transformation*, a fact that is hard to recognize if throughput is absent. R is that which is being transformed from raw material to finished product and waste (the latter symptomatically is not listed as an output in production functions). R is a flow. K and L are agents of transformation, stocks (or funds) that effect the transformation of input R into output Q—but which are not themselves physically embodied in Q. There can be substitution between K and L, both agents of transformation, and there can be substitution among parts of R (aluminum for copper), both things undergoing transformation. But the relation between agent of transformation (efficient cause) and the material undergoing transformation (material cause), is fundamentally one of complementarity. Efficient cause is far more a complement than a substitute for material cause! This kind of substitution is limited to using a little extra labor or capital to reduce waste of materials in process—a small margin soon exhausted.[20]

Language misleads us into thinking of the production process as multiplicative, since we habitually speak of output as "product" and of inputs as "factors." What could be more natural than to think that we multiply the factors to get the product! That, however, is mathematics, not production! If we recognized the concept of throughput we would speak of "transformation functions," not production functions.

V.   OPPOSITE PROBLEMS: NON-ENCLOSURE OF THE SCARCE AND ENCLOSURE OF THE NON-SCARCE

Economists have traditionally considered nature to be infinite relative to the economy, and consequently not scarce, and therefore properly priced at zero. But nature is scarce, and becoming more so every day as a result of throughput growth. Efficiency demands that nature's services be priced, as even Soviet central planners eventually discovered. But to whom should this price be paid? From the point of view of efficiency it does not matter who receives the price, as long as it is charged to the users. But from the point of view of equity it matters a great deal who receives the price for nature's increasingly scarce services. Such payment is the ideal source of funds with which to fight poverty and finance public goods.

Value added belongs to whoever added it. But the original value of that to which further value is added by labor and capital should belong to everyone. Scarcity rents to natural services, nature's value added, should be the focus of redistributive efforts. Rent is by definition a payment in excess of necessary supply price, and from the point of view of market efficiency is the least distorting source of public revenue.

Appeals to the generosity of those who have added much value by their labor and capital are more legitimate as private charity than as a foundation for fairness in public policy. Taxation of value added by labor and capital is certainly legitimate. But it is both more legitimate and less necessary after we have, as much as possible, captured natural resource rents for public revenue.

The above reasoning reflects the basic insight of Henry George, extending it from land to natural resources in general. Neoclassical economists have greatly obfuscated this simple insight by their refusal to recognize the productive contribution of nature in providing "that to which value is added." In their defense it could be argued that this was so because in the past economists considered nature to be non-scarce, but now they are beginning to reckon the scarcity of nature and enclose it in the market. Let us be glad of this, and encourage it further.

Although the main problem I am discussing is the non-enclosure of the scarce, an opposite problem (enclosure of the non-scarce) should also be noted. There are some goods that are by nature non-scarce and non-rival, and should be freed from illegitimate enclosure by the price system. I refer especially to knowledge. Knowledge, unlike throughput, is not divided in the sharing, but multiplied. There is no opportunity cost to me from sharing knowledge with you. Yes, I would lose the monopoly on my knowledge by sharing it, but we economists have long argued that monopoly is a bad thing because it creates artificial scarcity that is both inefficient and unjust. Once knowledge exists, the opportunity cost of sharing it is zero and its allocative price should be zero. *Consequently, I would urge that international development aid should more and more take the form of freely and actively shared knowledge, and less and less the form of interest-bearing loans.* Sharing knowledge costs little, does not create unrepayable debts, and it increases the productivity of the truly scarce factors of production.

Although the proper allocative price of existing knowledge is zero, the cost of production of new knowledge is often greater than zero, sometimes much greater. This of course is the usual justification for intellectual property rights in the form of patent monopolies. Yet the main input to the production of new knowledge is existing knowledge, and keeping the latter artificially expensive will certainly slow down production of the former. This is an area needing much reconsideration. I only mention it here, and signal my skepticism of the usual arguments for patent monopolies, so emphasized recently by the free-trading globalizers under the gratuitous rubric of "trade-related intellectual property rights." As far as I know, James Watson and Francis Crick receive no patent royalties for having unraveled the structure of DNA, arguably the most basic scientific discovery of the twentieth century. Yet people who are tweaking that monumental discovery are getting rich from monopolizing their relatively trivial contributions that could never have been made without the free knowledge supplied by Watson and Crick.

Although the main thrust of my remarks is to bring newly scarce and truly rival natural capital and services into the market enclosure, we should not overlook the opposite problem, namely, freeing truly nonrival goods from their artificial enclosure by the market.

VI.   PRINCIPLES AND POLICIES FOR SUSTAINABLE DEVELOPMENT

I am not advocating revolutionary expropriation of all private property in land and resources. If we could start from a blank slate I would be tempted to keep land and minerals as public property. But for many environmental goods, previously free but increasingly scarce, we still do have a blank slate as far as ownership is concerned. We must bring increasingly scarce yet unowned environmental services under the discipline of the price system, because these are truly rival goods the use of which by one person imposes opportunity costs on others.[21] But for efficiency it matters only that a price be charged for the resource, not who gets the price. The necessary price or scarcity rent that we collect on newly scarce environmental public goods (e.g., atmospheric absorption capacity, the electromagnetic spectrum) should be used to alleviate poverty and finance the provision of other public goods.

The modern form of the Georgist insight is to tax the resources and services of nature (those scarce things left out of both the production function and GDP accounts)—and to use these funds for fighting poverty and for financing public goods. Or we could simply disburse to the general public the earnings from a trust fund created by these rents, as in the Alaska Permanent Fund, which is perhaps the best existing institutionalization of the Georgist principle. Taking away by taxation the value added by individuals from applying their own labor and capital creates resentment. Taxing away value that no one added, scarcity rents on nature's contribution, does not create resentment. In fact, failing to tax away the scarcity rents to nature and letting them accrue as unearned income to favored individuals has long been a primary source of resentment and social conflict.

Charging scarcity rents on the throughput of natural resources and redistributing these rents to public uses can be effected either by ecological tax reform (shifting the tax base away from value added and on to throughput), or by quantitative cap-and-trade systems initiated by a government auction of pollution or depletion quotas. In differing ways each would limit throughput and expansion of the scale of the economy into the ecosystem, and also provide public revenue. I will not discuss their relative merits, having to do with price versus quantity interventions in the market, but rather emphasize the advantage that both have over the currently favored strategy. The currently favored strategy might be called "efficiency first" in distinction to the "frugality first" principle embodied in both of the throughput-limiting mechanisms mentioned above.[22]

"Efficiency first" sounds good, especially when referred to as "win–win" strategies or more picturesquely as "picking the low-hanging fruit." But the problem of "efficiency first" is with what comes second. An improvement in efficiency by itself is equivalent to having a larger supply of the factor whose efficiency increased. The price of that factor will decline. More uses for the now cheaper factor will be found. We will end up consuming more of the resource than before, albeit more efficiently. Scale continues to grow. This is sometimes called the "Jevons effect." A policy of "frugality first," however, induces efficiency as a secondary consequence; "efficiency first" does not induce frugality—it makes frugality less necessary, nor does it give rise to a scarcity rent that can be captured and redistributed.

I am afraid I will be told by some of my neoclassical colleagues that frugality is a value-laden concept, especially if you connect it with redistribution of scarcity rents to the poor. Who am I, they will ask, to impose my personal elitist preferences on the democratic marketplace, blah, blah, etc., etc. I am sure everyone has heard that speech. The answer to such sophistry is that ecological sustainability and social justice are fundamental objective values, not subjective individual preferences. There really is a difference, and it is past time for economists to recognize it.

VII.   CONCLUSION

Reducing poverty is indeed the basic goal of development, as the World Bank now commendably proclaims. But it cannot be attained by growth for two reasons. First, because growth in GDP has begun to increase environmental and social costs faster than it increases production benefits. Such uneconomic growth makes us poorer, not richer. Second, because even truly economic growth cannot increase welfare once we are, at the margin, producing goods and services that satisfy mainly relative rather than absolute wants. If welfare is mainly a function of relative income then aggregate growth is self-canceling in its effect on welfare. The obvious solution of restraining uneconomic growth for rich countries to give opportunity for further economic growth, at least temporarily, in poor countries, is ruled out by the ideology of globalization, which can only advocate global growth. We need to promote national and international policies that charge adequately for resource rents, in order to limit the scale of the macroeconomy relative to the ecosystem and to provide a revenue for public purposes. These policies must be grounded in an economic theory that includes throughput among its most basic concepts. These efficient national policies need protection from the cost-externalizing, standards-lowering competition that is driving globalization. Protecting efficient national policies is not the same as protecting inefficient national industries.

NOTES

1. Invited Address, World Bank, April 30, 2002, Washington, DC. Previously published in Marco Keiner, ed., *The Future of Sustainability*, Springer, Dordrecht, The Netherlands, 2006.
2. Natural capital is the capacity of the ecosystem to yield both a flow of natural resources and a flux of natural services. Keeping natural capital constant is often referred to as "strong sustainability" in distinction to "weak sustainability" in which the sum of natural and manmade capital is kept constant.
3. To a lesser degree because knowledge must be actively learned anew each generation. It cannot simply be passively inherited.
4. It also puts the future at a disadvantage—the present could bequeath an ever smaller throughput, and claim that this is sufficient for non-declining utility if only the future takes full advantage of foreseeable possibilities of substitution in both production and utility functions. But if these substitution possibilities are so easy to foresee, then let the present take advantage of them now, and thereby reduce its utility cost of a given throughput bequest.
5. The throughput is not only measurable in principle but has been measured for several industrial countries in the pioneering physical accounting studies published by WRI in collaboration with Dutch, German, Japanese, and Austrian research institutes. See *Resource Flows* (1997), and *The Weight of Nations* (2000).
6. Science tells us the physical world will end either in the big cooling or the big crunch. "Forever" requires a "new creation"—death and resurrection, not perpetual extension. Economics is not eschatology.
7. Investing nonrenewable resource rents in renewable substitutes is a good policy, with impeccable neoclassical roots, for sustaining the throughput over a longer time.
8. The prices used in calculating this value index are of course affected by the distributions of wealth and income, as well as by the exclusion of the demand of future generations and non-human species, and by the failure to have included other external costs and benefits into prices. It is hard to give a normative meaning to an index constructed with such distorted relative prices.

9. Evidence that growth in the US since the 1970s has likely been uneconomic is presented in H. Daly and J. Cobb, *For the Common Good*, Beacon Press, Boston, MA, 1989, 1994. See appendix on the Index of Sustainable Economic Welfare.

10. If welfare is a function of relative income, and growth increases everyone's income proportionally, then no one is better off. If growth increases only some incomes, then the welfare gains of the relatively better off are canceled by the losses of the relatively worse off.

11. "Illth" is John Ruskin's useful term for the opposite of wealth, i.e., an accumulated stock of bads as opposed to a stock of goods.

12. Instead of "deluding themselves" perhaps I should say "being deluded" by IMF and World Bank economists who require this misleading system of national accounts of them.

13. Macroeconomists do recognize that the economy can grow too *fast* when it causes inflation, even though the economy can never be too *big* in their view.

14. How might capital flows be restricted? A Tobin tax; a minimum residence time before foreign investment could be repatriated; and most of all something like Keynes's International Clearing Union in which multilateral balance on trade account is encouraged by charging interest on both surplus and deficit balances on current account. To the extent that current accounts are balanced, then capital mobility is correspondingly restricted.

15. Note that GDP does not value resources (that to which value is added). Yet we all pay a price in the market for gasoline. That gasoline price, however, reflects the labor and capital expended in drilling, pumping, and refining the petroleum, not the value of petroleum in situ, which is taken as zero. Your uncle in Texas discovered oil on his ranch and Texaco is paying him for the right to extract it. Is that not a positive price for petroleum in situ? It looks like it, but the amount Texaco will pay your uncle is determined by how easy it is to extract his oil relative to marginal deposits. Thus it is labor and capital saved in extraction that determines the rent to your uncle, not the value of oil in situ itself. The latter is still counted as zero.

16. Nicholas Georgescu-Roegen, *The Entropy Law and the Economic Process*, Harvard University Press, Cambridge, MA, 1971.

17. *Microeconomics* (second edition) by Jeffrey M. Perloff, Addison Wesley.

18. Some readers may rush to the defense of the textbook and tell me that the production function is only describing value added by L and K and that is why they omitted material inputs. Let me remind such readers that on the previous page they included material inputs, and further that the production function is in units of physical quantities, not values or value added. Even if expressed in aggregate units of "dollar's worth," it remains the case that a "dollar's worth" of something is a physical quantity.

19. I should say that I am thinking of the unit process of production—one laborer with one saw and one hammer converts lumber and nails into one doghouse in one period of time. We could of course multiply the unit process by ten and get ten doghouses made by ten laborers, etc. My point is that the unit process of production, which is what the production function describes, involves no multiplication.

20. Of course one might imagine entirely novel technologies that use totally different resources to provide the same service. This would be a different production function, not substitution of factors within a production function. And if one wants to induce the discovery of new production functions that use the resource base more efficiently, then it would be a good idea to count resources as a factor of production in the first place, and to see to it that adequate prices are charged for their use! Otherwise such new technologies will not be profitable.

21. For example, rents can be collected on, atmospheric sink capacity, electromagnetic broadcast spectrum, fisheries, public timber and pasture lands, offshore oil, rights of way, orbits, etc. . . .

22. By "frugality" I mean "non-wasteful sufficiency," rather than "meager scantiness."

5. The illth of nations: comments on World Bank *World Development Report, 2003*[1]

The *WDR 2003* draft is a welcome improvement over the *WDR 1992* treatment of the same theme, namely "sustainable development."[2] The discussions of complementarity of assets, limits to substitution, and the non-rival, non-excludable nature of many environmental services were especially welcome. The stated intention to include a final chapter on "open questions which could not be resolved" is an excellent idea, and should be a feature of all future *WDR*s.

There are some important ways in which the draft fails to deal adequately with its important topic. Seven such shortcomings are briefly discussed below.

1. The *WDR 2003*, insofar as it attempts a definition of sustainable development at all, seems much more committed to the utility-based definition, rather than the throughput-based definition. Exactly what is it that is supposed to be *sustained* in "sustainable" development? Two broad answers have been given: First, *utility* should be sustained; that is, the utility of future generations is to be non-declining. The future should be at least as well off as the present in terms of its utility or happiness as experienced by itself. Utility here refers to average per capita utility of members of a generation. Second, physical *throughput* should be sustained, that is, the entropic physical flow from nature's sources through the economy and back to nature's sinks, is to be non-declining. More exactly, the capacity of the ecosystem to sustain those flows is not to be run down. Natural capital[3] is to be kept intact. The future will be at least as well off as the present in terms of its access to biophysical resources and services supplied by the ecosystem. Throughput here refers to total throughput flow for the community over some time period (i.e., the product of per capita throughput and population).

    It would be better to adopt the throughput definition and reject the utility definition, for two reasons. First, utility is non-measurable. Second, and more importantly, even if utility were measurable it is still

50

not something that we can bequeath to the future. Utility is an experience, not a thing. We cannot bequeath utility or happiness to future generations. We can leave them things, and to a lesser degree knowledge.[4] Whether future generations make themselves happy or miserable with these gifts is simply not under our control. To define sustainability as a non-declining intergenerational bequest of something that can neither be measured nor bequeathed strikes me as a non-starter.[5] I hasten to add that I do not think economic theory can get along without the concept of utility. I just think that throughput is a better concept by which to define sustainability.

2. The throughput approach defines sustainability in terms of something much more measurable and transferable across generations—the capacity to generate an entropic throughput from and back to nature.[6] Moreover this throughput is the metabolic flow by which we live and produce. The economy in its physical dimensions is made up of things—populations of human bodies, livestock, machines, buildings, and artifacts. All these things are what physicists call "dissipative structures" that are maintained against the forces of entropy by a throughput from the environment. An animal can only maintain its life and organizational structure by means of a metabolic flow through a digestive tract that connects to the environment at both the source and sink ends. So too with all dissipative structures and their aggregate, the human economy. Although the *WDR 2003* draft has adopted the vocabulary of environmental "sources" and "sinks," it does not yet connect them by a throughput, much less recognize the entropic nature of the throughput and its economic consequences. This is a major failure.

3. There is still no recognition in *WDR 2003* that throughput growth (or even GDP growth as currently measured) might conceivably generate illth faster than wealth, and thus be *uneconomic* growth. There is no concept of the optimal physical scale of the economy as subsystem relative to its containing ecosystem. There is not even the concept of a maximum ecologically sustainable scale of the macroeconomy, which for a report on "sustainable" development is a major failure.

4. At a policy level there is still too much emphasis on "efficiency-first," as opposed to "frugality-first." Frugality-first induces efficiency; efficiency-first makes frugality less necessary.[7] Efficiency-first sounds good, especially when referred to as "win–win" strategies or more picturesquely as "picking the low-hanging fruit." But the problem of efficiency-first is with what comes second. An improvement in efficiency by itself is equivalent to having a larger supply of the factor whose efficiency increased. The price of that factor will decline. More uses for the now cheaper

factor will be found. We will end up consuming more of the resource than before, albeit more efficiently. Scale continues to grow. This is sometimes called the "Jevons effect." A policy of frugality-first, however, induces efficiency as a secondary consequence; efficiency-first does not induce frugality—it makes frugality less necessary.

5. While the importance of enclosing truly scarce environmental services in the market rather than treating them as a "free goods" is recognized, the opposite problem of imprisoning truly free goods (e.g., knowledge) in the market and treating them as if they were scarce, is not recognized. There is no discussion of the problem of freeing the non-scarce from the artificial scarcity required by the market—for example, intellectual property rights in biotechnology are rather uncritically reaffirmed.

6. The *WDR 2003* should at least question whether global economic integration is an adequate institutional context for policies of enhancing net wealth creation and poverty alleviation. The role of rich countries in sustainable development should be addressed. Which action should rich countries take to help poor countries: (a) grow faster to provide bigger markets and more capital investment for poor countries, or (b) restrict their own growth in throughput to free up carrying capacity and ecological space for poor countries to use? Globalization opts for (a), and so apparently does *WDR 2003*, but without raising the question, much less making the case. But if throughput is the limiting factor should not the answer be (b)?

7. Globalization, when not offered as the solution to problems of development, is at least assumed as the inevitable context. Yet the World Bank and the IMF were founded as international federations of independent nations, not as pushers of global economic integration. The distinction is worth emphasizing. *Internationalization* refers to the increasing importance of relations between nations: international trade, international treaties, alliances, protocols, and so on. The basic unit of community and policy remains the nation, even as relations among nations, and among individuals in different nations, become increasingly necessary and important. *Globalization* refers to global economic integration of many formerly national economies into one global economy, by free trade, especially by free capital mobility, and also, as a distant but increasingly important third, by easy or uncontrolled migration. *Globalization is the effective erasure of national boundaries for economic purposes.* National boundaries become totally porous with respect to goods and capital, and increasingly porous with respect to people, viewed in this context as cheap labor, or in some cases cheap human capital. In sum, globalization is the economic integration of the globe. But exactly what is "integration"? The word derives from

"integer," meaning one, complete, or whole. Integration means much more than "interdependence"—it is the act of combining separate albeit related units into a single whole. Since there can be only one whole, only one unity with reference to which parts are integrated, it follows that global economic integration logically implies national economic *dis*integration—parts are torn out of their national context (disintegrated), in order to be reintegrated into the new whole, the globalized economy. As the saying goes, to make an omelet you have to break some eggs. The disintegration of the national egg is necessary to integrate the global omelet. This obvious logic, as well as the enormous cost of national disintegration, is frequently met with denial. It is hard to imagine how nations can be expected to pursue policies for sustainable development, or anything else, when their economic borders have been erased. The *WDR* cannot even conceive of such issues.

If the *WDR 2003* is too ideologically blindfolded to deal with these issues, then at a minimum they should be listed in the proposed chapter on "open questions that were not resolved."[8]

NOTES

1. Previously published as "The IIIth of Nations: When Growth Becomes Uneconomic", in *Managing Sustainability World Bank-Style* (An Evaluation of the World Development Report 2003), Heinrich Boell Foundation, Washington, DC, August 2002.
2. For comments on the *1992 WDR*, see pp. 5–10 in H. Daly, *Beyond Growth*, Beacon Press, Boston, 1996.
3. Natural capital is the capacity of the ecosystem to yield both a flow of natural resources and a flux of natural services. Keeping natural capital constant is often referred to as "strong sustainability" in distinction to "weak sustainability" in which the sum of natural and manmade capital is kept constant.
4. To a lesser degree because knowledge must be actively learned anew each generation. It cannot simply be passively inherited.
5. It also puts the future at a disadvantage—the present could bequeath an ever smaller throughput, and claim that this is sufficient for non-declining utility if only the future takes full advantage of foreseeable possibilities of substitution in both production and utility functions. But if these substitution possibilities are so easy to foresee, then let the present take advantage of them now, and thereby reduce the utility it sacrifices in making a given throughput bequest.
6. The throughput is not only measurable in principle but has been measured for several industrial countries in the pioneering physical accounting studies published by WRI in collaboration with Dutch, German, Japanese, and Austrian research institutes. See *Resource Flows* (1997), and *The Weight of Nations* (2000).
7. Related to this is a focus on "patterns" of consumption rather than total volume of consumption. But it is the total volume that is limited by sustainability considerations, not the pattern. Let markets determine the pattern of consumption, but not the total volume (scale of throughput). Trying to control pattern (allocation) rather than volume (scale) is perverse from the perspectives both of the market and the environment.

While I am being cranky let me also complain about the *WDR*'s frequent use of the word "change" when what they mean is "improvement." Perhaps the same mindset that sees growth as always "economic" must also see change as always "improvement."

8.   This promised "chapter" turned out to be two pages (pp. 196–7 in *Sustainable Development in a Dynamic World*, World Bank 2003 World Development Report, Washington, DC) in the published report. They basically listed four topics needing further research. (1) Is there really such a thing as overconsumption? Preliminary answer, no, the problem is not the overall level of consumption, but rather a problem of misallocation due to externalities. (2) Agriculture and genetically modified organisms? Answer is to press ahead cautiously. (3) Intellectual Property Rights? Balance the interests of users, owners, and creators. (4) Global migration? Not a clue—it is a global challenge.

6. Can we grow our way to an environmentally sustainable world?[1]

I have a short answer and a long answer.

Short answer: My short answer is "No."

But suppose some of you think the short answer should be "Yes." My question to you then would be—After you grow your way to an environmentally sustainable world, then what? Would you then be willing to stop growing? Or would you want to keep on growing? Is it a state of the world, or the process of economic growth, that you want to sustain? I think the World Bank wants to sustain growth—that is, a process, not a state of the world. I would like to sustain that subsystem of the world called the "economy" in a state compatible with human well-being. I contend that the attempt to sustain growth will be inimical to that end.

When the economy grows it does not grow into the void, displacing nothing and incurring no opportunity costs. Rather it grows into the finite, non-growing ecosystem and incurs the opportunity cost of displaced natural capital and ecological services. Beyond some point growth in production and population will begin to increase social and environmental costs faster than it increases production benefits, thereby ushering in an era of uneconomic growth—growth that on balance makes us poorer rather than richer, that increases "illth" faster than wealth, and that is likely to be ecologically unsustainable. There is evidence that the US has already reached such a point.

That is my short answer. But it would be more productive to debate the longer, more nuanced, answer.

Long answer: A longer answer requires consideration of three subsidiary questions:

1. Growth in what? Exactly what is it that is supposed to be growing when we say "grow our way to an environmentally sustainable world . . ."?
2. What is environmental sustainability? Is it just a pair of words that make a rhetorically soothing sound, or does it have an operational definition?; and
3. Who is "we."

Let us consider each question.

Growth in what?—throughput, GNP, or welfare? Let's take the easy ones first—continual growth in physical throughput in a finite, non-growing, and entropic world is impossible, and beyond some point throughput growth becomes the main reason for environmental unsustainability by overwhelming environmental source and sink capacities. At or before that point throughput growth becomes "uneconomic growth."

What about growth in welfare? That is easy too. Welfare is a psychic magnitude, not a physical one; an experience, not a thing. Maybe welfare can grow forever, but if it can there is no problem since it is non-physical, and the environment is only disturbed by physical throughput. If welfare can grow forever with a constant throughput that is wonderful. Ecological economists usually call that "development" (qualitative improvement) rather than growth (quantitative increase), but that usage, although authorized by most dictionaries, has not caught on with neoclassicals. Most economists use growth and development as near synonyms, conflating quantitative and qualitative change—two very different things.

What economists usually mean by "growth" is growth in GNP. And GNP is the difficult case—is it physical or non-physical; quantitative or qualitative? It is the conflation of both. GNP is measured in value units. Value is price times quantity—$P \times Q$. Now Q is certainly physical—goods are physical, and even services are always of some thing or some body for some period of time, and therefore have a physical dimension. Relative price changes can reflect qualitative improvement in particular goods, but not for goods in general, since the relative price of all goods cannot increase. The absolute price level could increase forever with a constant Q, but that would be inflation, and I am sure no one wants to count inflation as growth. Economists take pains to calculate real GNP in order to eliminate aggregate changes in P and capture only changes in Q.

Certainly J.M. Keynes, one of the founders of the World Bank, defined the growth of the world economy, to which the World Bank would be dedicated, in physical terms—"by expansion we should mean increase of resources and production in real terms, in physical quantity, accompanied by a corresponding increase in purchasing power." This is the overwhelmingly dominant meaning of "growth." We can increase GNP to some extent without increasing throughput, but by how much? Just how tight the coupling is between GNP growth and throughput growth is a debatable question—some (Amory Lovins) think GNP can grow tenfold or more with a constant throughput—that is, a tenfold increase in resource efficiency. I tend to doubt it, to believe that the coupling is tighter than that, but if Amory is right that is fine with me—let GNP grow forever as long as throughput is held constant.

In general ecological economists think the throughput–GNP coupling is relatively tight, while neoclassicals tend to think it is loose. Indeed, neoclassicals frequently omit natural resources altogether from their production functions—implying no coupling at all! The coupling may well be a bit loose at the margin in rich countries, but in poor countries (most relevant to World Bank) the throughput intensity of GNP is likely to remain high for some time, since food, clothing, and shelter are resource-intensive. The Global South needs food on the plate—not 10,000 recipes on the Internet.

The other important growth coupling is the one between GNP and welfare. Here neoclassicals think the coupling is relatively tight, while ecological economists think it is loose, or even non-existent beyond a sufficiency threshold. Beyond that threshold welfare is overwhelmingly a function of relative income, and of quality of social relationships and ecological services, not a function of the absolute quantity of commodities consumed. GNP growth reflects only the last, the least important component of welfare beyond the threshold.

What is environmental sustainability? To be an operational concept it has to be defined in terms of throughput—the metabolic flow through the economy from environmental sources of useful, low entropy matter-energy to environmental sinks for waste, high entropy matter-energy.

Neoclassicals try to define sustainability in terms of non-declining utility between generations. This is a non-operational non-starter for three reasons: first, it is throughput, not utility, that directly impinges on the environment; second, utility is unmeasurable; and third, utility cannot be bequeathed. Even if we could measure utility well enough to judge whether it is non-declining, we still could not pass it on from one generation to the next. As any parent knows you can only pass on things, not happiness. Future generations are always free to make themselves miserable or content with whatever we give them. We do not owe the future their happiness, but we do owe them an intact resource base.

A more reasonable and operational definition of environmental sustainability requires that the throughput be within the regenerative capacities of renewable natural resources, and within the assimilative capacities of natural sinks. For non-renewable resources there is no regenerative capacity, and strictly speaking no ecologically sustainable use rate. However, quasi-sustainability may sometimes be attained by depleting non-renewables at a rate equal to the development of renewable substitutes. What is bequeathed is not utility, but productive capacity, capital in the broad sense, including especially natural capital. Sustainability means maintaining capital intact, avoiding the mistake of consuming capital and counting it as income. Weak sustainability means maintaining intact the sum of natural and manmade capital on the assumption that the two are largely substitutes. Strong sustainability means maintaining natural capital intact on the assumption that the two categories are largely complements, and that natural capital has generally become the limiting factor. For example, the fish catch is no longer limited by the manmade capital of fishing boats, but by the natural capital of remaining fish stocks and suitable habitats. Efficiency requires that investment should focus on the limiting factor.

We are very far from meeting these sustainability conditions at present, so it may sound utopian even to state them. But it is more utopian to think that we can continue to ignore them, or avoid the issue with non-operational definitions that allow "sustainability" to mean growth forever.

Throughput growth is the problem, not the solution—we will not "grow our way to environmental sustainability" as long as growth means either throughput growth or GNP growth. Welfare growth with constant throughput is all to the good and would help us bear the burden of limiting throughput to a sustainable level. But this is definitely not what economists and the World Bank have so far meant by growth.

Who is "we"? Is "we" both the North and the South? The South only? The poorest of the poor? An average of rich and poor, and if so do we choose the mean, the median, or the mode as our measure of central tendency? I think the World Bank has viewed the problem of sustainable development as mainly a problem for the South. The South has yet to develop, and they are now told to do it sustainably. The North has already developed, and is falsely assumed to be sustainable now that it has reached a developed state and presumably has climbed down the far slope of the "environmental Kuznets curve," a relationship that has absolutely nothing to do with Simon Kuznets, whose name is used only to lend the patina of credibility to a shaky concept.

Let me end with a multiple-choice question: From the viewpoint of sustainable development, what is the best growth policy for the North to adopt for itself in order to help the South overcome poverty?

a.   The North should grow its GNP as fast as possible to provide markets in which the South can sell its exports, and to accumulate capital to invest in the South. A rising tide lifts all boats, and it doesn't matter if the North grows faster than the South.

b.   The North should continue its welfare and efficiency development, but stop its throughput growth, in order to free up resources and ecological space for the South to grow into—at least enough to eliminate absolute poverty, and ideally enough to catch up with the North. If the latter is ecologically impossible, then the North should reduce its throughput.

It is clear that the World Bank has effectively opted for (a), although without, to my knowledge, ever explicitly asking the question. The World

Bank should explicitly ask the question. The closest they have come to doing so, I believe, is the question we have been asked to debate today. This is therefore an event worth celebrating!

By the way, the correct answer to the multiple-choice question is (b).

China, although considered a part of the Global South, is replacing the US as the world's largest absolute consumer of resources, even though per capita consumption is much lower. Therefore the frugality and efficiency of China's development strategy is even more critical to sustainability than that of the US. However, the rich cannot preach frugality and efficiency to the poor unless they practice these virtues themselves. And the sequence is also important: frugality first induces efficiency second; efficiency first dissipates itself by making frugality appear less necessary. Frugality keeps the economy at a sustainable scale; efficiency of allocation helps us live better at any scale, but does not help us set the scale itself.

NOTE

1. World Bank, Washington, DC, March 2, 2004, Debate.

PART 3

Issues in Ecological Economics and
Sustainable Development

This section, the longest in the book, deals with what I consider the major conceptual and theoretical questions facing ecological economics today. The effort is to show that ecological economics has deep historical roots in classical economics (Adam Smith, Thomas Robert Malthus, David Ricardo, and especially John Stuart Mill). These roots are obscured by the neoclassical revolution and the overwhelming dominance of neoclassical economics in universities today. But neoclassical economics is not without its strong points and provides such basic concepts as "optimal scale," (albeit never applied to the macroeconomy), and complementarity (as well as substitutability), and the important distinctions between rival and non-rival, excludable and non-excludable goods. Ironically, lack of attention to these latter concepts has led neoclassical economists into two opposite errors: treating the truly rival (natural capital) as if it were non-rival and consequently non-scarce, and therefore correctly priced at zero; and treating the truly non-rival (knowledge) as if it were scarce and required a positive price. The first is the traditional "tragedy of the open access commons," and the second might be called the "tragedy of unwarranted enclosure."

Also considered is the sorry history of stonewalling by the mainstream to avoid confrontation with the critique of the neoclassical production function by Nicholas Georgescu-Roegen. Some chastise ecological economics for not challenging standard economics from within the fold. This was indeed the approach of Georgescu-Roegen, Kenneth Boulding, E.F. Schumacher, and other early ecological economists. But the reaction of neoclassical economists was to ignore them to the extent possible, or else simply to redraw the boundaries of economics so as to exclude their critique. Thus Boulding is considered really a philosopher, not an economist, and Georgescu-Roegen is said to have gone off into physics and biology, and while his work may be interesting, it is no longer really economics. One result of this strategy of circling the wagons ever tighter is that standard economics has become narrower and ever more barren in its silly but unending attempt to substitute mathematical formalism for physical, social, and moral content.

7. Consumption and welfare: two views of value added[1]

Any discovery which renders consumption less necessary to the pursuit of living is as much an economic gain as a discovery which improves our skills of production. (Kenneth Boulding, 1945)

I. INTRODUCTION

The total of resource consumption (throughput), by which the economic subsystem lives off the containing ecosystem, is limited—because the ecosystem that both supplies the throughput and absorbs its waste products is itself limited. The earth-ecosystem is finite, non-growing, materially closed, and while open to the flow of solar energy, that flow is also non-growing. Historically these limits were not generally binding, because the subsystem was small relative to the total system. The world was "empty." But now it is "full," and the limits are more and more binding—not necessarily like brick walls, but more like stretched rubber bands.

The total flow of resource consumption is the product of population times per capita consumption. Many people have for a long time urged the wisdom of limiting population growth—few have recognized the need to limit consumption growth. In the face of so much poverty in the world it seems "immoral" to some to even talk about limiting consumption. But populations of cars, buildings, TVs, refrigerators, livestock, and yes, even of trees, fish, wolves, and giant pandas, all have in common with the population of human bodies that they take up space and require a throughput for their production, maintenance, and disposal. Nevertheless, some think the solution to human population growth lies in increasing the growth of populations of all the commodities whose services we consume. The "demographic transition" will automatically stop population growth if only per capita consumption grows fast enough. Arguing that one term of a product will stop growing if only the other term grows faster, is not very reassuring if it is the product of the two terms that is limited. Will the average Indian's consumption have to rise to that of the average Swede before Indian fertility falls to the Swedish level? Can the eroding and crowded country of India support that many cars, power plants, buildings, and so on?

Never fear, the same people who brought you the demographic transition are now bringing you the Information Reformation, a.k.a. the "dematerialized economy." McDonald's will introduce the "info-burger," consisting of a thick patty of information between two slices of silicon, thin as communion wafers so as to emphasize the symbolic and spiritual nature of consumption. We can also dematerialize human beings by breeding smaller people—after all if we were half the size there could be twice as many of us—indeed we would have to dematerialize people if we were to subsist on the dematerialized GNP! The Information Reformation, like the demographic transition before it, expands a germ of truth into a whale of a fantasy.

While all countries must worry about both population and per capita consumption, it is evident that the South needs to focus more on population, and the North more on per capita consumption. This fact will likely play a major role in all North/South treaties and discussions. Why should the South control its population if the resources saved thereby are merely gobbled up by Northern overconsumption? Why should the North control its overconsumption if the saved resources will merely allow a larger number of poor people to subsist at the same level of misery? Without for a minute minimizing the necessity of population control, it is nevertheless incumbent on the North to get serious about consumption control. Toward this end, a reconsideration of the meaning of consumption is offered below.

II.   CONSUMPTION AND VALUE ADDED

When we speak of consumption what is it that we think of as being consumed? Alfred Marshall reminded us of the laws of conservation of matter/energy and the consequent impossibility of consuming the material building blocks of commodities.

> Man cannot create material things—his efforts and sacrifices result in changing the form or arrangement of matter to adapt it better for the satisfaction of his wants—as his production of material products is really nothing more than a rearrangement of matter which gives it new utilities, so his consumption of them is nothing more than a disarrangement of matter which destroys its utilities. (Marshall, 1961, pp. 63-4)

What we destroy or consume in consumption is the improbable arrangement of those building blocks, arrangements that give utility for humans, arrangements that were, according to Marshall, made by humans for human purposes. This utility added to matter/energy by human action is not production in the sense of creation of matter/energy, which is just as impossible as destruction by consumption. Useful structure is added to matter/energy (natural resource flows) by the agency of labor and capital stocks. The value of this useful structure imparted by labor and capital is called "value added" by economists. This value added is what is "consumed"; that is, used up in consumption. New value needs to be added again by the agency of labor and capital before it can be consumed again. That to which value is being added is the flow of natural resources, conceived ultimately as the indestructible building blocks of nature. The value consumed by humans is, in this view, no greater than the value added by humans—consumption plus savings equals national income—which in turn is equal to the sum of all value added. In the standard economist's vision we consume only that value which we added in the first place.[2] And then we add it again, and consume it again, and so on. This vision is formalized in the famous diagram of the isolated circular flow found in the initial pages of every economics textbook.

For all the focus on value added one would think that there would be some discussion of *that to which value is being added*. But modern economists say no more about it than Marshall. It is just "matter," and its properties are not very interesting. In fact they are becoming ever less interesting to economists as science uncovers their basic uniformity. As Barnett and Morse (1963) put it:

> Advances in fundamental science have made it possible to take advantage of the uniformity of matter/energy—a uniformity that makes it feasible, without pre-assignable limit, to escape the quantitative constraints imposed by the character of the earth's crust.

That to which value is being added are merely homogeneous, indestructible building blocks—atoms in the original sense—of which there is no conceivable scarcity. That to which value is added is therefore inert, undifferentiated, interchangeable, and superabundant—very dull stuff indeed, compared to the value-adding agents of labor with all its human capacities, and capital that embodies the marvels of human knowledge. It is not surprising that value added is the centerpiece of economic accounting, and that the presumably passive stuff to which value is added has received minimal attention (Daly and Cobb, 1994, Chapter 10).

Three examples will show how little attention is given to that to which value is added, which for brevity I will refer to as "resources." Some philistines ("non-economists" as they are now called) have questioned whether there are enough resources in the world for everyone to use them at the rate Americans do. This ignorant fear is put to rest by Professor Lester Thurow (1980, p. 118), who points out that the question assumes that the rest of the world is going to achieve the consumption standards of the average American without at the same time achieving the productivity standards of the average American. This of course is algebraically impossible. The world can consume only what it can produce.

You can only disarrange matter (consume) if you have previously arranged it (produced). Resources are totally passive recipients of form added by labor and capital. Value added is everything, and it is impossible to subtract value that was never added. So if you are consuming it you must have produced it, either recently or in the past. More and more high consuming people just means more and more value was added. Where else could the arrangements of matter have come from? It is "algebraically impossible" for consumption to exceed value added, at least in the economist's tight little abstract world of the circular flow of exchange value.

A second example comes from Professor William Nordhaus (*Science*, 1991), who said that global warming would have only a small effect on the US economy because basically only agriculture is sensitive to climate, and agriculture is only 3 percent of total value added, of GNP. Evidently it is the value added to seeds, soil, sunlight, and rainfall by labor and capital that keeps us alive. Older economists might have asked about what happens to marginal utility, price, and the percentage of GNP going to food when food becomes very scarce, say, due to a drought? What about the inelasticity of demand for necessities? Could not the 3 percent of GNP accounted for by agriculture easily rise to 90 percent during a famine? But these considerations give mere stuff a more than passive role in value, and diminish the dogmatic monopoly of value added by human agents of labor and capital.

The importance of mere stuff is frequently downplayed by pointing out that the entire extractive sector accounts for a mere 5 or 6 percent of GNP. But if the 95 percent of value added is not independent of the 5 percent in the extractive sector, but rather depends upon it—is based on it—then the impression of relative unimportance is false. The image this conjures in my mind is that of an inverted pyramid balanced on its point. The 5 or 6 percent of the volume of the pyramid near the point on which it is resting represents the GNP from the extractive sector. The rest of the pyramid is value added to extracted resources. That 5 percent is the base on which the other 95 percent rests, that to which its value is added. Value cannot be added to nothing.

Indeed, since the value of the extracted resources themselves (the 5 or 6 percent of GNP) represents mostly value added in extraction, practically the entire pyramid of value added is resting on a tiny point of near zero dimension representing the *in situ* value of the resources. This image of a growing and tottering pyramid makes me want to stop thinking exclusively about value added and think some more about that to which value is being added. What, exactly, is holding up this pyramid of value added?

A third example comes from the theory of production and the customary use of a multiplicative form for the production function, the most popular being the Cobb–Douglas. Frequently production is treated as a function of capital and labor alone—resources are omitted entirely. But now economists have taken to including resources. However, the welcome step toward realism thus taken is very small, because, although resources are now necessary for production, the amount of resources needed for any given level of output can become arbitrarily small, approaching zero, as long as capital or labor are substituted in sufficient quantities. Georgescu-Roegen (1979, p. 98) referred to this "paper and pencil exercise" as Solow's and Stiglitz's "conjuring trick."[3]

III.   CONSUMPTION AND PHYSICAL TRANSFORMATION

The vision sketched above, that of Marshall, of Barnett and Morse, and of all textbooks founded on the circular flow of value added, is entirely consistent with the first law of thermodynamics. Matter/energy is not produced or consumed, only transformed. But this vision embodies an astonishing oversight—it completely ignores the second law of thermodynamics (Georgescu-Roegen, 1971; Soddy, 1922). Matter is arranged in production, disarranged in consumption, rearranged in production, and so on. The second law tells us that all this rearranging and recycling of material building blocks takes energy, that energy itself is not recycled, and that on each cycle some of the material building blocks are dissipated beyond recall. It remains true that we do not consume matter/energy, but we do consume (irrevocably use up) the *capacity to rearrange* matter/energy. Contrary to the implication of Barnett and Morse, matter/energy is not at all uniform in the quality most relevant to economics—namely its capacity to receive and hold the rearrangements dictated by human purpose, the capacity to receive the imprint of human knowledge, the capacity to embody value added. The capacity of matter/energy to embody value added is not uniform, and it wears out and must be replenished. It is not totally passive. If the economic system is to keep going it cannot be an isolated circular flow. It must be an open system, receiving matter and energy from outside to make up for that which is dissipated to the outside. What is outside? The environment. What is the environment? It is a complex ecosystem that is finite, non-growing and materially closed, while open to a non-growing flow of solar energy.

Seeing the economy as an open subsystem forces us to realize that consumption is not only rearrangement within the subsystem, but involves rearrangements in the rest of the system, the environment. Taking matter/energy from the larger system, adding value to it, using up the added value, and returning the waste, clearly alters the environment. The matter/energy we return is not the same as the matter/energy we take in. If it were, we could simply use it again and again in a closed circular flow. Common observation tells us, and the entropy law confirms, that waste matter/energy is qualitatively different from raw materials. Low-entropy matter/energy comes in, high-entropy matter/energy goes out, just as in an organism's metabolism. We irrevocably use up not only the value we added by rearrangement, but also the pre-existing arrangement originally imparted by nature, as well as the very energetic capacity to further arrange, also provided by nature. We not only consume the value we add to matter, *but also the value that was added by nature before we imported it into the economic subsystem*, and that was necessary for it to be considered a resource in the first place. Capacity to rearrange that which is used up within the subsystem can be restored by importing low-entropy matter/energy from the larger system and exporting high-entropy matter/energy back to it. But the rates of import and export, determined largely by the scale of the subsystem, must be consistent with the complex workings of the parent system, the ecosystem. The scale of the subsystem matters.

From this perspective value is still being added to resources by the agents of labor and capital. But that to which value is added is not inert, indifferent, uniform building blocks or atoms. Value is added to that matter/energy which is most capable of receiving and embodying the value being added to it. That receptivity might be thought of as "value pre-added by nature." Carbon atoms scattered in the atmosphere can receive value added only with the enormous expenditure of energy and other materials. Carbon atoms structured in a tree can be rearranged much more easily. Concentrated copper ore can hold value added, atoms of copper at average crustal abundance cannot. Energy concentrated in a lump of coal can help us add value to matter; energy at equilibrium temperature in the ocean or atmosphere cannot. The more work done by nature, the more concentrated and receptive the resource is to having value added to it, the less capital and labor will have to be expended in rearranging it.

From a utility or demand perspective value added by nature ought to be valued equally with value added by labor and capital. But from the supply or cost side it is not, because value added by humans has a real cost of disutility of labor and an opportunity cost of both labor and capital use. We tend to treat natural value added as a subsidy, a free gift of nature. The greater the natural subsidy, the less the cost of labor and capital (value added) needed for further arrangement. The less the humanly added value, the lower the price, and the more rapid the use. Oil from East Texas was a much greater net energy subsidy from nature to the economy than is offshore Alaskan oil. But its price was much lower precisely because it required less value added by labor and capital.[4] The larger the natural subsidy, the lower the price we put on it!

Thanks in part to this natural subsidy, the economy has grown relative to the total ecosystem to such an extent that the basic pattern of scarcity has changed. It used to be that adding value was limited by the supply of agents of transformation, labor and capital. Now, value added is limited more by the availability of resources subsidized by nature to the point that they can receive value added by us. Mere knowledge means nothing to the economy until it becomes incarnate in physical structures. Low-entropy matter/energy is the restricted gate through which knowledge is incorporated in matter and becomes manmade capital. No low-entropy matter/energy, no capital— regardless of knowledge.[5] Of course, new knowledge may include discovery of new sources of low-entropy resources, and new methods of transforming them to better serve human needs. New knowledge may also discover new limits, and new impossibility theorems.

The physical growth of the subsystem is the transformation of natural capital into manmade capital. A tree is cut and turned into a table. We gain the service of the table; we lose the service of the tree. In a relatively empty world (small economic subsystem, ecosystem relatively empty of human beings and their artifacts) the service lost from fewer trees was nil, and the service gained from more tables was significant. In today's relatively full world fewer trees mean loss of significant services, and more tables are not so important if most households already have several tables, as in much of the world they do. Of course continued population growth will keep the demand for tables up, and we will incur ever greater sacrifices of natural services by cutting more and more trees, as long as population keeps growing. The size or scale of the economic subsystem is best thought of as per capita consumption times population (which of course is the same as total consumption). The point is that there is both a cost and a benefit to increasing the scale of the subsystem (total consumption). The benefit is economic services gained (more tables); the cost is ecosystem services sacrificed (fewer trees to sequester CO_2, provide wildlife habitat, erosion control, local cooling, etc.). As scale increases, marginal costs tend to rise, marginal benefits tend to fall. Equality of marginal costs and benefits define the optimal scale, beyond which further growth in scale (total con- sumption) would be uneconomic.

As we come to an optimal, or mature scale, production is no longer for growth but for maintenance. A mature economy, like a mature ecosystem (Odum, 1969), shifts from a regime of growth efficiency (maximize P/B, or production per unit of biomass stock) to a regime of maintenance efficiency (maximize the reciprocal, B/P, or the amount of biomass stock maintained per unit of new production). Production is the maintenance cost of the stock and should be minimized. As Boulding (1945) argued almost fifty years ago,

> Any discovery which renders consumption less necessary to the pursuit of living is as much an economic gain as a discovery which improves our skills of production. Production—by which we mean the exact opposite of consumption, namely the creation of valuable things—is only necessary in order to replace the stock pile into which consumption continually gnaws.

IV. CONSUMPTION AND WELFARE

Welfare is the service of want satisfaction rendered by stocks of capital, both manmade and natural. The proper economic objective is to transform natural into manmade capital to the optimal extent—that is, to the point where total service (the sum of services from natural and manmade capital) is a maximum. As discussed in the previous section, this occurs where the marginal benefit of services of more manmade capital is just equal to the marginal cost of natural services sacrificed when the natural capital that had been yielding those services is transformed into manmade capital. The theoretical existence of an optimal scale of the economic subsystem is clear in principle. What remains vague are the measures of the value of services, especially of natural capital, but also of manmade capital. But if economic policy is anything it is the art of dialectically reasoning with vague quantities in the support of prudent actions. We can have reasons for believing that an optimum scale exists, and that we are either above it or below it, without knowing exactly where it is. For policy purposes a judgment about which side of the optimum we are on is what is critical. Reasons are offered below for believing that we (both the US and the world as a whole) have overshot the optimal scale—that is, that the marginal benefits of growth are less than commonly thought; that the marginal costs are greater than commonly thought; and that the marginal costs are for some countries greater than the marginal benefits.

Welfare is not a function of consumption flows, but of capital stocks. We cannot ride to town on the maintenance costs, the depletion and replacement flow of an automobile, but only in a complete automobile, a member of the current stock of automobiles. Once again Boulding (1949) got it right fifty years ago,

I shall argue that it is the capital stock from which we derive satisfactions, not from the additions to it (production) or the subtractions from it (consumption): that consumption, far from being a desideratum, is a deplorable property of the capital stock which necessitates the equally deplorable activities of production: and that the objective of economic policy should not be to maximize consumption or production, but rather to minimize it, i.e., to enable us to maintain our capital stock with as little consumption or production as possible.

This shift from maximizing production efficiency toward maximizing maintenance efficiency is the exact economic analog of the shift in ecosystems mentioned earlier, as they reach maturity—that is, from maximizing P/B to maximizing the reciprocal, B/P. As a mature scale is reached, production is seen more and more as a cost of maintaining what already exists rather than the source of additional services from added stock. The larger something has grown, the greater, ceteris paribus, are its maintenance costs. More new production, more throughput, is required just to keep the larger stock constant against the entropic ravages of rot, rust, and randomization.

Boulding's and Odum's insights can be expressed in a simple identity (see Daly, 1991 for discussion and elaboration):

$$\frac{\text{Service}}{\text{Throughput}} = \frac{\text{Service}}{\text{Stock}} \times \frac{\text{Stock}}{\text{Throughput}}$$

Stocks are at the center of analysis. On the one hand it is the stock that yields service; on the other it is the stock that is regrettably consumed and consequently requires maintenance by new production, which in turn requires new throughput and new sacrifices of natural capital with consequent reductions of the service of natural capital. We can define *growth* as increase in throughput, holding the two right-hand ratios constant. Service thus increases in proportion to throughput as a result of growth. *Development* can be defined as an increase in service from increases in the two right-hand efficiency ratios, holding throughput constant. "Economic growth," growth in GNP, is a conflation of these two processes: (1) growth (physical increase) and (2) development (qualitative improvements that allow more stock maintenance per unit of throughput, and more service per unit of stock). Since physical growth is limited by physical laws, while qualitative development is not, or at least not in the same way, it is imperative to separate these two very different things. Failure to make this distinction is what has made "sustainable development" so hard to define. With the distinction it is easy to define sustainable development as "development without growth—without growth in throughput beyond environmental regenerative and absorptive capacities."[6] So far the politicians and economists are so wedded to growth that they insist that economic growth is itself the main characteristic of sustainable development, albeit growth that is supposed to be more respectful of the environment (e.g., the President's Council on Sustainable Development).[7]

If we accept that it is the stock of capital that yields service (capital in Irving Fisher's sense, including the stock of consumer goods as well as producer goods), then we still must ask how much extra welfare do we get from extra manmade capital stock, say in the US at the present time? How much extra cost in terms of sacrificed service of natural capital is required by the transformation of natural capital into the extra manmade capital?[8]

Our empirical measures of the value of natural capital services (enjoyed or sacrificed) are virtually non-existent. Even the concept barely exists in standard economic theory because the natural functions of source and sink have been considered free goods, as was reasonable when the world was relatively empty. But now the world is relatively full. Also, contrary to what many think, we have only piecemeal measures of the value of services of manmade capital. Our national income accounts overwhelmingly measure throughput, not service of capital stock. Furthermore, the throughput is valued by market prices that are based on marginal utility and consequently omit consumer surplus, by far the larger part of welfare. Also, diminishing marginal utility is ignored—a dollar used to satisfy basic needs counts the same as a dollar used to satisfy velleities. Yet diminishing marginal utility is the keystone of economic theory. National income, when considered a measure of welfare, adds up the utilities of different people, which is not allowed in standard economic theory. National income ignores the value of leisure, of household work, of working conditions, of security . . . and so on. The point is that even if we were able to construct accounts for valuing natural capital services which were *as good as* our accounts for valuing manmade capital services, we still would not have accomplished much because the latter has itself only been done to a very limited extent. And it is universally acknowledged that it is much harder to evaluate natural capital than manmade capital.

The quest for empirical measures always requires some sacrifice of conceptual purity, but so many sacrifices have been made in standard national income accounting that the number no longer bears any relationship to welfare. Indeed, what is worse, welfare was not even the concept that the statisticians were, for the most part, aiming to approximate. Politicians made that interpretation after the fact, and economists acquiesced in it because it enhanced their political importance. It is better to reason via correct welfare-related concepts to the theoretical existence of an optimal scale, and then figure out by dead reckoning from the north star and familiar landmarks which side of the optimum we are on, than to rely on a compass whose needle we know is not magnetized.

What then are our commonsense, dead reckoning judgments about whether we are at, below, or above the optimal scale? I suggest we are beyond the optimal scale. To show that we have exceeded the optimum it is *not* necessary to show that growth is physically impossible, nor that it has catastrophic costs; nor that it would have negative or zero marginal benefit, even if free. It is only necessary to show that marginal costs are greater than marginal benefits. It is quite logical and reasonable to argue that on the whole, up to the present time, the total benefits of growth have been greater than the total costs, and yet to hold that growth should cease because at the margin costs have now begun to outweigh benefits. Economists, of all people, surely understand this! They apply this logic to the micro level every day. Why it suddenly becomes inapplicable at the macro level has never been explained.

What "dead reckoning judgments" can we make about the marginal benefits of growth in manmade capital? (Note that benefits from *development* are not in question, just those from *growth*.) For rich, full countries the marginal utility of extra growth is surely low. Great sums of money have to be spent on advertising to cajole people into buying more. As we have become goods-rich we have become time-poor. In rich countries people die more from stress and overconsumption than from starvation (Linder, 1970). Relative, rather than absolute, income seems to be the main determinant of self-evaluated welfare, and growth is powerless to increase everyone's relative income. The effect of aggregate growth on welfare in rich countries is largely self-canceling.

What about the poor? An increase in wealth up from subsistence to middle class comforts surely increases welfare, if all other things are equal. Should these high marginal utility uses by the poor be paid for by cutting low marginal utility luxury consumption of the rich, or by converting more natural capital into manmade capital? The rich favor the latter, and perhaps the poor do also because they want to emulate the rich, or because they doubt the political likelihood of redistribution or limits to the takeover of natural capital. Inequality is converted into pressure for growth.

The growth that often results from inequality does not go to the poor. Consider for a moment what, exactly, is growing in a growth economy. It is the reinvested surplus that grows in the first instance. Who controls the surplus? Not the poor. They get only the trickle down from growth, and their relative position is more likely to worsen than improve as a result of growth. This is especially so in light of the far more rapid rate of population growth of the poor than of the rich. A large and growing supply of labor will keep wages from ever rising, and thereby also keep profits up.

What are the marginal costs of further growth? How serious are the ecosystem services lost as a result of transformation of more natural into manmade capital? Here one can recite the by now familiar litany of CO_2 build-up, biodiversity loss, stratospheric ozone depletion, acid rain, topsoil depletion, aquifer depletion, chemical pollution—in sum an overall reduction of the capacity of the earth to support life. Loss of natural capital is not deducted from GNP (nor NNP). Only the value added in the process of transforming the natural capital into manmade capital is counted. A large part of our GNP is regrettably necessary defensive expenditure that we are forced to make to protect ourselves from the unwanted side effects of increasing production and consumption—for example health care from tobacco and alcohol consumption, chemical and radioactive poisoning, clean-up costs of oil spills, longer commuting times, and so on. This should be subtracted as an intermediate cost of the goods (or "anti-bads") whose production or consumption imposed these regrettably necessary activities—but instead we add them, and politicians, along with their academic magicians and media jesters, rejoice in the improvement.

Add to these considerations the corrosive effects of economic growth on community and on moral standards. Capital and labor mobility rip communities apart in the name of growth. Also, an economy that must grow must also sell. It is easier to sell in a community with low standards—if anything goes, then nearly anything will sell, no matter how tawdry or shoddy. Common prudence is now referred to negatively as "sales resistance." We have plenty of landmarks to suggest that the marginal costs of growth are very high. Even a dead reckoning comparison of the low marginal benefits with the high marginal costs should be enough to convince us that it is time to redirect our economy away from growth and toward development. As a north star, we may occasionally check our course by the principle that if we are reducing the capacity of earth to support life, then we are going the wrong way.

IV. POLICY IMPLICATIONS

A fundamental economic principle is to maximize the productivity of the limiting factor in the short run and to invest in its increase in the long run. If factors are good substitutes then neither factor can be limiting. But if they are complements, then the one in short supply is limiting. From the foregoing it is clear that the relationship between value added (labor and manmade capital) and that to which value is added, natural resources (the material flow produced by the stock of natural capital) is one of complementarity. Even if manmade and natural capital were good, but imperfect, substitutes the process of transforming the latter into the former would still reach an optimum extent. But if manmade and natural capital are complements that optimum extent will be reached much sooner and more dramatically, since the scarcity of the factor in shortest supply will limit the usefulness of the other more abundant factor. In the empty world economy of the past manmade capital was the limiting factor. In today's full-world economy it is remaining natural capital that is scarce and therefore limiting. The fish catch is limited, not by fishing boats, but by the remaining populations of fish in the sea. Cut timber is limited not by number of sawmills or lumberjacks, but by the remaining standing forests and our desire to preserve the non-timber services of forests (wildlife habitat, flood control, recreation, etc.).

As we move into an era in which natural capital is limiting, we need to economize on it more. That means its price must go up relative to manmade capital. But since much natural capital is common property, outside the market, and since the market itself is very short-sighted temporally, it is necessary to raise the price of natural capital by public policy. This can be done in a general way by shifting the tax base from value added (labor and capital are no longer limiting) on to that to which value is added (the natural resource flow yielded by natural capital). In short, tax throughput, not income. Income and employment are things we want more of, so we should stop taxing them. Depletion and pollution (throughput) are things we want less of, so we should tax them. We have to raise public revenue somehow, and nearly all taxes are "distortionary" relative to a perfect market. So why not tax ourselves in a way that induces "distortions" that correct other market imperfections instead of adding to them? In the interest of progressivity the income tax could be retained for very high incomes, along with a negative income tax for very low incomes. The shift could be revenue neutral and introduced gradually according to an announced schedule. The tax should take the form of a severance tax levied on basic resources, especially energy, at the wellhead or mine mouth. Also emissions taxes on pollutants and waste materials in general would be included. Resulting higher prices for throughput (for the regenerative and absorptive services of natural capital) would induce levels and patterns of consumption, and new technologies, that use resources more efficiently.

Consumption limits will be set by differing *national* policies—not by a single global policy. Nations can limit their total consumption by a strategy of low population and high per capita consumption; or by a strategy of high population and low per capita consumption. Different nations will make different choices. Some will not even limit aggregate consumption, and those that do will make different choices regarding per capita consumption vs number of "capitas." These differences cannot be maintained in a world of free trade, free capital mobility, and free (or uncontrolled) migration. Compensating tariffs will be necessary. National policies of controlling consumption and population, and of counting external costs, are more important than the tenuous gains from comparative advantage and free trade, which are currently celebrated beyond reason. This does not imply autarky, but it does throw cold water on global economic integration as an unquestioned good. "Globalization" ranks with "dematerialization"[9] as a false panacea—another germ of truth that has been allowed to grow into a whale of a fantasy in order to protect the dominant myth of our culture—that of an ever-growing economy.

V. SUMMARY AND CONCLUSIONS

Everyone accepts the idea that value is added to raw material by labor and capital. The issue is whether or not raw material must contain value previously added by nature, or can it be simply inert indestructible building blocks? Can humanly added value substitute for value added by nature? If the answer were yes, it should be possible, since matter-energy is not destroyed in consumption, to substitute the waste flow of matter-energy for the flow of fresh natural resources (raw materials). But this would contradict the second law of thermodynamics. The quality of low entropy is what differentiates raw material from waste, and we know of no process whose net effect is to lower the entropy of the total system on which we depend. The consequences of the two different views about value added are far-reaching.

1. Consider first the traditional view—we produce and consume only value added by labor and capital—production is arrangement of inert passive matter, consumption is disarrangement. Production and consumption are mechanical, reversible processes. To the extent that nature contributes anything beyond indestructible building blocks, it is easily substituted for by manmade capital and ingenuity (value added). So value added is everything, the sole source of value, if not actually in every case, at least potentially.
2. The view here advocated is that nature adds value to indestructible building blocks before they can be considered resources, and without which they are waste. We still add further value by labor and capital, but that to which value is being added is not passive, inert, building blocks, but highly structured raw materials and services of natural capital stocks. Consumption disarranges the order and structure imparted by nature (nature's value added) as well as that imparted by human labor and capital (traditional value added). Disordered, high-entropy matter and energy are returned to the environment as waste, some of which is reconstituted into resources by slow biogeochemical cycles.

What are the practical consequences of these different views for economic development?

a. The traditional value added view of income would lead one to reject the very notion of a "global pie" of income to be divided justly or unjustly among nations and people. There is no given pie—there are only a lot of separate tarts that some statistician has stupidly aggregated into an abstract pie (Kenneth Boulding's image). The separate tarts are the product of value added by the labor and capital of the nations that produced them, and nothing more. If nation A is asked to share some of its large tart with nation B who baked a small tart, the appeal should be made to nation A's generosity, and not to any notion of distributive justice, much less exploitation.

   If you believe that all value comes from labor and capital, and that nature contributes only a material substratum which is non-destructible and superabundant, and hence valueless, then this is a quite reasonable view. Are you poor? Well, just add more value by your own labor and capital. There are no limits from nature. Stop whining and get busy—and shut up about this imaginary pie. This view is common among neoclassical economists. And given its presuppositions it is not unreasonable. In fact it is a corollary to John Locke's justification of private property—to claim something as one's property requires that one has mixed one's labor with the materials of which it is made—that is, added value to it.

b. The alternative view that nature too adds value can also reject the imaginary global pie. But look carefully at the tarts different peoples have baked. Is the tart really only the product of the cook's labor and the kitchen's capital adding value to random, substitutable atoms? Certainly not. You need flour, and sugar, and butter, and apples. Before that you needed wheat, sugar cane, milk, and apple trees. And before that you need gene pools for wheat, sugar cane, cows, and apples, with some minimal degree of diversity, and soil whose fertility is maintained by all sorts of worms and microbes and minerals, and sunlight without too much ultraviolet, and rainfall that is not too acidic, and catchment areas to keep that rain from eroding topsoil, and predictable seasonal temperatures regulated by the mix of gasses in the atmosphere, and so on. In other words we need natural capital and the flow of resources and services that it renders—a whole lot more than indestructible building blocks! Our dowry of natural capital is more or less given, and is not the product of human labor and capital. Parts of that dowry are highly systemic and indivisible among nations and individuals. And the part that is divisible was divided by geologic, not economic, processes.

This distinction is why I want to shift attention from traditional value added to "that to which value is added." While one may argue that value added by labor and capital rightly belongs to the laborer and the capitalist (let them fight over how to divide it), one cannot distribute nature's value added so easily, especially the systemic life support services of natural capital. In this latter sense there really is a global pie, and the demands for justice regarding its division and stewardship cannot be subsumed under the traditional notion that value belongs to whomever added it.

To deal with this problem a North/South bargain will have to be struck in which the South gets very serious about limiting population growth, and the North gets very serious about limiting consumption growth. But the North will not get serious about limiting consumption as long as our economists and some philosophers trumpet the view that all wealth comes from value added, that we can only consume what we have produced. In this view growth in labor supply and capital stock simply means more value added in the next period, and is therefore welcome. We have to recognize that we can and do (and indeed must) consume a lot more value than we add, and that what we consume over and above conventional value added is value added by nature. To make matters worse, we even consume the very natural capital by which nature adds value to the indestructible building blocks. But at least we are consistent—if the flow of natural resources and services have no value, then neither does the stock of natural capital that yields these flows!

The policy implications are that we must economize on and invest in natural capital, because it has become the limiting factor (replacing manmade capital in that role) as we have moved from an empty world to a full world. To force ourselves to economize on natural capital we must raise its price above the market level. One concrete policy suggestion is that of ecological tax reform. Shift the tax base off income and employment (things we want more of), and on to the throughput flow that begins with depletion and ends with pollution (things we want less of). This at least puts a positive price on value added by nature and forces us to economize on its use.

If we refrain from consuming natural capital then the resulting sustainable flow of consumption will for some time be less than what we are currently used to. This will make more urgent: (1) sharing; (2) population control; (3) development in the qualitative sense of improving efficiency of resource use.

Economists who tell us not to worry because it is algebraically impossible for us to consume more value than we added have studied too much algebra and not enough biology and physics. Consumption; that is, the transformation of natural capital into manmade capital and then ultimately into waste, leads to the basic question of what is the optimal extent of this transformation. What is the optimal scale of the economic subsystem, the scale beyond which further conversion of natural into manmade capital costs us more (in terms of natural capital services lost) than it benefits us (in terms of manmade capital services gained). Growing beyond the optimum is by definition uneconomic. Currently growth is uneconomic, as indicated by our "dead reckoning" considerations about marginal costs and benefits of growth. The future path of progress therefore is not growth, but development—not an increase in throughput, but increases in the efficiency ratios (maintenance efficiency and service efficiency). Individual nations, not the globe, will control consumption by limiting both population and per capita consumption. Different national strategies for limiting consumption cannot coexist in an integrated world economy dominated by free trade, free capital mobility, and free migration. The use of tariffs and a general backing away from global integration toward relative self-sufficiency will be necessary.

The consumer society must pay attention to what Al Gore (1992, p. 220) said in his excellent, but too soon forgotten book, *Earth in the Balance*: "our civilization is, in effect, addicted to the consumption of the earth itself." We absolutely must break that addiction. Economists can help break the addiction by remembering and finally taking seriously what Kenneth Boulding (1949, p. 81) taught us fifty years ago: "Consumption is the death of capital, and the only valid arguments in favor of consumption are the arguments in favor of death itself."

NOTES

1. "Consumption and Welfare: Two Views of Value Added", *Review of Social Economy*, Vol. LIII, No. 4 (Winter 1995), pp. 451–73. This essay is dedicated to the memory of Kenneth Boulding (1910–93)—great economist, inspiring teacher, and generous friend.
2. We may have added the value consumed in the current year, or in the past. In the latter case, of course, this year's consumption can be greater than this year's value added because value added and saved in the past is being consumed this year—i.e., capital is being consumed.
3. This is discussed further in the article "How Long Can Neoclassical Economists Ignore the Contribution of Georgescu-Roegen?"
4. Differential rent would equalize the price of both oil sources if demand were sufficient for them to be used simultaneously. But if they are used sequentially, the differential rent is never charged against the earlier subsidy. The energy rate of return on investment in petroleum has been declining, so that the real subsidy to the economy has been declining, even while the contribution of higher priced petroleum to the GNP has been rising (see Gever et al., 1986; and Cleveland et al., 1984).
5. As geologist Earl Cook (1982, p. 194) wrote: "without the enormous amount of work done by nature in concentrating flows of energy and stocks of resources, human ingenuity would be onanistic. What does it matter that human ingenuity may be limitless, when matter and energy are governed by other rules than is information?"
6. This is the definition of a sustainable scale. Sustainability does not imply optimality— we may prefer another sustainable scale, one with more or less natural capital, but still sustainable. I think it would be reasonable to consider sustainability as a necessary but not sufficient condition of optimality. But in current economic theory sustainability is not implied by optimality—maximizing present value at positive discount rates implies

writing off the future beyond some point and liquidating it for the benefit of the present and near future.

7. Although Clinton and Gore won on a rather conventional growth platform, Al Gore's book, *Earth in the Balance*, shows a deep understanding of the problems with growth. From the other end of the political spectrum, a former member of the Reagan administration, Fred Charles Ikle (1994), has argued cogently against his fellow conservatives who consider growth the summum bonum.

8. Reasoning in terms of broad aggregates has its limitations. Converting natural into manmade capital embraces both the extravagant conversion of tropical hardwoods into toothpicks, and the frugal conversion of pine trees into shelters for the homeless. The point is not that all conversions of natural into manmade capital simultaneously cease being worthwhile, but rather that ever fewer remain worthwhile as growth continues.

9. As much as I dislike the term "dematerialization" I hasten to acknowledge that some people who use it mean by it nothing more than increased resource efficiency, and that excellent work has been done by people who use the term in this sense.

REFERENCES

Barnett, Harold and Chandler Morse (1963), *Scarcity and Growth*, Baltimore: Johns Hopkins University Press.

Boulding, Kenneth (1945), "The Consumption Concept in Economic Theory", *American Economic Review*, **35**(2) May, 1–14.

Boulding, Kenneth (1949), "Income or Welfare?", *Review of Economic Studies*, **17**, 77–86.

Cleveland, C., R. Costanza, C.A.S. Hall and R. Kaufmann (1984), "Energy and the US Economy: A Biophysical Perspective", *Science*, **225**, 890–97.

Cook, Earl (1982), "The Consumer as Creator: A Criticism of Faith in Limitless Ingenuity", *Energy Exploration and Exploitation*, **1**(3), 194.

Daly, H. (1991), *Steady-State Economics*, 2nd edn, Washington, DC: Island Press.

Daly, H. and J. Cobb (1994), *For the Common Good*, 2nd edn, Boston: Beacon Press.

Georgescu-Roegen, N. (1971), *The Entropy Law and the Economic Process*, Cambridge, MA: Harvard University Press.

Georgescu-Roegen, N. (1979), "Comments. . .", in V. Kerry Smith (ed.), *Scarcity and Growth Reconsidered*, Baltimore: RfF and Johns Hopkins Press.

Gever, J. et al. (1986), *Beyond Oil*, Cambridge, MA: Ballinger.

Gore, Al (1992), *Earth in the Balance*, Boston: Houghton Mifflin Co.

Ikle, Fred Charles (1994), "Growth Without End . . . Amen?", *National Review*, March 7, 36–44.

Linder, S. (1970), *The Harried Leisure Class*, New York: Columbia University Press.

Marshall, Alfred (1961) (originally 1920), *Principles of Economics*, 9th edn, New York: Macmillan.

Odum, E.P. (1969), "The Strategy of Ecosystem Development", *Science*, **164**(877), April 18, 262–70.

Science, September 14 (1991), p. 1206; *Science*, October 18 (1981), p. 358, Letter, "Ecological Economics".

Soddy, Frederick (1922), *Cartesian Economics* (The Bearing of Physical Science upon State Stewardship), London: Hendersons.

Thurow, Lester (1980), *The Zero-Sum Society*, New York: Penguin Books.

8. Ecological economics: the concept of scale and its relation to allocation, distribution, and uneconomic growth[1]

INTRODUCTION

My discussion is in five parts. First, I look at ecological economics from the outside by summarizing the views of some scholars from other disciplines who have recently taken an interest in ecological economics and compared it quite favorably to neoclassical economics. Second, a look at the main features and issues in ecological economics, noting differences and questions under debate with mainline neoclassical economics. Third, a look at the meanings of economic growth, and the specific issue of economic growth versus uneconomic growth in the scale of the physical economy. Fourth, some policy implications from ecological economics about avoiding uneconomic growth by seeking a steady-state economy at or near the optimum scale. Fifth, I consider some alternative formulations on why optimal allocation presupposes a given scale, as well as a given distribution.

I. ECOLOGICAL ECONOMICS AS VIEWED FROM THE OUTSIDE

Although neoclassical economists persist, by and large, in ignoring ecological economics, we have, nevertheless, recently received some very sympathetic attention from historians of the recent past. I cite three examples below.

1.   J.R. McNeill, *Something New Under the Sun* (An Environmental History of the Twentieth Century World), W.W. Norton, New York, 2000.

> The growth fetish, while on balance quite useful in a world with empty land, shoals of undisturbed fish, vast forests, and a robust ozone shield, helped create a more crowded and stressed one. Despite the disappearance of ecological buffers and mounting real costs, ideological lock-in reigned in both capitalist

and communist circles. No reputable sect among economists could account for depreciating natural assets. The true heretics, economists who challenged the fundamental goal of growth and sought to recognize value in ecosystem services, remained outside the pale to the end of the century [these heretics are explicitly identified by McNeill as ecological economists in his footnote 21]. Economic thought did not adjust to the changed conditions it helped to create; thereby it continued to legitimate, and indeed indirectly to cause, massive and rapid eco-logical change. The overarching priority of economic growth was easily the most important idea of the twentieth century. (p. 336)

2.   Peter Hay, *Main Currents in Western Environmental Thought*, Indiana University Press, Bloomington, IN, 2002. In his Chapter 8 on economic thought and the environment, Hay clearly distinguishes ecological eco-nomics from environmental economics, and devotes more space to dis-cussing the former, including the contributions of many individual ecological economists.

[Ecological economics] is problem-focused rather than concerned with abstract modeling, and, in contrast to conventional neo-classicism, ecological econom-ics shifts the focus from micro to macro and relevant time frames from the very short term to deep time. Ecological economics complements the relational and synergistic realities of ecology. It is, therefore, a holistic rather than a reduction-ist endeavor and gives due weight to process, change and flux, rather than stasis. Such an economics also incorporates an ethical and visionary dimension—nec-essary because grounding economic thought within a broader and prior context requires strictures of "ought" to govern contextual relationships. (p. 233)

3.   Robert L. Nadeau, *The Wealth of Nature* (How Mainstream Economics Has Failed the Environment), Columbia University Press, 2003.

What the ecological economists have to say about the inherent flaws of neoclas-sical economic theory from an ecological perspective is, as we shall see, quite dev-astating, and many of their proposed economic solutions to environmental problems are carefully reasoned, beautifully conceived, and utterly appropriate. But if this is the case, why is there virtually no dialogue between the ecological economists and the mainstream economists who sit at the right hand of global planners? (p. 10)

Why indeed?

4.   In addition to these historians, a professor of Law at Cornell University, Douglas A. Kysar, has recently given a fair hearing to ecological economics (see "Sustainability, Distribution, and the Macroeconomic Analysis of Law", *Boston College Law Review*, Vol. XLIII, No. 1, December, 2001, pp. 1–71; see also "Law, Environment, and Vision", *Northwestern University Law Review*, Vol. 97, No. 2, Winter 2003, pp. 675–729):

> This Article introduces the field of ecological economics and analyzes its potential use as a macroeconomics for legal analysis . . . As will be seen the implications could be quite broad. Traditionally legal economists have given little attention to macroeconomic subject matter. If the tenets of ecological economics are to be believed, this narrowness of focus may rest on unfounded assumptions about the nature of human economic activity and its relationship to the environment. Indeed, if the ecological economic understanding of this relationship is correct, the impact of legal rules on the macroeconomy could become an issue of central concern to legal scholars . . . Ecological economics offers this potential because it is built around a more complex understanding of human economic goals than traditional economic analysis. (p. 6, "Sustainability . . .")

Professor Kysar then proceeds to introduce ecological economics to legal scholars with a highly competent 50-page summary of its basic ideas. One certainly wishes him success in redirecting the attention of "law and economics" away from its founding fixation on microeconomics (Chicago-style), and toward macroeconomics (ecological economics-style)!

5.   Theologian Sallie McFague ("New House Rules: Christianity, Economics, and Planetary Living", *Daedalus*, fall 2001) argues that "a persuasive case can be made that there is an intrinsic connection between the ecological economic model and Christianity. Distributive justice and sustainability, as goals for planetary living, are pale reflections, but reflections nonetheless, of what Jesus meant by the kingdom of God." However, "presently Christianity is supporting the neoclassical economic paradigm to the degree that it does not speak against it and side publicly with the ecological view." The main problem with neoclassical economics, she argues, is that "distributive justice to the world's inhabitants and the optimal scale of the human economy within the planet's economy—are considered 'externalities' by neoclassical economics. In other words, the issues of who benefits from an economic system and whether the planet can bear the system's burden are not part of neoclassical economics." Therefore it is hard to consider neoclassical economics as even a pale reflection of the Kingdom of God. Ecological economics at least offers a better set of "house rules" for the human and biospheric community.

6.   Economist and media expert Robert E. Babe (*Culture of Ecology: Reconciling Economics and Environment*, University of Toronto Press, 2006) writes that,

> ecological economics . . . is clearly distinguished from environmental economics through its holism, its insistence that the human economy is a subset of a finite and non growing ecosystem, its refusal to consider price strategies as adequate to resolve environmental issues, its penchant for proposing that human

economies conform to ecosystem principles, its consideration and incorporation of entropy into its analysis, and its understanding that events are not reversible. An evolving ecological economics will be an important component of a culture of ecology. (p. 140)

Since these scholars are more disinterested observers of ecological economics than are mainstream economists, I think we are justified in taking some satisfaction in their relatively favorable evaluation of our work, even if they, like us, may not be representative of the majority of their disciplines. Occasionally it is good to try to see ourselves as others see us. While it remains true that a small fraction of all economists agree with ecological economics, we must remember that the large denominator mainly responsible for the smallness of this fraction contains many economists who have never given a moment's thought to the issues that have called ecological economics into being. If we eliminate them from the denominator as irrelevant then the fraction is not nearly so small!

II. ECOLOGICAL ECONOMICS IN GENERAL AND COMPARED TO NEOCLASSICAL ECONOMICS

Ecological economics is mainly about three issues: allocation of resources, distribution of income, and scale of the economy relative to the ecosystem—especially the third. A good allocation of resources is *efficient* (Pareto optimal); a good distribution of income or wealth is *just* (a limited range of acceptable inequality); a good scale does not generate "bads" faster than goods, and is also ecologically *sustainable* (it could last a long time, although nothing is forever).

Allocation and distribution are familiar concepts from standard economics—for any given distribution of income there is a different optimal efficient allocation of resources with its corresponding optimal set of prices. A Pareto optimal allocation is one in which it is impossible to reallocate resources in a way that makes someone better off without making someone else worse off—a very minimalist definition of efficiency. Standard economics focuses primarily on the allocation issue, but pays secondary attention to distribution, first because a given distribution is logically necessary for defining efficient allocation, and second because distributive justice is important in its own right. It is fair to say, however, that ecological economists consider the issue of distributive justice more pressing than do most neoclassical economists.

The third issue of "scale," by which is meant the *physical* size of the economy relative to the containing ecosystem, is not recognized in standard economics, and has therefore become the differentiating focus of ecological economics.

Ecological economists' pre-analytic vision of the economy as an open subsystem of a larger ecosystem that is finite, non-growing, and materially closed (though open with respect to solar energy), immediately suggests several analytical questions regarding scale: How large *is* the economic subsystem relative to the earth's ecosystem? How large *could* it be; that is, what is its maximum scale? And most importantly, How large *should* the subsystem be relative to the ecosystem? Is there an optimal scale (less than the biophysical maximum) beyond which physical growth of the economic subsystem (even if possible) begins to cost more at the margin than it is worth, in terms of human welfare? You will not find these questions in standard economics textbooks.

If the economy grew into the Void it would encroach on nothing, and its growth would have no opportunity cost. But, since the economy in fact grows into and encroaches upon the finite and non-growing ecosystem, there *is* an opportunity cost to growth in scale, as well as a benefit. The costs arise from the fact that the physical economy, like an animal, is a "dissipative structure" sustained by a metabolic flow from and back to the environment. This flow, called "throughput," begins with the depletion of low-entropy, useful resources from the environment and ends with the return of high-entropy polluting wastes. Depletion and pollution are costs—"bads" rather than goods. Not only does the growing economy encroach spatially and quantitatively on the ecosystem, it also qualitatively degrades the environmental sources and sinks of the metabolic throughput by which it is maintained.[2]

The scale of the economy has two measures: (1) the throughput flow of physical resources that constitute the material component of the annual flow of goods and bads, and (2) the accumulated stock of goods in the form of wealth, and of bads in the form of "illth" (to employ a useful word coined by John Ruskin to designate the opposite of wealth). The throughput flow measure is emphasized because it is what affects ecosystem sources (depletion) and sinks (pollution) at the margin.

We would of course prefer not to produce bads or allow them to accumulate in illth, but since we live in a finite world governed by the laws of thermodynamics, and since we and the artifacts we produce are dissipative structures, we cannot avoid producing bads along with goods. If we stop depleting, we and our economy die of starvation; if we stop polluting, we die of constipation. If, however, we keep the throughput within the natural capacity of the ecosystem to absorb wastes and regenerate depleted resources, then the scale of the economy is ecologically "sustainable." There are many sustainable scales. The particular sustainable scale that maximizes the difference between wealth and illth (i.e., equates marginal goods produced with marginal bads), is the optimal scale. If we grow beyond this point then growth becomes uneconomic, and GNP becomes, in Ruskin's terms, "a gilded index of far-reaching ruin."

As growth pushes us from an empty world to a full world the limiting factor in production will increasingly become natural capital, not manmade capital—for example, the fish catch today is no longer limited by manmade capital of fishing boats, but by the complementary natural capital of fish populations in the sea; irrigated agriculture is limited not by the manmade capital of pumps and pipes, but by the natural capital of aquifers and rivers, and so on. As we move from the empty world into a full world, economic logic remains the same, namely to economize on and invest in the limiting factor. But the identity of the limiting factor changes from manmade capital to remaining natural capital, and our economizing efforts and policies must change accordingly. Therefore it becomes more important to study the nature of natural capital, of environmental goods and services—are they rival or non-rival, excludable or non-excludable—in order to know the extent to which they can be allocated by markets.

Ecological economics has no quarrel with the standard analysis of allocative efficiency, given prior social determination of the distribution and scale questions. Although the main difference has been the focus on scale, that difference has entailed more attention to distribution, especially to two often neglected dimensions of distribution: namely intergenerational distribution of the resource base, and distribution of places in the sun between humans and all other species (biodiversity). Also as more vital natural resources and services cease being free goods, and are allocated by the market whenever possible, the fairness of the assumed distribution underlying efficient market allocation becomes more critical.

One question sure to be asked is: What is the relation between ecological economics and the fields of resource economics and environmental economics? The difference is that the latter two are both subfields of neoclassical economics, do not consider scale an issue, have no concept of throughput, and are focused on efficiency of allocation. Resource economics deals with the efficiency of allocation of labor and capital devoted to extractive industries. It develops many useful concepts, such as scarcity rent, user cost, and Hotelling's rule. Likewise, environmental economics also focuses on efficiency of allocation and how it is disrupted by pollution externalities. Concepts of internalizing externalities by Pigouvian taxes or Coasian property rights are certainly useful and policy-relevant, but their aim is allocative efficiency via right prices, not sustainable scale. Ecological economics connects resource and environmental economics by connecting depletion with pollution by the concept of throughput.[3] It also pays much more attention to impacts on, and feedbacks from, the rest of the ecosystem induced by economic activities that cause depletion, pollution and entropic degradation, chief among which is the growing scale of the human economy.

Within this overall context of a difference in basic vision, there are in addition some specific issues of debate between ecological and neoclassical economists. Below I list seven important ones.

1. *Whether natural and manmade capital are primarily substitutes or complements*. Ecological economics sees them as basically complements, substitutable only over a very limited margin. Neoclassical economics regards them as overwhelmingly substitutes. If complements, the one in short supply is limiting; if substitutes, there is no limiting factor. The phenomenon of limiting factor greatly increases the force of scarcity. For example, the scarcity of fish in the sea reduces the value of complementary capital of fishing boats.

2. *The degree of coupling between physical throughput and GNP*. Ecological economics sees this coupling as by no means fixed, but not nearly as flexible as neoclassicals believe it to be—in other words, the "dematerialization" of GNP and the "information economy" will not save growth economics by forever reducing material intensity of GNP. We can certainly eat lower on the food chain, but we cannot eat recipes! While throughput per dollar of GDP has recently declined somewhat in some OECD countries, the absolute level of throughput continues to increase as GDP increases.

3. *The degree of coupling between GNP and welfare*. Here ecological economists consider the coupling very loose, at least beyond some minimum amount. Since many non-economic sources of welfare are damaged by growth in GNP, yet are not subtracted from GNP, the gap between welfare and GNP widens as we move from the empty world to the full world. Neoclassical economists invariably advocate policies based on the assumption that welfare increase is rigidly coupled to GNP growth, even though in theory they allow themselves a few doubts. *In sum, ecological economists see GNP as tightly coupled to throughput and loosely coupled to welfare, while neoclassicals believe that GNP is only loosely coupled to throughput but tightly coupled to welfare.* There is clearly room for empirical work here!

4. A deeper philosophical issue is the *relative importance in production of "value added" versus "that to which value is added."* Value is added *to* the throughput flow of natural resources, and it is added *by* the transforming services of labor and capital. In Aristotle's terms labor and capital are the *efficient cause* of production (transforming agent), while

natural resources are the *material* cause (that which is transformed). Neoclassical economists evidently do not believe in material causation because their production functions usually say that output is a function only of labor and capital inputs—a recipe that includes the cook and her kitchen, but no list of ingredients. When they occasionally do include resources as an input in the production function, they almost always do it in a way that contradicts the first law of thermodynamics.[4]

This error is repeated with admirable logical consistency in national income accounting where GNP is defined as the sum of all value added by labor and capital. *No valuable contribution from nature is recognized.* Natural resources in the ground are of zero value. When extracted they are valued by the marginal cost of capital and labor needed to extract them. Yes, there are royalties paid to resource owners, and that seems like a price for resources in the ground, but royalties are determined by savings on labor and capital costs of extraction whenever the owner's mine or well is richer or more accessible than the marginal mine or well. Resources are considered a free gift of nature, but some free gifts are easier to unwrap than others, and earn a rent determined by their relative ease of "unwrapping" or extraction, as measured by labor and capital costs saved. Labor and capital remain the source of all value, nothing is attributed to nature.

Ecological economics recognizes that it is a lot easier to add value to low-entropy natural resources than to high-entropy waste, and that this extra receptivity to the addition of value by labor and capital should count as "nature's value added." Low-entropy matter/energy is our ultimate means without which we cannot satisfy any of our ends, including that of staying alive. We cannot produce low entropy in net terms, but only use it up as it is supplied by nature. It is scarce and becoming more so. To omit this necessary contribution from nature both from our theory of production and from our accounting of value is a monumental error.

5. Growth has been treated as a macroeconomic issue, and frequently justified in terms of *GNP accounting*. If macro policies are designed to promote growth in GNP, then *ex post* accounting issues become relevant to *ex ante* policy in the next time period. Ecological economists have argued that whole categories being measured in GNP are mistakenly conceived, even if the prices by which the value of the category is measured are correct. I consider three such category mistakes in GNP accounting in the next section.

6. Although ecological economics focuses on the physical or real economy, *monetary issues* are also relevant. Under our current fractional reserve banking system, favored by the neoclassical mainstream,

the money supply is a by-product of private commercial activities of lending and borrowing, rather than a public utility for effecting exchange. Over 95 percent of our money supply is created by the private banking system (demand deposits) and bears interest as a condition of its existence. Unless loans are repaid at interest and renewed, the money supply will shrink and transactions will be more difficult. Fractional reserve money is therefore not neutral with respect to the scale of the physical economy—it requires growth of GDP to keep the money supply from declining. And GDP growth correlates positively with throughput growth. Furthermore the seigniorage (profit to the issuer of fiat money) now goes largely to the private sector (banks and their customers), rather than to the public sector, the government, the legitimate supplier of the public utility of money. A public good has been subjected to "enclosure"—converted to a private good—just like the common pastures of England. Ecological economists also welcome the local reclaiming of money as a public utility by the various supplementary local currency movements. Local currencies allow people, especially in depressed areas, to make local exchanges (to employ each other) without first having to compete or be employed in the national economy just to get the money that allows them to avoid the enormous inconvenience of even local barter. Also seigniorage from local money can be used to finance local public goods.

7. Ecological economists' preference for the local is also expressed by its advocacy of internationalization and opposition to the globalization so favored by neoclassicals. *Internationalization* refers to the increasing importance of relations between nations: international trade, international treaties, alliances, protocols, and so on. The basic unit of community and policy remains the nation, even as relations among nations, and among individuals in different nations, become increasingly necessary and important. *Globalization* refers to global economic integration of many formerly national economies into one global economy, by free trade, especially by free capital mobility, and also, as a distant but increasingly important third, by easy or uncontrolled migration. Globalization is the effective erasure of national boundaries for economic purposes. As nations encounter limits to the scale of their national economies they seek to grow into the global commons, and into the ecological space of other nations. Global integration is an attempt by all economies to expand their national scale simultaneously. Global boundaries are of course not erased, and the result is that all countries now integrated will hit the limits to growth more simultaneously and less sequentially than before, with less opportunity to learn from the experience of others.

There are other issues, of course, but these seven illustrate the range and importance of the differences, and provide a research agenda for at least several years.

III. ECONOMIC GROWTH AND UNECONOMIC GROWTH

Economic growth is the major goal of most countries today. But what exactly do we mean by economic growth? Usually growth in GNP. But is economic growth so measured a holy icon of the *summum bonum*, or a statistically graven image of Mammon? It can be either—because there are two very different meanings of economic growth in common usage, often confused, and certainly conflated in the measure of GNP:

1. "Economic growth" in sense (1) is simply the expansion of what we call "the economy," i.e., production and consumption of goods and services. The economy is basically the human niche within the ecosystem, what we have called its scale. It is measured either by the stock of people and their artifacts, or by the flow of resources necessary to maintain and add to this stock. That, in physical terms, is the economy. When it gets bigger in scale we have growth of the economy, and refer to it in quite normal English usage as "economic growth."
2. "Economic growth" in sense (2) is any change in the economy for which extra benefits are greater than extra costs. Benefits and costs are not physical concepts, but refer to psychic experiences of increased or decreased welfare or enjoyment of life. The changes in the economy that cause changes in costs and benefits may themselves be either physical or non-physical. Whatever profits us, whatever yields net benefits, is "economic growth." In public discourse we shift easily from one meaning of "economic growth" to the other, and thereby introduce a lot of confusion. Quantitative increase in size and qualitative improvement in well-being are very different things, and should not be lumped together, as done in calculating GNP.

As discussed earlier, there are *three* economic problems (allocation, distribution, and scale), not just one (allocation). Let us consider each in its relation to the two meanings of economic growth.

Economic growth as physical expansion of the economy (sense 1) clearly refers to the third problem (scale). Economic growth occurs when the economy gets physically larger, as measured either in its stock or its flow dimensions. Since the economy grows into the rest of the finite ecosystem, not into the infinite Void, the economy becomes larger not only absolutely, but relative to its enveloping ecosystem. That is what is meant by scale increase, the first of the two common senses of "economic growth." The second sense of "economic growth"—an increase in net benefit—may or may not result from growth in the first sense. More on that later.

Net benefit can result from an improvement in allocative efficiency— redirecting the same scale of resource use from low-value uses to high-value uses—this is economic growth in sense (2), but not in sense (1). Ecological economists have no problem with this kind of growth. But GNP does *not* distinguish growth based on greater allocative efficiency from growth based on larger scale.[5]

Let us turn now from scale and allocation to distribution—what is the relation of distribution to economic growth? Redistribution does not involve growth in sense (1)—scale stays the same. But does it involve economic growth in sense (2)—an improvement in net benefit? It does not involve a Pareto improvement because someone is made worse off in any redistribution, so neoclassical economists would disallow redistribution as a source of net social benefit.

But Vilfredo Pareto was not God, and many people, including some economists, think it perfectly reasonable to say that a dollar redistributed from the low marginal utility uses of the rich to the high marginal utility uses of the poor increases total social utility—that is, signals an increase in net social benefit (economic growth in sense (2)).

The conclusion is inescapable if we assume the law of diminishing marginal utility, and the democratic principle that everyone's utility counts equally. Carried to its extreme this argument implies complete equality in the distribution of income, which is why many economists backed off from it. But principles need not be carried to extremes. For that matter, the Pareto principle has its own extreme—one person could have all the surplus and everyone else live at subsistence (or die for that matter!), and there would still be no case for arguing that redistribution would increase net social benefit. Within limits, therefore it is reasonable to say that redistribution can give us economic growth in sense (2), but not in sense (1)—another reason why ecological economists pay more attention to distribution than do neoclassicals.

Does economic growth in sense (1) (scale) imply economic growth in sense (2) (net benefit)? No, absolutely not! Growth in the economy, sense (1) (expansion), *can be* economic growth in sense (2) (net benefit), but does not have to be. It can be, and in some countries probably already is, "*uneconomic growth*"—physical expansion that increases costs by more than benefits, thus reducing net benefit. Or, to recall John Ruskin's more colorful language, the economy becomes a net producer of "illth," not wealth, and GNP would become, in Ruskin's terms, "a gilded index of far-reaching ruin." I think this is more than a logical possibility—it is a reasonable characterization of the actual state of affairs in some countries.

One will surely ask: What makes you think that growth has become uneconomic, say in the US? Some empirical evidence is referenced below,[6] but an equally fair question is to ask what makes economists think that benefits of growth are greater than costs at the current margin? GNP measures only benefits and not costs. Moreover GNP accounting commits several category mistakes—mistakes that count as benefits what are in fact costs. Three examples are discussed below.

Regrettably necessary defensive expenditures are what national income accountants call those expenditures we make to defend ourselves from the unwanted side effects of production and consumption by others. To escape the congestion and pollution of the city one buys another car and more gasoline to commute from the suburbs. This is a voluntary expenditure, but regrettable. Alternatively, one can remain in the city and regrettably spend more on soundproof windows, security services, and air filters. Regrettably necessary defensive expenditures are more coerced than voluntary, even though they are, strictly speaking, voluntary in the sense that no one had a gun at your head. Some reject such a distinction, arguing that all expenditure is defensive—food defends us against hunger, clothes defend us against cold, and so on. True, but hunger and cold are not the consequences of other people's production and consumption—they are natural background default conditions. Defensive expenditures are *"anti-bads"* rather than goods. They counteract or neutralize the negative effects of other production. They *should be* counted as a cost of production of the activity that made them necessary, thereby increasing the price and reducing the amount purchased of that activity, and reducing scale. Instead we count them as purely voluntary purchases and *add* them to GDP. This may be economic growth in sense (1) (expansion), but not in sense (2) (net benefit).

Monetization of previously non-monetized production. A young colleague told me that he and his wife must make more money so that they can pay the woman who looks after their children enough to enable her to pay someone to look after her children while she is caring for theirs, and so on. Childcare, housekeeping, cooking, and other household production used to be non-monetized. Now they have largely been shifted to the monetary sector and thus counted in GDP. Simply counting what was previously uncounted, even though it existed, is likely not to be economic growth in either sense (1) or (2).

Counting consumption of capital as income. Running down stocks of natural capital reduces future capacity to produce, even while increasing current consumption. Depleting non-renewables is like running down an inventory without replacing it; consuming renewable stocks beyond sustainable yield is like failing to maintain and replace depreciating machinery. The same applies to failure to maintain social overhead capital such as roads, bridges, and so on. Some would consider the costs of dishonesty, whether Enron or local robbery, as the cost of having allowed the depletion of traditional social standards of honesty, or "moral capital." Mis-counting capital consumption as income increases economic growth in sense (1), but not in sense (2), at least in the long term.

The above cases are examples of uneconomic growth in GNP even with correct prices—they involve accounting category mistakes[7] rather than measurement errors—counting intermediate as final production, counting traditional but newly monetized production as if it were new production, and treating capital drawdown as if it were income. Each of these categories may be priced correctly, but the categories are misused. A job not worth doing is not worth doing well.

More convincing to me than empirical measures, which I along with others have attempted, is the simple theoretical argument that as the scale of the human subsystem (the economy) expands relative to the fixed dimensions of the containing and sustaining ecosystem, we necessarily encroach upon that system and must pay the opportunity cost of lost ecosystem services as we enjoy the extra benefit of increased human scale.

As rational beings we presumably satisfy our most pressing wants first, so that each increase in scale yields a diminishing marginal benefit. Likewise, we presumably would sequence our takeovers of the ecosystem so as to sacrifice first the *least* important natural services. Obviously we have not yet begun to do this because we are just now recognizing that natural services are scarce. But let me credit us with capacity to learn. Even so, that means that increasing marginal costs and decreasing marginal benefits will accompany growth in human scale. At some point increasing marginal cost will equal declining marginal benefit. That is the optimum scale. Beyond that point growth becomes uneconomic in sense (2)—the economy becomes a net producer of a current flow of bads and an accumulating stock of illth.

If we add to the limits of finitude and non-growth of the total system the additional limits of entropy and ecosystem complexity, then it is clear that the optimal scale will be encountered sooner rather than later. Additionally, if we expand our anthropocentric view of the optimum scale to a more biocentric view, by which I mean one that attributes not only instrumental but also some degree of intrinsic value to other species, then it is clear that the optimal scale of the human presence will be further limited by the duty to reserve a place in the sun for other species, even beyond what they "pay for" in terms of their instrumental value to us. "Biodiversity" is an empty slogan unless we are willing to limit human scale. And of course the whole idea of "sustainability" is that the optimal scale should exist for a very long time, not just a few generations. Clearly a sustainable scale will be smaller than an unsustainable scale. For all these reasons I think that, for policy purposes, we do not really need exact empirical measures of the optimal scale.

Consider a thought experiment. Imagine an economy in which all prices were right—at the initial scale of the economy air and water are free goods so their right price is zero. Now suppose scale increases—population and per capita resource use both triple, so scale goes up nine-fold (roughly what has happened in my lifetime). Now air and water are scarce, so their right prices are no longer zero, but positive numbers, which are, let us assume, accurately set. In both cases right prices give us a Pareto optimal allocation and the neoclassical economist is happy. But are people indifferent between the two cases? Should they be? Some will agree with John Stuart Mill (1857, p. 325) that:

> It is not good for a man to be kept perforce at all times in the presence of his species . . . Nor is their much satisfaction in contemplating a world with nothing left to the spontaneous activity of nature; with every rood of land brought into cultivation . . . every flowery waste or natural pasture plowed up, all quadrupeds or birds which are not domesticated for man's use exterminated as his rivals for food, and every hedgerow or superfluous tree rooted out, and scarcely a place left where a wild shrub or flower could grow without being eradicated as a weed in the name of improved agriculture.

To bring Mill up to date we need only extend the predicament of the wildflower to the traditional agricultural crops that replaced it. These crops are now in danger of being eradicated by their genetically engineered cousins, designed to grow faster and be more resistant to both pests and pesticides.

The difference between Mill's view and that of his opposites, such as Julian Simon and Peter Huber, runs deep. Some will consider Mill old fashioned and agree with Huber, who says:

> Cut down the last redwood for chopsticks, harpoon the last blue whale for sushi, and the additional mouths fed will nourish additional human brains, which will soon invent ways to replace blubber with olestra and pine with plastic. Humanity can survive just fine in a planet-covering crypt of concrete and computers . . . There is not the slightest scientific reason to suppose that such a world must collapse under its own weight or that it will be any less stable than the one we now inhabit.[8]

Huber does admit that such a world might not be as pretty, but it is clear that on balance he likes it better than Mill's world.

Neither side will be comforted by the neoclasssical economist pointing out that in both cases right prices will give us a Pareto optimal allocation. Some will want a larger scale, some a smaller—but it seems that only the neoclassical economist is indifferent.

Some say that it is idle to talk about maintaining a steady state at some limited scale unless we first know the optimal scale at which to be stable. On the contrary, unless we first know how to be stable, it is idle to know the optimal scale. Such knowledge would only enable us to recognize and wave goodbye to the optimal scale as we grew through it! If one jumps from an airplane one needs a parachute more than an altimeter.

IV.   TOWARD POLICY

So let us begin to search for some parachutes to arrest the free-fall of growth in scale.

We measure growth of the macroeconomy by GNP. Does that measure reflect economic growth in sense (1) (scale) or in sense (2) (net benefit)? As we have seen it conflates the two. But by historical design and intention it mainly reflects sense (1), growth in the physical scale of aggregate production. However, economists soon began to treat GNP also as a measure of growth in sense (2), any change yielding net benefits. They reasoned that for something to count in GNP, someone had to buy it, and consequently that person must have judged that the item benefited her more than it cost her, so its production must represent economic growth in sense (2) as well as in sense (1). Consequently, for most economists the concept of "*un*economic growth in GNP" makes no sense. There is no separate problem of scale. The free market is thought to optimize scale and allocation simultaneously.[9] Presumably you could temporarily have uneconomic growth in the scale of the economy (sense (1)), but if it were truly uneconomic growth (sense (2)), it would cost people more than it was worth and they would learn not to buy it, and therefore it would not be counted in GNP, and whoever was making it would go out of business, and scale would decline.

This individualistic, consumer-sovereign judgment of costs and benefits has its obvious strengths, but also some less obvious weaknesses. It assumes that *individual* costs and benefits coincide with *social* costs and benefits—in other words that the prices faced by the consumer are a good measure of opportunity cost, not just to the individual consumer, but to society as a whole. However, our economy has a bias toward privatizing or internalizing benefits and socializing or externalizing costs, in the interest of maximizing private profits, thus driving a wedge between private and social.

Collecting and selling poisonous mushrooms no doubt has greater social costs than benefits. But if the costs fall on the public who cannot distinguish poisonous from non-poisonous varieties, while the benefits all accrue to me, then I will find the activity privately profitable. Frequently the prices individuals pay are an underestimate of full social opportunity cost, so it is true that much stuff is purchased only because the prices are wrong—too low. Therefore some growth in GNP is uneconomic due to wrong prices. The economists' answer is admirably straightforward—get the prices right! I certainly agree. But note that getting prices right does not mean that GDP can grow forever—it means that growth as measured by GDP based on right prices would presumably have stopped sooner, when it became uneconomic—when it began to cost more than it was worth as measured by corrected prices—when the price of my poisonous mushrooms was high enough to pay wrongful death claims to my customers' survivors. By then I would be out of business. Right prices are all to the good. However, whether right prices are by themselves *sufficient* to avoid uneconomic growth requires further consideration.

Indifference to scale is only one neoclassical reaction. Somewhat contradictorily neoclassical economists frequently argue that scale will automatically be optimized along with allocation. The first view, indifference to scale, is logically consistent with neoclassical theory, but inconsistent with the facts (people are not indifferent to scale). The second view, that scale is automatically solved along with allocation, is either logically inconsistent or requires absurd premises to be consistent.

Regarding the second view, it is inconsistent for neoclassicals to claim that the same set of prices that optimizes allocation would also optimize scale. That would sin against the mathematical condition that we cannot maximize simultaneously for two independent variables, as well as against Jan Tinbergen's policy rule that for every independent policy goal we need a separate policy instrument. If we use relative prices to solve the allocation problem, we cannot simultaneously use prices to solve the scale problem (or the distribution problem).

The only way out of this logical difficulty, and a way taken by some economists, is to claim that the allocation and scale problems are not independent, but merely the same problem. The way to reduce scale to allocation is to assume that scale is total. Everything is economy, nothing is environment. Everything in creation, every whale and every amoeba, is conceptually yoked to pull the human wagon, and their services are allocated according to pecuniary calculation of present value maximization. The scale of the economy would not be a separate issue because there is nothing that is external to the economy. This is the result of carrying the principle of internalization of costs and benefits to its extreme. When everything is internalized, then nothing is external, the scale of the economy is 100 percent by definition.

One of the saving graces of neoclassical economists has been their humility when faced with the information requirements of a centrally planned economy. The information requirements of "centrally planning" the entire biosphere, even with liberal use of markets, is so utopian that honest neo-classicals will blush at the very thought.

Given prior social decisions on scale and distribution, the market can, as always, determine allocatively efficient prices. Indirectly these prices would then reflect socially imposed scale and distributive limits and therefore may be thought of as, in a sense, "internalizing" the values of sustainability and justice that have been previously decided politically, independently of prices.

Another way to make the point is to distinguish *price-determining* from *price-determined* policy actions. Allocation is price-determined. Distribution and scale are, or should be, price-determining. What then determines distribution and scale? Social values of justice and of sustainability. Once these social values are reflected in constraints on the market, then the allocative prices calculated by the market will reflect, and in a sense "internalize" these external constraints. We cannot use these corrected allocative prices to calculate the cost and benefit of a change in scale or distribution, because we first had to set the distribution and scale to get the corrected allocative prices.

The way to get prices to reflect the values of just distribution and sustainable scale is to impose quantitative restrictions on the market that limit the degree of inequality in distribution of income and wealth to a just range; and that limit the scale of physical throughput from and back to nature to a sustainable volume. These imposed macro scale limits reflect the social values of justice and sustainability, which are not personal tastes and cannot be reflected in the market by individualistic actions. The market can, however, recalculate allocative prices that are consistent with the *imposed* scale and distribution constraints, thereby in a sense "internalizing" these social values into prices. Scale and distribution limits are our "parachutes." Allocative prices are more like an altimeter.

Finally it is worth emphasizing a general policy consequence of these considerations: namely, "frugality first, efficiency second." By frugality I mean limiting scale by limiting quantity of throughput. Limited throughput will drive up resource prices (the rents can be captured as public revenue and used to finance the reduction of other taxes). Higher resource prices will induce greater efficiency. If on the other hand we continue to follow the usual policy of "efficiency first" we do not induce frugality as a secondary consequence. Instead, efficiency improvements make frugality less necessary. A more efficient car is equivalent to discovering more oil. It will have the same consequence, namely reducing the price of oil. That will induce more use of oil than before. True, the oil will be burned more efficiently, but more will be used. We will have become more efficient and less frugal. We must become *more* frugal. If we seek frugality first by limiting scale, we will get efficiency as a bonus.

Standard economics strains out the gnat of allocative inefficiency while swallowing the twin camels of unjust distribution and unsustainable scale. As distribution becomes more unjust big money buys political power and uses it to avoid any redistribution. A favorite political ploy for avoiding redistribution is to emphasize economic growth. Growth in sense (1) leads to an unsustainable scale and uneconomic growth in sense (2). But if growth is uneconomic then it makes us poorer, not richer. Growth is then no longer the cure for poverty and cannot substitute for redistribution. Consequently, the concepts of uneconomic growth, accumulating illth, and unsustainable scale have to be incorporated in economic theory if it is to be capable of expressing what is happening in the world. This is what ecological economists are trying to do.

V. SOME ADDITIONAL THOUGHTS AND ALTERNATIVE FORMULATIONS

Ecological economics claims that sustainable scale and fair distribution are both problems whose solutions are logically prior to determining efficient allocation. Scale determines what is scarce and what is free. Distribution determines who owns what is scarce. Only after these two issues have been determined is the market able to effect exchanges, determine prices, and allocate resources efficiently. Economists have long accepted that an optimal allocation of resources (Pareto optimum), with its resulting set of prices, requires a given distribution of income. In other words, there is a different Pareto optimal allocation for each possible distribution of income. Efficiency is only defined with reference to a given distribution of income. This point is not in dispute.

But does a Pareto optimal allocation assume a given scale as well as a given distribution? That is a disputed question—ecological economists say yes; neoclassical economists seem to say no—to the limited extent they have thought about it in view of their traditional neglect of scale. As discussed, it would seem very inconsistent for neoclassicals to claim that the same set of prices that optimizes allocation would also optimize scale.

And there are further problems. If we take the concept of scale literally, as in the scale model of a house, to mean a proportional change in all linear (scalar) dimensions, then we might say that a scale change is simply an increase or decrease in which all proportions remain constant. All *relative* quantities would also remain constant. But even so an increased scale would change relative scarcities because the marginal utilities of different goods decline at different rates.[10] Nevertheless, as long as the proportions are right the absolute size doesn't matter. This seems to be what standard economists often have in mind. Growth can go on forever as long as the proportions are right—allocation is all, scale is nothing (see Note 3 again).

But is it possible to have everything grow in proportion? No, for two reasons. First, if something is fixed, then it obviously cannot grow proportionally to everything else. What is fixed from the ecological economist's perspective is the size of the total ecosystem. As the economic subsystem grows, albeit proportionally in terms of its internal dimensions, the ecosystem itself does not grow. The economy becomes larger as a proportion of the total system—what we have called an increase in its scale. Natural capital becomes more scarce relative to manmade capital. That fact has enormous consequences, especially if natural and manmade capital are more complementary than substitutable—as ecological economists, contrary to standard economists, believe is the case.

The second difficulty, long noticed by biologists and some economists, is that if you scale up anything (increase all linear dimensions by a fixed factor), then you will inevitably change the relative magnitudes of non-linear dimensions. Doubling length, width and height will not double area—it will increase area by a factor of four, and will increase volume by a factor of eight. Biologists have long noted "the importance of being the right size." If a grasshopper were scaled up to the size of an elephant it could not jump over a house. It would not even be able to move, because its weight (proportional to volume) would have increased by the cube, while its strength (proportional to cross-sectional area of muscle and bone) would have increased only by the square of the scale factor.

Returning to our example of a house, doubling the scale will increase surfaces and materials by four-fold, and volumes to be heated, cooled, and supported by eight-fold. Relative demands, scarcities, and prices of resources cannot remain the same. So the answer to our question, Does the notion of Pareto optimal allocation assume a given scale as well as a given distribution, appears to be "yes." Scale cannot increase "in proportion" because (a) there is a fixed factor, namely the size of the total ecosystem, (b) it is mathematically impossible even for all relevant internal dimensions of the subsystem to increase in the same proportion, and (c) even if quantities of all commodities could increase proportionally their relative prices would still change because marginal utilities decline at different rates for different goods. A different scale requires a different set of relative prices to be Pareto efficient.

If we recognize the importance of scale, and want to calculate the optimal scale, how do we do it? Can we measure the cost and benefit of a change in scale by the metric of prices? The initial allocative prices, even correct prices, to be used in the calculation depend on the given, initial scale. We cannot know what new prices would correspond to optimal scale unless we already know the optimal scale. But it is exactly the optimal scale that we were trying to calculate! It is circular to calculate the optimal scale on the basis of equating marginal costs and benefits measured by prices, which assume that we are already at the optimal scale to begin with. Known initial prices correspond to the initial scale, and would be different at any other scale, including the optimal scale. To correct those initial prices to reflect the conditions of an optimal scale requires that we already know the optimal scale from independent considerations.

Furthermore, and more basically, the prices under consideration are tools for solving the problem of efficient allocation. Prices, exchange values, are simply not the relevant metric for measuring costs and benefits in terms of justice (distribution), or sustainability (scale). Prices are specific tools for attaining allocative efficiency. They are not adequate to the separate and higher level problem of determining optimal trade-offs among allocative efficiency, distributive justice, and sustainable scale. The circular reasoning encountered when this attempt is made is a symptom of a basic conceptual confusion.

If in the name of perfect internalization we insist that prices should optimally balance the "external" costs and benefits of different scales, why not likewise insist that prices should optimally balance the costs and benefits of different distributions? We would run into the same problem of circularity. If we tried to use prices based on a given distribution as the means of measuring the costs and benefits of a change in distribution in order to calculate the optimal distribution, we are again being circular—assuming we know the optimal distribution in advance. Here economists have clearly recognized the circularity and insisted that just distribution is one thing, efficient allocation is another. They do not appeal to "perfect information" and advocate raising the price of things poor people sell, or lowering the price of things poor people buy, in order to internalize the external cost of poverty into prices.[11] Instead they say redistribute income directly to attain a more just distribution, and let prices adjust to attain a new efficient allocation subject to the new distribution. They do not always say this loudly enough, but they do say it. Ecological economists insist on the same logical treatment for scale as for distribution.

We need some metric of benefit and cost other than prices, other than exchange value, other than ratios of marginal utilities. As already suggested this metric is the value of justice in the case of distribution; it is ecological sustainability, including intergenerational and interspecies justice, in the case of scale. These are collective values, not individual preferences. If we follow mainstream economists in reducing all value to the level of aggregated subjective personal taste, then we will not be able to capture or bring to bear on the market the real weight of objective social values, such as distributive justice and ecological sustainability. Value transcends subjective individual preferences. Economists need to (re)learn this.

NOTES

1. Keynote address, Canadian Society for Ecological Economics, October 16–19, 2003, Jasper, Alberta, Canada.
2. See Nicholas Georgescu-Roegen, *The Entropy Law and the Economic Process*, Harvard University Press, Cambridge, MA, 1972.
3. Curiously the World Bank in WDR 2003, *Sustainable Development in a Dynamic World*, has adopted the ecological economists' vocabulary of "sources" and "sinks," but does not tie them together by the concept of throughput—the entropic flow from source to sink. Much less do they consider the scale of the throughput or its entropic directionality. In dismissing the idea of overconsumption they say, "But the overall level of consumption is not the source of the problem. It is the combination of the specific consumption mix and the production processes that generates the externality. And for these there are well-established policy prescriptions from public finance" (p. 196). So much for scale—it is not important—allocative efficiency via right prices is everything!
4. That is, as a multiplicative form that analytically describes the process of production as the multiplication of capital times labor times resources (each factor is raised to an exponent, but that is not important to the point I am making). In this representation we can hold output constant and reduce resources as much as we wish (though not to zero), as long as we increase labor or capital by the required amount. We can supposedly make a hundred-pound cake with only five ounces of flour, sugar, eggs, etc., if only we stir hard enough, and bake in a big enough oven! In mathematics a "product" is yielded by multiplying "factors." In production there is no multiplication, only transformation of resources (material cause) by labor and capital (efficient cause) into a final good. Have we been misled by the mathematical terms of "factors" and "products" to see a process of multiplication where there is none?
5. Indeed, GNP does not reflect efficiency very well. Greater efficiency by itself leads to lower cost and lower price. This would by itself reduce GNP, unless the quantity sold of the good increases sufficiently to offset the price decline—i.e., unless the demand for the good were elastic. Similarly, a fall in efficiency and an increase in price for a good with inelastic demand will perversely register an increase in GNP.
6. For critical discussion and the latest revision of the ISEW see Clifford W. Cobb and John B. Cobb, Jr. et al., *The Green National Product*, University Press of America, New York, 1994. For a presentation of the ISEW see Appendix of *For the Common Good*, H. Daly and J. Cobb, Beacon Press, Boston, 1989; second edition 1994. See also Clifford W. Cobb et al., "If the GDP is Up, Why is America Down?", *Atlantic Monthly*, October 1995; Manfred Max-Neef, "Economic Growth and Quality of Life: A Threshold Hypothesis", *Ecological Economics*, 15, 1995, pp. 115–18; Phillip A. Lawn, *Toward Sustainable Development* (An Ecological Economics Approach), Lewis Publishers, Boca Raton, FL, 2001; Clive Hamilton, *Growth Fetish*, Allen and Unwin, NSW, Australia, 2003.
7. My favorite personal experience with a category mistake occurred in Federal District Court in New Orleans concerning a Corps of Engineers cost–benefit study being used to justify dredging deep canals in the marshlands along the Louisiana coast. One category

of benefit was "hurricane refuge benefits" for submersible drilling rigs in the Gulf of Mexico. The rigs, it was argued, could henceforth ride out hurricanes in the now deeper inland canals of nearby Louisiana, rather than be transported all the way to Texas. That transport savings was a significant part of total benefits of canal dredging. It sounded logical until the plaintiff pointed out that submersible drilling rigs were designed to withstand hurricanes, and the last thing you would want to do if there were a hurricane in the forecast would be to move one anywhere—neither to Texas nor Louisiana. Therefore inclusion of such a benefit was spurious, a category mistake. The lawyers for the Corps kept saying, "if you disagree with our numerical estimate, give us your estimate." The plaintiff replied that the number would obviously be zero, no calculation required, because it was a category mistake, not an error of measurement. The defense did not, or pretended not, to understand. The plaintiff lawyer clarified: "you might as well count hurricane refuge benefit for whales as a category of benefits and claim to be saving all the world's whales. If you tell me that whales do not need hurricane refuge, then I will tell you that neither do submersible drilling rigs. It is not a matter of miscalculation—it is a category mistake." Even the judge seemed to have a hard time understanding this, so the example is probably worth recounting. The judge eventually did understand and disallowed the hurricane refuge benefits. Curiously the Corps of Engineers redid their cost–benefit analysis eliminating this mistaken benefit, but discovered an overlooked benefit whose inclusion resulted in exactly the same required cost–benefit ratio as was originally (mis)calculated! The result was that the Corps got what it wanted.

8. *Hard Green: Saving the Environment from the Environmentalists* (A Conservative Manifesto), Peter Huber, Basic Books (A Manhattan Institute Book), 2000, p. 81. This book is reviewed in Part 5 of this volume.

9. In spite of the fact that mathematicians tell us that we cannot maximize a function for more than one variable!

10. The marginal utility curves for different goods drop off at different rates. Even though the world is happy at an exchange rate of 5 bananas to 1 coconut, if we double the world's supply of both, people might tire of coconuts faster than they do of bananas. So the price of coconuts might fall, to 4 bananas, say. Even though the relative proportion of bananas and coconuts in the world has remained the same, the relative scarcity of the two has not. All of which is to say that even if you could scale things up linearly (which is not possible), prices would still change! So too would the allocation. In other words, an efficient allocation presupposes a given scale.

11. To do so would be to return to the "just price" doctrine of the Middle Ages.

REFERENCE

Mill, J.S. (1857), *Principles of Political Economy*, Vol. 2, London: John W. Parker.

9.   Sustaining our commonwealth of nature and knowledge[1]

This chapter addresses issues of sustainability in the context of two somewhat opposite difficulties in managing our commonwealth: the problem of non-enclosure of the truly scarce (nature); and that of enclosure of the truly non-scarce (knowledge). Policy reforms respecting both the capacities and limitations of the market in each case are considered. In closing a third type of commonwealth, neither nature nor knowledge but institutions, is briefly discussed in terms of the example of fiat money.

By sustaining I mean using without using up, to use while keeping intact, while maintaining or replacing the capacity for future use. What is being sustained is ultimately the capacity to produce income. Income is in turn the maximum that a community can consume this year and still produce the same amount next year—that is, income is consumption that leaves productive capacity (capital in the broad sense) intact. Income is by definition sustainable consumption (Sir John Hicks). "Unsustainable income" is not income at all but capital drawdown. A large part of our capacity to produce, sometimes consumed and falsely counted as income, is our commonwealth, social wealth as opposed to privately owned wealth. In a free society individuals have the right to draw down or consume their private wealth, but not the commonwealth. I want to consider mainly two categories of our commonwealth: nature and knowledge, with brief mention of a third category, institutions. How can we use these forms of social wealth sustainably, as well as efficiently and justly?

To address this question I will make use of some distinctions familiar to economists, but probably not to the general public. Goods can be rival or non-rival. My shirt is a rival good because if I am wearing it you cannot wear it at the same time. The warmth of the sun is non-rival because my enjoyment of it does not preclude the same enjoyment by others. Rivalness is a physical property of a good that precludes its simultaneous use by many people. Goods are also excludable or non-excludable. Excludability is a legal right to prevent another from using your property. For example you could wear my shirt if I let you, but that is up to me because it is my property. My shirt is thus both rival and excludable, as are most market goods. The warmth of the sun is both non-rival and non-excludable. We cannot buy and sell solar warmth. The categories that cause problems and will be of interest to us are the remaining combinations: rival and non-excludable, and non-rival and excludable.

Knowledge is easy to use sustainably because it is a non-rival good. If I use the Pythagorean theorem I don't use it up, and I don't prevent you or any number of other people from using it at the same time. We can all use it as much as we want without using it up. The problem of sustainable use of knowledge is trivial—sustainability is guaranteed by the fact that knowledge is non-rival. Knowledge is multiplied among users, not divided. However, expenditure of rival resources in the pursuit of new knowledge, or the teaching of old knowledge, may indeed be unsustainable—but not existing knowledge itself. *Once it exists*, knowledge is non-rival, has zero opportunity cost, and its efficient allocation requires that its price be zero.

Certainly new knowledge has a cost of production, sometimes substantial, sometimes negligible. New knowledge may cost a lot, as with the space program's discovery of no life on Mars, or with the discovery of yet another elementary particle resulting from smashing other particles in a billion dollar accelerator. On the other hand, a new insight could occur to you while you are lying in bed idly staring at the ceiling—as was the case for Rene Descartes' invention of analytic geometry. Accident also plays a large role in discovery. Or the joy and excitement of research may delight and motivate you to work hard, independently of material incentives.

Nevertheless, in spite of these elementary facts, the idea has somehow grown up that new knowledge would never be discovered unless some people were paid a great deal of money to provide them with the incentive to undergo the drudgery, pain, and expense of discovery. Patent monopolies, intellectual property rights, are urged as the way to provide an extrinsic reward for knowledge production. The dominant view is that knowledge, a non-rival good, must be made artificially rival; that is, legally excludable, so that it will command a market price, which in turn will stimulate its production.

James Maitland, Earl of Lauderdale, a classical economist, noted in 1819 an important distinction between "public wealth" and "private riches." Public wealth "consists of all that man desires that is useful or delightful to him." Private riches consist of "all that man desires that is useful or delightful to him, which exists in a degree of scarcity." Scarcity is a necessary condition for something to have exchange value and be counted as private riches. In the Garden of Eden (no scarcity) private riches were zero, but public wealth was at its maximum. Creating scarcity indeed may increase private riches, but at the expense of diminishing public wealth. Lauderdale felt that, "the common sense of mankind would revolt at a proposal for augmenting wealth by creating a scarcity of any good generally useful and necessary to mankind." Nevertheless, it seems we create a scarcity of knowledge precisely to give it a positive price so it can be counted as private riches, which we mistakenly consider to represent an increase rather than a decrease in public wealth.

Likewise for nature. It also starts to be counted as private riches when it becomes scarce. Costanza's et al.'s estimate of 33 trillion dollars for the value of global ecosystem services would have been zero in the Garden of Eden. So 33 trillion dollars is really a measure of how far we are from the Garden of Eden. Yet a reporter who called me about that estimate asked, "How do you think we should use all that newly discovered wealth? What should we spend it on?" So much for Lauderdale's faith in the "common sense of mankind."

The justification offered for this violation of common sense is that unless knowledge is kept scarce enough to have a significant price, no one in the market will have an incentive to produce it. The justifiers cannot conceive of anything being produced other than for the market. But even within that restricted vision keeping knowledge scarce makes little sense because the main input to the production of new knowledge is existing knowledge, and making that key input more expensive will surely make the production of new knowledge more expensive. This is why the production of new knowledge has traditionally either been financed publicly or by private philanthropy, rather than as a profit-making market venture.

Another problem with profit-driven knowledge production, noted by Sismondi in 1837, is that not all new knowledge is equally beneficial, and private profit does not provide the best social filter for selecting what kind of knowledge should be developed. For example, the profit filter will select research that gives us liposuction, Viagra, and Cialis, with its grave warning that erections lasting more than four hours require medical attention. A cure for AIDS or malaria would not be nearly as profitable.

Nature, in the form of natural resources, is rival. The timber cut to make a table for me cannot be used to make a chair for you. In the form of natural services nature is sometimes rival and sometimes non-rival. Even when it is rival it is sometimes so plentiful relative to the existing scale of demand that it is effectively treated as non-rival (i.e., legally non-excludable), even though physically it is rival. For example, drinking water is rival, but may be so plentiful as to be non-excludable and command no price. Yet, unlike the Pythagorean theorem, if enough people use it, its inherently rival nature will become apparent. Solar energy provides natural services of light and warmth that are non-rival. But if your photovoltaic panel shades mine, then it is rival, at least during part of the day or year. Furthermore, some resources are rival within a generation but may be either rival or non-rival between generations. For example, renewable resources like timber and fish, while rival at a given time, are non-rival over time if exploited at sustainable yields, but rival over time if exploited beyond sustainable yield. Metals are rival within generations but largely non-rival between generations through recycling. Fossil fuels, however, are rival both within and between generations.

The point is that goods differ in the fundamental physical characteristic of degree of rivalness. The price system, the market, works only for rival goods that are sufficiently scarce to command an opportunity cost, and to have also been declared excludable by a legal system. My shirt is inherently rival, but unless I have exclusive use rights to it then you may take it from me—it would not really be *my* shirt, it would be a loose shirt up for grabs. So for market exchange to replace conquest, rival goods must also be legally excludable. But if a good is physically non-rival, is there any point in making it legally excludable? I think not, at least not in the case of knowledge. Many people disagree, and I would have to admit that when knowledge is specific to the production of bads, then I would favor making it excludable, if possible. For example, the knowledge of how to make an atomic bomb. But even here I think our efforts should be directed at controlling access to critical ingredients, plutonium and uranium, which are rival goods, rather than to trying to keep secret the recipe for a bomb.

However, for rival goods that are only now becoming scarce and are consequently still treated as non-excludable—the open access commons—it *does* make sense to institute a regime of excludability, thereby enclosing the resource in the market domain. This combination of rival and non-excludable gives rise to tragedy of the open access commons (overuse and unsustainability). The opposite combination, non-rival and excludable, gives rise to what might be called "the tragedy of artificial or self-inflicted scarcity"—for example, the inefficient under-use of knowledge due to intellectual property and patent monopoly. This is also a tragedy because treating what is non-scarce as if it were scarce is at least as big an error as treating what is scarce as if it were non-scarce.

It is curious that Watson and Crick received no royalties for the discovery of the structure of DNA, yet second-rate gene jockeys are getting royalties by tweaking the monumental discovery of their scientific betters. Nor did Gregor Mendel get any royalties for discovering the principles of heredity—but then he was a monk, motivated by pious curiosity about how God's creation works—however politically incorrect that may be today! Even secular economists, however, work hard in spite of being unable to patent supply and demand, or national income accounts. So why not cut back on intellectual property—why not rely more on public finance and joy of discovery as the means, motivation, and filter for producing new knowledge? How many important discoveries can you name that would not have been made without the incentive of profit guaranteed by patent monopolies?

The relation of profit to new knowledge is nevertheless an important issue in economics. Joseph Schumpeter's theory of profit holds that new knowledge, by virtue of its novelty, confers a temporary monopoly on the firm discovering it, and consequently temporary monopoly profits. These monopoly profits are competed away as the new knowledge gradually spreads to other firms. It is the continuing stream of new invention, followed by temporary monopoly profits, that Schumpeter argued was the source of profit in a competitive market whose tendency is to compete profits down to zero in equilibrium (a necessary condition for efficient allocation, you will remember!). The benefit of new knowledge does not disappear as it spreads, but rather that benefit is maximized. The benefit from the increased use of the non-rival good (knowledge) is realized in higher productivity of the rival goods (labor, capital, and resources).

It is silly to enclose non-rival goods in the market and impose artificial scarcity (excludability) on what is inherently non-rival. Let me just note in passing that much recent trade legislation dealing with so-called "trade-related intellectual property rights" (TRIPS) is an effort not so much to promote free trade as to police US intellectual property rights worldwide by using the sanction of trade restriction. Also, if we thought clearly about it, it would be apparent that international development aid should consist more of freely shared knowledge, accompanied by small grants—and less of interest-bearing loans for large projects that require rival goods that create unrepayable debts and dependency.

In sum, my conclusion regarding the sustainable use of the common-wealth of knowledge is that it is in no danger whatsoever of unsustainable overuse, but is in fact grossly underused. Knowledge is both inefficiently allocated and unjustly distributed as a result of excessive reliance on intellectual property. The fundamental error is to treat a non-rival good as if it were rival in order to fit the Procrustean bed of free-market ideology. This has led both to converting a non-rival good into an artificially rival good, and to converting a commonwealth into private property, essentially by "enclosure" or "silent theft," as David Bollier calls it in his insightful book of that title. Abolishing all intellectual property tomorrow would be draconian, but a minimum policy implication is that fewer discoveries should be eligible for patent monopolies, and these should be granted for shorter periods of time. Unfortunately, both trends are in the opposite direction.[2]

Let us turn now to focus on the commonwealth of nature. Those natural goods and services that are rival, and have so far remained non-excludable, should be enclosed in the market to avoid the tragic incentives for unsustainable use. The excludability can be in the form of individual private property or collective social property. What needs to be avoided is open access. Access can be restricted to a community and managed by the community, or it can by restricted at the individual level by private property. How that new property is distributed among individuals then becomes an important issue.

Consider a market-based institution for dealing with this broad class of rival but non-excludable goods—the cap-and-trade system. It merits consideration not only for its practical value, but also for the light it sheds on a fundamental problem in economics.

The cap-and-trade system is often illegitimately taken as the paradigm institution of so-called "free market environmentalism." Traditionally some environmental assets, say fishing rights or rights to emit SO_2, have been treated as non-excludable free goods. Then, as economic growth increases the scale of the economy relative to the biosphere, it is recognized that these goods are in fact rival and impose an opportunity cost at the new larger scale of use. The first step is to cap the scale of use at a level deemed environmentally sustainable. The cap, or quota, may be placed at the source or sink end of the resource throughput, whichever is more scarce, or easier to control. Setting the cap at a sustainable level is a social-ecological decision, not a market decision. Second, the right to extract or emit up to the cap is now a scarce asset, no longer a free good, and consequently has an opportunity cost and a price. Who owns this newly created asset? This also must be decided politically outside the market. Ownership could be social with yearly quotas to deplete or emit auctioned to the highest bidder and proceeds entering the public treasury. Or rights could be given to the historical private users for nothing—a bad idea, but frequently done under the benevolent label of "grandfathering." Someone must own the assets before they can be traded in a market, and who owns them is an issue of distribution. Only after the scale question is answered, and then the distribution question is answered, are we able to have exchange in a "free" market that answers the allocation question.

The practical problem of cap-and-trade policies confronts us squarely with the logically separate issues of scale, distribution, and allocation. The cap-and-trade system is not "free market environmentalism" as frequently labeled—it is "social market environmentalism." Social constraints on scale (sustainability), and on distribution (fairness) must be politically imposed *before* markets are allowed to trade permits and determine prices.

Allocation, distribution, and scale are separate problems. Neoclassical economics has dealt mainly with allocation (the apportionment of scarce resources among competing commodity uses—how many resources go to produce beans, cars, haircuts, etc.). A good allocation is efficient—in the sense that no reallocation can increase anyone's welfare without decreasing the welfare of someone else. Properly functioning markets allocate resources efficiently in this sense (called Pareto optimality). But this

concept of efficient allocation presupposes a given distribution (the apportionment of goods and resources among different people—how many
resources embodied in beans, cars, etc. go to you, how many to me). A good
distribution is one that is just. A third issue is scale (the physical size of the
economy relative to the ecosystem that sustains it—how many of us are
there and how many beans, cars, etc. do we each get on average, and how
large are the associated matter-energy flows relative to natural cycles). A
good scale is sustainable. A sustainable scale, like a just distribution, cannot
be determined by the market—both are conditions which the market must
take as given, which must be politically imposed on the market, and subject
to which the market finds the efficient allocation and corresponding prices.
Economists' legitimate concern with efficient allocation should not be
allowed to obscure the critical presuppositions regarding just distribution
and sustainable scale.[3]

I believe it is fair to say that neoclassical economists accept this reasoning as far as distribution is concerned, but not for scale. If someone urges
lower energy prices as a way to help the poor, economists rightly say no that
will distort the allocative function of prices—better to help the poor by
redistribution of income to them. Yet economists seem to think that
manipulating prices will solve the scale problem—if we just get prices right
then the market will move us to the optimal scale. But then why not apply
the same logic of just "getting prices right" to distribution—for example,
let's internalize the cost of poverty by subsidizing wage goods and taxing
luxury goods, and let the "right prices" lead us to the optimal distribution.
There are good reasons for not trying to solve the distribution question by
"right prices," but those reasons also prevent right prices from solving the
scale problem.

What are the "right prices," anyway? Are they the ones that give us the
optimal allocation, the optimal distribution, and the optimal scale, all at
the same time? That would be lovely, but it runs afoul of logic. Nobel
economist Jan Tinbergen set forth a basic princple: for every independent
policy goal, we need an independent policy instrument. The logic is analogous to that of simultaneous equations. For every variable to be solved for,
we need a separate equation. Is our goal optimal allocation? Fine, then
supply equals demand pricing in competitive markets can be our policy
equation. We also want just distribution? Fine, but we need a second policy
instrument (not prices again). We also want a sustainable scale? Fine, now
we need a third policy instrument (not prices yet again). Let us by all means
keep prices and markets for solving the allocation problem. Now what are
our independent instruments for solving the distribution and scale problems? Following the logic of cap-and-trade, which conforms nicely to
Tinbergen's rule, scale is set by ecological criteria of sustainability effected

by setting aggregate quotas (caps); distribution is set by ethical criteria of fairness effected by distribution of ownership of the quotas; and that leaves only allocation to be settled by efficiency criteria effected through market prices.

How is it that economists accept the distributive precondition for efficient prices, but apparently not the analogous scale precondition? That may simply be because they have not thought much about scale. Sometimes scale is treated as infinitesimal—the economy is thought to be very small relative to the ecosystem, which consequently is considered infinite and non-scarce. Alternatively economists sometimes seem to consider scale as total, the economy is the whole. If everything is economy then nothing is left over as environment, and scale disappears as an issue with allocation taking its place—atoms and amoebas and wild tigers must all be hitched to pull the human wagon in an efficient way. The program then becomes one of putting a price on everything, calculating so-called "shadow prices" for things not traded in markets, which includes most things in the world. This creates an information problem that overwhelms even that faced by the old Soviet central planners. So economists resort to "contingent valuation" studies, a kind of full-employment act for economists, to come up with a shadowy number for these shadow prices.

A further advantage of the cap-and-trade system is that, if the ownership of the quotas is public, they can be auctioned off for public revenue. The resource scarcity rents, unearned income, from the newly scarce part of the natural commonwealth, can go to the public, not privileged private parties. This is in the spirit of Henry George's basic idea of taxing away scarcity rent.

Another good policy for managing our commonwealth of nature is "ecological tax reform." Ecological tax reform advocates shifting the tax base away from value added (income earned by labor and capital) and on to "that to which value is added," namely the throughput flow of resources, preferably at the depletion end (at the mine-mouth or well-head, the point of "severance" from the ground). Many states have severance taxes. Taxing the origin and narrowest point in the throughput flow, induces more efficient resource use in downstream production and consumption, and facilitates monitoring and collection. Taxing what we want less of (depletion and pollution), and ceasing to tax what we want more of (income) would seem reasonable—as the bumper sticker puts it, "tax bads, not goods." The shift could be revenue neutral and gradual. Begin for example by forgoing $x revenue from the worst income tax we have (payroll tax, perhaps). Simultaneously collect $x from the best resource severance tax we could devise (perhaps a carbon tax). Next period get rid of the second worst income tax, and substitute the second best resource tax, and so on. Such a policy would raise resource prices and induce efficiency in resource use, while encouraging value added and employment.

The regressivity of such a consumption tax could be offset by spending the proceeds progressively, and by instituting a sumptuary tax, or retaining an income tax on high incomes. Also offsetting the regressivity of a consumption tax is its advantage of bringing the underground economy into the tax base. Illegal and unreported income from drug dealers and other income tax cheaters at least would get taxed when they buy their beach condos, Mercedes, and gasoline. Cap-and-trade systems can also increase government revenue, replacing some taxes, if the initial quotas are auctioned to users rather than given away.

Admittedly, any change in the tax system, except more loopholes for the wealthy, is politically very difficult. However, people resent having their earned income, value added, taxed away, and they also resent seeing unearned income in the form of scarcity rents accrue to people who added no value. Ecological tax reform would remove much of the cause of these two justified resentments, while raising public revenue. That is a substantial political advantage to set against the political opposition of the extractive industries.

Ecological tax reform increases the efficiency in using our commonwealth of nature, and makes distribution of its ownership fairer by, in effect, taxing unearned scarcity rent while reducing taxes on earned income. However, unlike the cap-and-trade system, ecological tax reform exerts only an indirect and relatively weak limit on scale, while improving allocation and distribution.

To summarize, managing the commonwealths of nature and knowledge present us with two rather opposite problems and solutions. *For nature*, the truly scarce is often treated as non-scarce. Therefore we must recognize the scarcity of natural resources and enclose the resource commons as public property from which we capture the scarcity rent as public revenue. Examples of natural commons are: mining, logging, and grazing rights on public land, the electromagnetic spectrum, and absorptive capacity of the atmosphere, orbital locations of satellites, and so on. *For knowledge*, we often treat the truly non-scarce as if it were scarce, enclosing a non-rival good in the prison of excludability. Instead we must free knowledge from this perverse enclosure, allowing it to be allocated efficiently as a non-rival good at its proper price of zero. Especially knowledge financed by government and university research should quickly be freed from enclosure, and even privately financed knowledge should be granted shorter monopoly protection, and eventually be recognized as a non-rival good.[4]

Are there other dimensions of commonwealth besides nature and knowledge? Yes, and in fact a national economy itself constitutes a commonwealth and used to be referred to as such.[5] The resources, customs, laws, division of labor, distribution of purchasing power, labor markets, and so on, of a nation constitute a community, cohesive internally, but with strict limits to access from the outside. Imports of goods and services are controlled, imports of capital are controlled, and immigration of people is controlled, all in the internal interests of citizens of the commonwealth. Traditionally national markets have not been thought of as an open access commons. Globalization aims to change that—to erase national boundaries for economic purposes (free trade, free capital mobility, and free, or at least uncontrolled, immigration). The consequence of open access is the tragedy of the commons, the disintegration of the national commonwealth, which is welcomed by many in the questionable pursuit of an integrated global economy. In the absence of world government, however, such a global economy is not a commonwealth writ large, but a kind of global feudalism in which corporate individualism has free reign.

More narrowly, social institutions such as legal systems, language, moral codes, and monetary systems also constitute a kind of social wealth or commonwealth, that is different from knowledge and nature, and that, like knowledge, seem to be inherently non-rival. I would like to consider only one of these in closing, namely money.

Money, at first glance, may seem to be rival, since if I have a dollar you cannot simultaneously have it. Yet the only reason for having a dollar is to be able to give it in exchange for something else, and so its value depends on the willingness of everyone to accept it in exchange and hold it at least temporarily. The more people use a dollar, the more useful it is, and in that sense it is non-rival. We use money without using it up. But is money a commonwealth? Indeed, is it wealth at all? It depends—if it is commodity money, then it circulates at its commodity value, and is a rival commodity that can be privately produced and owned, for example gold—then it is not really commonwealth. It is private wealth that serves a social function. However, token or fiat money is different. Its commodity value is nil (it has only a trivial cost of production), but it circulates at an exchange value independent of its commodity value. The amount of token money that people are willing to hold rather than exchange it for real commodities is the "virtual wealth" of the community. People are willing to hold token money balances to avoid the inconvenience of barter. They can convert their money balances into real wealth at any time, and thus reasonably count these balances as part of their personal wealth. Yet if everyone tried to convert their money balances into real wealth at once it could not be done, because someone would have to end up holding the money. Thus the aggregate of individuals in a community considers itself as if it were richer than it really is by the amount of virtual wealth, which is equal to the exchange value of stock of token money.

Although we all benefit from the convenience of money, the issuer of token money, the one who creates and first spends it, gets a transfer of real wealth from the rest of the community. He pays the negligible cost of production of token money, but receives the full exchange value when he spends it. Everyone else must give the full exchange value's worth of something in exchange for money. The profit to the issuer of fiat money is called "seigniorage" and really should be public income since it derives from the socially created commonwealth of token money.

Seigniorage used to accrue to the king. The privilege largely passed, not to the State, the legitimate heir of the king, but to the private banking sector via the institution of fractional reserve banking. Seigniorage on currency still goes to the government, but that on demand deposits, over 95 percent of our money supply, goes to the commercial banks in the first instance, and is probably in large part competed away to the rest of the private sector (commercial banks' customers).

One hundred percent reserves would eliminate the ability of the commercial banks to create money, and put our money supply back under the control of the government rather than the private banking sector. Money would be a true public utility, rather than the by-product of commercial lending and borrowing in pursuit of growth. Under the fractional reserve system the money supply expands during a boom, and contracts during a slump, reinforcing the cyclical tendency of the economy. Demand deposits are loaned into existence at interest, and a new loan will only be taken if the project it finances is expected to grow at a rate greater than the interest rate. Therefore it would seem that under fractional reserve banking, economic growth is required just to keep the money supply from shrinking as old loans are repaid.

The seigniorage from creating and being the first to spend token money would, with 100 percent reserve requirements, accrue to the government rather than the private sector. It could be used for interest-free financing of public goods. The reserve requirement, something the Fed manipulates anyway, could be raised gradually to 100 percent. Commercial banks would make their income by financial intermediation (lending savers' money for them), and by service charges on checking accounts, and so on, rather than by lending money they simply create. Lending only pre-existing money that someone has actually saved brings about a greater discipline in lending, and enforces the classical balance between marginal time preference and marginal productivity of capital.

The two leading American economists of the 1920s, Irving Fisher of Yale and Frank Knight of Chicago, both strongly advocated 100 percent reserves. Why this issue disappeared from the policy agenda is an interesting question for historians of economic thought—if there are any left. And why there are so few left is another interesting question.

In sum—I have argued that the commonwealth of nature should be enclosed as property, to the extent possible as *public* property, and administered so as to capture scarcity rents for public revenue. The commonwealth of knowledge should be freed from enclosure as property and be treated as the non-rival good that it is. A third category of commonwealth, the institutional, was mentioned in closing with the example of the institution of fiat money and the suggestion of capturing seigniorage for public wealth through 100 percent reserve requirements. These three policies establish basic directions in which to move. How fast we should move in each direction is an important question that I have not attempted to answer. However, the policies advocated in each case (fewer and shorter patent monopolies; cap-and-trade plus ecological tax reform; and 100 percent reserve requirements) can all be imposed with varying speeds and to varying degrees. We can try them out a little at a time.

If what I have argued is even more or less correct, then I am faced with a difficult question. Why do so many neoclassical economists continue to teach, by and large, the opposite—namely, that nature is not really scarce; that knowledge must be made scarce in order to increase it; and that the private banking institutions must create money out of nothing and lend it at interest as a necessary part of the economic order?

They may be right—I may be crazy. But crazy people should be easy to refute, shouldn't they? So let's see what happens!

NOTES

1. Originally presented in Forum on Social Wealth, University of Massachusetts, Amherst, September 29, 2005. Published in *International Journal of Ecodynamics*, Vol. 1, No. 3, 2006, pp. 1–9.
2. The big danger to the sustainability of knowledge is not overuse, but the incomplete and biased transfer between generations. Witness the fact that few universities any longer offer a course in the history of economic thought.
3. Moreover, prices are tools to allocate resources efficiently, subject to an independently given scale and distribution. We cannot take the allocatively efficient prices and use them to calculate some "optimal scale" or "optimal distribution" because that would be circular—we had to have a given scale and distribution to get the prices in the first place, and if we used these prices to then calculate a different scale or distribution then that would change the prices that we just used in our calculation. Since allocative prices are determined subject to a given (just) distribution and a given (sustainable) scale, they can be thought of as, in a sense, internalizing the external costs of unsustainability and injustice into prices. But the danger in thinking this way is to believe that the causation can run from the cause of calculated "right shadow prices" to the effects of just distribution and sustainable scale, as well as to efficient allocation. The causation goes from given scale and given distribution to market prices that are allocatively efficient on the basis of those two givens. But the values of sustainability and justice are set politically, not by market prices.
4. A colleague told me a story that illustrates how far we have strayed. He was on a review panel for awarding large government research grants. In interviewing one of the final

candidates he asked for some specific information referred to vaguely in the proposal. The applicant replied that he was not allowed by his university to disclose that information since it was their intellectual property.

5. As defined by the *OED*, commonwealth = "the whole body of people constituting a nation or state, the body politic; a state, an independent community, esp. viewed as a body in which the whole people have a voice or an interest."

10. The steady-state economy and peak oil[1]

In classical economics (Smith, Malthus, Ricardo, Mill) the steady-state, or as they called it the "stationary state" economy was a real condition toward which the economy was tending as increasing population, diminishing returns, and increasing land rents squeezed profits to zero. Population would be held constant by subsistence wages and a high death rate. Capital stock would be held constant by a lack of inducement to invest resulting from zero profits thanks to rent absorbing the entire surplus which was itself limited by diminishing returns. Not a happy future—something to be postponed for as long as possible in the opinion of most classical economists. Mill, however, saw it differently. Population must indeed stabilize, but that could be attained by Malthus' preventive checks (lowering the birth rate) rather than the positive checks (high death rate). A constant capital stock is not static, but continuously renewed by depreciation and replacement, opening the way for continual technical and qualitative improvement in the physically non-growing capital stock. By limiting the birth rate, and by technical improvement in the constant capital stock, a surplus above subsistence could be maintained. Mill also believed that the surplus could be equitably redistributed. Unlike the growing economy, the stationary state economy would not have to continually expand into the biosphere and therefore could leave most of the world in its natural state. The stationary state is both necessary and desirable, but neither static nor eternal—it is a system in dynamic equilibrium with its containing, sustaining, and entropic biosphere. The path of progress would shift from bigger and more, toward better and longer lived.

In the late 1800s classical economics was replaced by neoclassical economics, and although the term "stationary or steady-state economy" was retained, its meaning was radically changed. It no longer referred to constant population and stock of capital, but to a situation of constant tastes and technology. In Mill's conception physical magnitudes (population and capital) were constant, and culture (tastes and technology) adapted. In the new version culture (tastes and technology) are constant and the physical magnitudes (population and capital stock) adapt. Given that our cultural tastes were assumed to reflect infinite wants, and that technical progress was considered unlimited, the way to adapt was by growth, so-called "steady-state growth" which means proportional growth of population and capital stock. The absolute magnitudes continue to grow while the ratio between them is supposed to remain constant. Furthermore the concept of a steady state is no longer thought of as a real state of the world, whether desirable or undesirable, but as an analytical fiction, like an ideal gas or frictionless machine. It is a short-run reference point for analyzing growth, and has neither normative nor ontological significance, whereas for Mill it had both. Mill's steady state was both necessary in the long run and desirable much sooner. It is not too much of an oversimplification to say that the classical economists were concerned with adapting the economy to the dictates of physical reality, while the neoclassicals want to adapt physical reality to the dictates of the economy. In an empty world the dictates of physical reality are not immediately binding on growth; in a full world they are. Consequently, and paradoxically, it is the older classical view of the steady state, Mill's version, that is more relevant today, even though the neoclassical view dominates the thinking of empty-world economists.

Another basis for the stationary state comes from the demographers' model of a stationary population, one in which birth rates and death rates are equal and both the total population size and its age structure are constant. This model is both an analytical fiction and also for some a normative goal. Indeed, a constant population is part of the classical view of the stationary state. A constant population requires only that the birth rate equals the death rate, and that could be the case at either high or low levels. Most of us[2] prefer lower levels, within limits, because we value longevity. Likewise, the constancy of the capital stock requires production rates equal to depreciation rates. Basically the preference here is also for equality at low rather than high levels. Greater life expectancy of capital (the total stock of durable goods) requires less depletion and pollution (lower rates of throughput). In this view new production is a maintenance cost of a capital stock that unfortunately depreciates as it is used to serve our needs. Like other costs it should be minimized, even though the idea of minimizing the flow of new production is strange to most economists. I have sometimes offered an alternative definition of the steady-state economy as one that maintains itself with a constant throughput that is within regenerative and absorptive capacities of the biosphere. Capital and population could then grow up to the limit imposed by the constant throughput.

Something similar to the classical stationary state was revived by Keynes in his concept of the "quasi stationary community." This was also a real state of the world rather than an analytical fiction, and was considered desirable by Keynes. It assumed population stability, no wars, and several generations of full employment and capital accumulation. Keynes believed that in the resulting world of abundant capital the "marginal efficiency of capital" would fall to zero, leading to a situation in which new investment would merely replace capital depreciation and the capital stock would cease growing. Capital would in effect no longer be scarce, leading to a near zero interest rate and the happy consequence that it would no longer be possible to live off interest on accumulated wealth—the "euthanasia of the rentier." As Keynes put it, "The owner of capital can obtain an interest rate because capital is scarce, just as the owner of land can obtain rent because land is scarce. But whilst there may be intrinsic reasons for the scarcity of land, there are no intrinsic reasons for the scarcity of capital" (*General Theory . . .*, p. 376, 1936). That Keynes's vision seems not to be coming true is due to many things, including destruction of capital by wars, dilution of capital by population growth, and an enormous increase in consumption in wealthy countries such as the US, stimulated by novel products, advertising, and financed not only by reduced savings and investment, but also by capital decumulation. In the US this decumulation takes the form of enormous consumer debt as well as huge continuing deficits in both the domestic budget and the international balance of trade. In addition, regardless of the marginal efficiency of capital, the Fed keeps the interest rate from falling too low because we must attract foreign investment from our surplus trading partners, as well as keep inflation under control. In addition the Fed's feelings for the rentier class are more tender than were Keynes's. Nevertheless, like Mill, Keynes saw a real possibility that was simply rejected by the growth obsession, to which, ironically, conventional "Keynesian economics" has itself contributed substantially.

The classical view of the steady-state economy was replaced by the neoclassical view for two historical reasons. First, the neoclassical subjective utility theory of value began to receive more emphasis than the classical real cost theory of value that emphasized labor and land. There are no obvious limits to growth in utility (a psychic experience), as there are to growth in labor and in the physical product that labor extracts from nature. Second, with the advent of the industrial revolution there came the enormous subsidy of fossil fuels. The annual flow of solar energy captured by land and harvested by labor was now supplemented by the concentrated sunlight of millions of Paleolithic summers accumulated underground. Growth now seemed limitless, and neoclassical economists attributed this bonanza not to nature's non-renewable subsidy, first of coal then of petroleum, but to human technological invention that was taken to be renewable and not limited by the particular resources being exploited. Indeed, a general presupposition of neoclassical economics is that nature does not create value. Peak oil signals the end of the bonanza with no alternative subsidy in sight, either from nature or human invention. And even before the source limit of global peak oil hits, we have begun to experience the sink limit of greenhouse-induced climate change. Not only are the sources emptying, but the sinks are filling up as well. A modernized classical view of the steady-state economy as a subsystem of a finite, non-growing, and entropic biosphere, as foreseen by Mill, must now replace the growth economy— even if the latter is misleadingly re-baptized as "steady-state growth economy."

Many will say that I am selling technology short, and that it will find a substitute for cheap oil. Even assuming this were true, should we not limit our depletion of petroleum now to drive its price up and provide an incentive for developing these new hoped-for technologies as soon as possible? Should not the technological optimists have the courage of their convictions and provide the incentives to develop the very technologies of which they are so confident? A policy of frugality first will induce efficiency as a secondary response: our currently favored policy of efficiency first does not induce frugality second, and in fact makes it less necessary, as often documented in the so-called "rebound" or "Jevons effect," whereby more efficient technology for using a resource simply makes it cheaper, leading us to increase its total usage. The most obvious policy response to peak oil, and to furthering the classical steady-state economy, is to put a cap on aggregate petroleum depletion and auction off the rights to deplete in divisible units up to that cap in each time period. Depletion is slowed, price of petroleum goes up, greater efficiency in use is stimulated, the rebound effect is blocked by the cap, and the government gets the windfall rents.

A second-best, but perhaps politically more viable policy, is to shift the tax burden from "*value added*" (income produced by labor and capital) and on to "*that to which value is added*," namely the resource throughput, especially fossil fuels. We need to raise public revenue somehow, so why not tax what is truly most scarce, and is not the product of anyone's labor, rather than tax labor and entrepreneurship? Why not tax resource rents, "unearned income" as the tax accountants so honestly call it, instead of earned income or value added in the form of wages and profits? This is not only fairer but also more efficient because it raises the relative price of the truly scarce and long-run limiting factor, the throughput of low-entropy matter-energy, natural resources. In addition to being the long-run limiting factor the resource throughput, principally fossil energy, is also the factor most responsible for external environmental costs—another reason to raise its price by taxation. The tax shift could be revenue neutral, taking the same amount from the public but in a different way. It would offer an opportunity to get rid of some of our worst taxes (e.g., the payroll tax) at the same time we add taxes with better incentives. To the extent that a tax tends to reduce its base, that is all to the good since throughput is depletion and pollution, both costs. However, such reduction is likely to be limited because resources are absolutely necessary for production and both demand and supply for them are inelastic. But taxing a factor with inelastic demand and supply is minimally distortionary, whereas the supply of labor and enterprise is more elastic, and taxing them is likely to reduce the supply of these value-adding services.

It is true that a resource tax, like any consumption tax, is regressive compared to an income tax. However, even the Mafia, drug dealers, crooked politicians, illegal aliens, and Enron executives would have to pay taxes on their resource consumption, whereas they currently manage to escape income taxes by off-shoring, complex cheating, bribed tax exemptions, or submersion in the cash economy. In any case, as neoclassical economists themselves have long correctly argued it is better to help the poor by direct income supplements than by indirectly lowering prices through tax subsidies. A subsidized price gives the biggest subsidy to the biggest consumer, who is usually not poor. However, in the absence of a quantitative cap there is no guarantee against the rebound effect, although higher prices for petroleum would surely limit it compared to the case of a "windfall" efficiency increase (one lacking the goad of higher prices).

Why is such a simple and obvious policy not advocated by neoclassical economists? Because for them natural resources are unimportant and ultimately non-scarce. If this sounds extreme remember that the usual neoclassical production function in microeconomics omits resources altogether—production is seen as a function of labor and capital only. And if sometimes neoclassicals do include R into the equation it makes little difference because the multiplicative form of the usual production functions implies that manmade capital is a good substitute for resources—you can bake a fifty-pound cake with only five pounds of flour, eggs, and sugar, if only you use a big enough oven and stir vigorously! And, with admirable consistency, macroeconomists calculate our national income without attributing value to resources in situ. Resources are valued according to their labor and capital costs of extraction (value added), and any royalty paid for resources in situ is simply a premium paid for access to a mine or well whose extraction costs are lower than the margin that it is currently profitable to exploit. All resources are free gifts of nature, but some gifts are easier to "unwrap" than others and therefore trade at a premium.

Paralleling the shift from the classical real cost (labor and capital) to the neoclassical subjective (utility) theory of value was a shift from commodity money (gold) to fiat money (paper). Just as value measured by subjective utility loses its connection to the objective factors of labor and land, so value symbolized by fiat money loses its connection to the real costs of mining gold, especially when amplified by fractional reserve banking. Both utility and fiat money are relatively unconstrained by the biophysical world of finitude and entropy that characterize resources, land, labor, and physical wealth. The token or "counter" of wealth, namely money, is now governed by laws different from those that govern real wealth. Fiat money can be created out of nothing and annihilated; physical wealth cannot. Money does not spoil or entropically disintegrate over time; real wealth does. Money does not take up space when accumulated; real wealth does. Money spontaneously grows at compound interest in a bank account; manmade capital does not—its spontaneous default tendency is to diminish. The world of money, debt, and finance becomes increasingly disjoined from the world of real wealth and physical resources. The financial world is built around debt and expectations of future growth in wealth to redeem the debt pyramid built by expansion of fiat money. Peak oil will disrupt the physical basis of those growth expectations and lead to a financial crash resulting in levels of real production that are even below physical possibility, as happened in the Great Depression.

The steady-state economy needs a monetary system more congruent with real wealth. M. King Hubbert in his early writings suggested an energy-based currency. The history I have sketched may suggest a return to gold or some other commodity money. I would favor a continuation of fiat money, but subject to the discipline of 100 percent reserve requirements, as suggested by Frederick Soddy, Irving Fisher, and Frank Knight—but that is another story.[3]

There is a bright side to peak oil if we can adapt to it. Obviously lower inputs of petroleum will, other things equal, reduce outputs of CO_2 and greenhouse effects, albeit with a lag. Also, higher prices for petroleum will act not only as an incentive for more efficient technology, but also as a tariff on all international and long-distance trade providing protection to national and local producers, thereby increasing local self-sufficiency and slowing down the lemming rush to globalization. Without the subsidy of cheap oil, the rates of exploitation and takeover of the natural world by mining, drilling, cutting, draining, filling, digging, blasting, paving, hauling, dredging, leaching, over-harvesting, mono-culturing, and so on, will all be slowed.

The big obstacle to the steady-state economy is our commitment to growth as the central organizing principle of society. Even as growth becomes uneconomic we think we must continue with it because it is the central myth, the social glue that holds our society together. Consider the *Washington Post*'s recent editorial, "The Case for Economic Growth" (April 2, 2006). They admit that the case for growth has been greatly weakened in the US by the fact that most of the GNP growth for over a decade has gone to the rich and little if any to the poor. They also acknowledge that even growth to the rich has produced little welfare in view of studies by psychologists and economists showing that beyond a threshold, already passed in the US, self-evaluated happiness ceases to rise with rising income. Despite these two blows, however, the *Washington Post* believes the case for growth remains strong, for two additional reasons. First, as Americans become richer they become more optimistic and tolerant, and therefore act more generously toward racial minorities, immigrants, and the poor. Second, only a richer America can continue making the world safe for free trade and democracy. If the mouthpiece of official Washington can't make a stronger case than that, then I think the growth ideology may finally be in trouble. But notice that even to make that weak case they had to assume that growth in GNP is in fact making us richer, when that is the very point most at issue in the growth debate! The evidence is that at the current margin growth increases environmental and social costs faster than it increases production benefits, making us poorer, not richer. Furthermore, by their own admission nearly all GNP growth has gone to the rich. Do they imagine that the portion of GNP redistributed to the poor through taxes and transfers has increased? In fact, GNP growth has not made us richer, and generosity has little to do with wealth in the first place. Nevertheless, the *Washington Post* editorial represents the level of reasoning that passes for serious economic discourse in Washington, DC. Does it reflect honest confusion, or cynical pandering to ruling class interests? In either case it falls far short of John Stuart Mill's 150-year-old analysis.

In the absence of a good substitute for petroleum, something currently not identifiable on the required scale, peak oil will signal an era of dwindling supplies and rising prices of the major energy source of industrial civilization, requiring a thorough adaptation of the economy to more severe geological and biological constraints. The classical steady-state economy is a way of thinking accustomed to adapting the economy to physical reality. The idea of a steady-state economy predates and is independent of peak oil—this is true even for M. King Hubbert[4] who wrote about the steady state well before his famous prediction of US peak oil. But the growing evidence that we are close to peak oil for the world should dramatically increase interest in the classical steady-state economy as a better fit for the real world than the current neoclassical perpetual growth model. Does someone have a better idea?

NOTES

1. Presented at Peak Oil Conference, George Washington University, Washington, DC, May 9, 2006, sponsored by the Program in Conservation Biology and Sustainable Development, University of Maryland.

2. Extreme neo-Darwinists sometimes seem to prefer high birth and death rates in order to exert greater selective pressure on the population, but I leave them for another discussion. Similarly one might argue for high depreciation rates to more quickly replace old capital with qualitatively better new capital.
3. See Afterword, "Money, Wealth, and Debt", in H. Daly and J. Cobb, *For the Common Good*, Beacon Press, Boston, MA, second edition, 1994.
4. Published on December 30, 2004 by Hubbertpeak.com. Archived on December 30, 2004. "Hubbert's Prescription for Survival, A Steady State Economy," by Robert L. Hickerson.

11.   How long can neoclassical economists ignore the contributions of Georgescu-Roegen?[1]

I.   INTRODUCTION

Some will immediately object to my title—Nicholas Georgescu-Roegen has not been ignored, they will point out. He was a Distinguished Fellow of the American Economic Association; Paul Samuelson, the pope of American economists, called him "a scholar's scholar, an economist's economist" (1965); and Mark Blaug (1985) included him in his book *Great Economists Since Keynes*. All true. What I mean is that Georgescu-Roegen has been ignored in the sense of not being taken seriously. Samuelson has said little about Georgescu-Roegen since his 1965 paean. Did he change his mind? Why? Certainly none of Georgescu-Roegen's ideas on the biophysical foundations of economics ever made it into the canon of Samuelson's famous textbook. Nor have Samuelson's colleagues and students at MIT paid Georgescu-Roegen the slightest attention. Little notice was taken of his death by the American Economic Association. Hardly a trace of his influence remains in the Economics Department of Vanderbilt University where he taught for twenty years. Did someone subsequently refute the "economist's economist"? Who? Where? Why this combination of temporary recognition followed by apparent amnesia? Mark Blaug (1985, p. 71) gives a partial answer:

> It is only fair to add that Georgescu-Roegen's later books have not been well received, or rather, have been respectfully received and quickly put away. For various complex reasons, not to mention the difficult style in which they are written and the intimidating references they contain to theoretical developments in physics and biology, these works have received virtually no critical discussion from economists.

It would seem that economists are allergic to physics and biology, and should be excused from any contact with such irritating and intimidating sciences! After all, the neoclassicals had just made a very heavy investment in learning mathematics, and that was thought sufficient to acquire scientific status, or at least the appearance thereof. Also if one starts encumbering mathematical growth models with biophysical dimensions one loses the analytical beauty and austere elegance of the pure mathematics. One also raises impolite political questions about biophysical limits to economic growth, and the sufficiency of economic growth as the panacea for poverty, unemployment, overpopulation, environmental degradation, and so on. One may even arrive at the very awkward conclusion that some very respected economists have been saying some very erroneous things for a very long time.

De Gleria (1995), in a thoughtful tribute to Georgescu-Roegen, argued that his was a mind that thought ahead of its time. If this is true, and I think it is, then the future should witness our catching up with his thinking. I believe this will eventually happen. Although it is ungracious to say so, Georgescu-Roegen's ideas may advance more rapidly now that he himself is no longer around to scare people away from them by his irascible nature and impatience to "suffer fools gladly." Some of Georgescu-Roegen's secret admirers may now openly take up his cause, no longer fearful that the master will disown them because of some minor difference.

In their excellent obituary essay and summary of Georgescu-Roegen's contributions, Maneschi and Zamagni (1997) remark that in spite of the recognition accorded him, "it is somewhat paradoxical that Georgescu seems to be better known outside than inside his adopted country, the United States" (p. 705). While in some ways adding to the puzzle, this remark also suggests a clue. European economists might have been more receptive because they learned from Georgescu-Roegen at a distance—more through his writings than in person. Also Europeans accord more respect to professors than do Americans, and that made personal relations with Georgescu-Roegen easier because, a European himself, he took the respectful deference of others as his due. Most importantly, Europeans are less under the domination of the MIT department of economics and its clones than are US economists. Samuelson's 1965 laudatio notwithstanding, the US neoclassicals found Georgescu-Roegen just too problematic to deal with. He was after all an accomplished mathematician who criticized the frequently excessive and pretentious use of mathematics in economics, and, as already emphasized, he was not an easy man to get along with. I once asked him why he thought that the neoclassical MIT "mafia" (his term) never referred to him or cited his work. He replied with a Romanian proverb to the effect that, "in the house of the condemned one must not mention the executioner." He was indeed something of an executioner, but usually a just one. A discussion of his critique of Solow/Stiglitz will provide an example of his justice, as well as of the neoclassical school's capacity to stonewall for thirty years. Georgescu-Roegen's ire was not always unprovoked—not by any means!

As Gowdy and Mesner (1998) pointed out, in the end Georgescu-Roegen gave up on the standard economists, and resigned from the American Economic Association. His own assessment of the situation was given in the following words,

> If I finally realized that I was running against one current or another, it was not from any crossing of intellectual swords with my fellow economists, who have systematically shunned such an encounter, but from their personal attitudes toward me. I was a darling of the mathematical economists as long as I kept contributing pieces on mathematical economics. (Georgescu-Roegen, 1992, p. 156)

That the systematic shunning of any intellectual encounter with Georgescu-Roegen continues to be the modus operandi of the neoclassical establishment, is evident from the forum discussion in *Ecological Economics* in September 1997. Parts of that discussion are repeated below.

II. GEORGESCU-ROEGEN'S CRITIQUE OF THE SOLOW/STIGLITZ NEOCLASSICAL VIEW OF PRODUCTION

In his Richard T. Ely Lecture to the American Economic Association, Robert Solow (1974, p. 11) stated that "If it is very easy to substitute other factors for natural resources, then there is in principle no 'problem'. The world can, in effect, get along without natural resources." As an "if–then" statement this is no less true than saying, "If wishes were horses then beggars would ride." But the facts are that wishes are not horses, and that natural resources and capital are generally not substitutes, but complements. While it is no doubt useful to state this conditional possibility for the sake of logical completeness in cataloging alternatives, one would expect that the production-without-resources case, once recognized, would be quickly set aside as unrealistic and unworthy of further analysis. However, Solow does not set it aside, but retains it as a real possibility. In fact, it is precisely this "real possibility" that has provided the foundation for a significant part of his previous work. His well-known work in growth theory is based on an aggregate production function in which resources do not appear at all, and which takes production to be a function only of capital and labor. That production function is a mathematically clear way of saying that "the world can, in effect, get along without natural resources."

What evidence does Solow offer for this remarkable affirmation about the way the world works? In the next paragraph he says, "Fortunately, what little evidence there is suggests that there is quite a lot of substitutability between exhaustible resources and renewable or reproducible resources." True enough, but irrelevant. The issue is not substitution between two types of natural resource, rather it is one of substitution of capital for resources—an entirely different matter. Easy substitution between two types of natural resource will not help the world to get along without natural resources!

Since the production function is often explained as a technical recipe, we might say that Solow's recipe calls for making a cake with only the cook and his kitchen. We do not need flour, eggs, sugar, and so on, nor electricity or natural gas, nor even firewood. If we want a bigger cake, the cook simply stirs faster in a bigger bowl and cooks the empty bowl in a bigger oven that somehow heats itself. Nor does the cook have any cleaning up to do, because the production recipe produces no wastes. There are no rinds, peel-ings, husks, shells, or residues, nor is there any waste heat from the oven to be vented. Furthermore, we can make not only a cake, but any kind of dish—a gumbo, fried chicken, a paella, bananas foster, cherries jubilee—all without worrying about the qualitatively different ingredients, or even about the quantity of any ingredient at all! Real recipes in real cookbooks, by contrast, begin with a list of specific ingredients and amounts.

A technical production recipe that contradicts both the first and second laws of thermodynamics, as well as best practice in cooking, is more than a little troubling. It led Georgescu-Roegen to the following verdict on Solow:

> One must have a very erroneous view of the economic process as a whole not to see that there are no material factors other than natural resources. To maintain further that "the world can, in effect, get along without natural resources" is to ignore the difference between the actual world and the Garden of Eden. (Georgescu-Roegen, 1975, p. 361)

Perhaps as an unacknowledged concession to Georgescu-Roegen's criti-cism, we find some years later a new version of the production function in which resources appear along with labor and capital, all multiplied together in a Cobb–Douglas function. Georgescu labeled this the "Solow–Stiglitz variant," and showed that including R (resources) in this type of produc-tion function simply sweeps the contradiction under the rug, without removing it.

Georgescu-Roegen deserves to be quoted at length on this point. He writes the "Solow–Stiglitz variant" of the Cobb–Douglas function as:

$$Q = K^{a1} R^{a2} L^{a3} \tag{1}$$

where Q is output, K is the stock of capital, R is the flow of natural resources used in production, L is the labor supply, and $a1 + a2 + a3 = 1$ and of course, $ai > 0$.

From this formula it follows that with a constant labor power, L_o, one could obtain any Q_o, if the flow of natural resources satisfies the condition

$$R^{a2} = \frac{Q_o}{K^{a1}L_o^{a3}} \tag{2}$$

This shows that R may be as small as we wish, provided K is sufficiently large. Ergo, we can obtain a constant annual product indefinitely even from a very small stock of resources $R > 0$, if we decompose R into an infinite series $\Sigma R = R_i$, with $R_i \rightarrow 0$, use R_i in year i, and increase the stock of capital each year as required by (2). But this "ergo" is not valid in actuality. In actuality, the increase of capital implies an additional depletion of resources. And if $K \rightarrow$ infinity, then R will rapidly be exhausted by the production of capital. Solow and Stiglitz could not have come out with their conjuring trick had they borne in mind, first, that any material process consists in the transformation of some materials into others (the flow elements) by some agents (the fund elements), and second, that natural resources are the very sap of the economic process. They are not just like any other production factor. A change in capital or labor can only diminish the amount of waste in the production of a commodity: no agent can create the material on which it works. Nor can capital create the stuff out of which it is made. In some cases it may also be that the same service can be provided by a design that requires less matter or energy. But even in this direction there exists a limit, unless we believe that the ultimate fate of the economic process is an earthly Garden of Eden.

The question that confronts us today is whether we are going to discover new sources of energy that can be safely used. No elasticities of some Cobb–Douglas function can help us to answer it. (Georgescu-Roegen, 1979, p. 98; see also Stiglitz, 1979, p. 41, fn 5)

To my knowledge neither Solow nor Stiglitz has ever replied to Georgescu-Roegen's critique. They were invited to do so in the above-mentioned September 1997 issue of *Ecological Economics*, and both chose to avoid even mentioning Georgescu-Roegen, much less reply to his specific criticism! What reply could they make? Let us consider a few possibilities that others have put forward in similar contexts.

First, it might be argued that resources can be left out of the production function because they are not really scarce. Air is usually necessary for production, but we do not explicitly enter it in the function because it is considered a free good. This argument loses plausibility as soon as we remember that most resources are not free goods. Furthermore, we cannot logically use price, even a zero price, as a coefficient of factors in the production function. The production function is a technical recipe with all terms in physical units, not value units. The fact that *aggregate* production functions must use prices as weights in calculating an aggregate quantity index (dollar's worth) of capital (or labor or resources) is a fundamental problem that limits the usefulness of aggregate production functions, not an answer to the difficulty just raised. Also, expressing the quantities of different factors in units of the same numeraire reflects an assumption, not a demonstration, that the factors are substitutes.

Second, it is sometimes argued that leaving resources out of the production function is justified by the implicit assumption that resources can be perfectly substituted by reproducible capital. Nordhaus and Tobin (1972) are quite explicit:

> The prevailing standard model of growth assumes that there are no limits on the feasibility of expanding the supplies of nonhuman agents of production. It is basically a two-factor model in which production depends only on labor and reproducible capital. Land and resources, the third member of the classical triad, have generally been dropped . . . the tacit justification has been that reproducible capital is a near perfect substitute for land and other exhaustible resources.

If that were the case then we could equally well leave out capital and include natural resources (substitution is reversible), yet no one suggests doing that (for related discussion, see Victor, 1991). To do that would run counter to the whole animus of neoclassical theory, which is to deny any important role to nature.

The Solow–Stiglitz variant includes resources explicitly, but implicitly makes a similar assumption about near perfect substitution of capital for resources—what Georgescu-Roegen aptly dismissed as a "conjuring trick." In the Solow–Stiglitz variant, to make a cake we need not only the cook and his kitchen, but also some non-zero amount of flour, sugar, eggs, and so on. This seems a great step forward until we realize that we could make our cake a thousand times bigger with no extra ingredients, if we simply would stir faster and use bigger bowls and ovens. The conjuring trick is to give the appearance of respecting the first law of thermodynamics (material balance) without really doing so.

Another argument for the unimportance of resources was offered in the influential book *Scarcity and Growth* (1963, p. 11) by Barnett and Morse, who argued that

> Advances in fundamental science have made it possible to take advantage of the uniformity of matter/energy—a uniformity that makes it feasible without pre-assignable limit, to escape the quantitative constraints imposed by the character of the earth's crust`. . . Nature imposes particular scarcities, not an inescapable general scarcity.

Just below the surface lies the alchemist's dream of converting lead into gold. All we need from nature are uniform, indestructible building blocks—the alchemical "quintessence" or "fifth essence" to which the traditional four essences (earth, air, fire, and water) are thought to be reducible, and through which they become convertible one into the other. Given the building blocks, all the rest is transmutation—value added by capital and labor (and perhaps a few magic words or symbols). Technical improvement enables labor and capital to add more value to the inert building blocks, but nature remains unnecessary beyond the initial provision of those blocks. This view at least respects the first law of thermodynamics, but unfortunately crashes headlong into the second law. While it may be technically possible to convert lead into gold thereby eliminating the particular scarcity of gold, we do not thereby remove general scarcity, because the potential for making such conversions is itself scarce. That potential must be continually used up by the economy and re-supplied by nature in the form of low-entropy natural resources.

Another possible reply would be to take off from Georgescu-Roegen's qualification that in some cases "the same service may be provided by a design that requires less matter or energy." This implicitly introduces a distinction between substitution among factors within a given set of technologies (existing state of the art), and substitution among factors made possible by a new technology (improved state of the art). Even the latter case is limited—future technologies must also conform to the laws of thermodynamics, Georgescu-Roegen insists—but he leaves it at that. Just how far new technology can ease the burden of scarcity, within the constraint of physical laws, remains an open question. But that really is another subject from the one at hand, since in constructing their aggregate production function Solow/Stiglitz aim to represent actual production processes of today and the recent past—not unknown future possibilities. It is as an empirically based representation of actual production processes that their production function is intended, and it is as such that it fails. That it would also fail to depict future technologies is an a fortiori criticism.

In an article otherwise critical of neoclassical theory, Ayers (1996, p. 12) offers a last-ditch defense of Solow/Stiglitz, in the absence of which he considers Georgescu-Roegen's critique "devastating." Ayers's too-generous defense is that, "in the distant future the economic system need not produce significant amounts of material goods at all." Further down the same page he implicitly conflates the production function with the utility function to make the claim that, "nobody can define a finite absolute minimum material input required to produce a unit of economic welfare." Maybe not, but we were talking about physical output, not welfare. Even production functions that yield services are producing a physical output—the use of something or somebody for some period of time. That is different from utility or welfare. The service of my physician may not increase my welfare at all, and could even reduce it—but it remains a measurable service for which I am charged. But even without this clarification Ayres found it necessary to immediately condition his statement questioning the existence of a minimum material input, by adding "with the obvious exception of food and drink." Are there not other obvious exceptions, for example clothing and shelter?

Maybe there are other replies to Georgescu-Roegen's criticism that are less unconvincing than those considered above, but if so then Solow or Stiglitz should break their silence and finally reply to Georgescu-Roegen's criticism of long standing. Of course Georgescu-Roegen is now deceased, but his critique did not die with him. Serious criticism and serious replies are both essential parts of science. When a fundamental critique from a very prominent economist goes for decades without a reply, we should worry about the health of our discipline!

Consider a further major difficulty resulting from the conjuring trick of just plugging R into a production function along with K and L. An immediate consequence is that the marginal physical products of K and L would have to be zero once R is included in the function. This is because the definition of marginal product of one factor requires that the amounts of all other factors be held constant as one more unit of the variable factor is added. But when resources are held constant then there can be no extra unit of output as labor or capital is increased because there is no extra physical substance for the extra output to be made from—it would have to be produced out of nothing, again fracturing the first law of thermodynamics. The point of course is not limited to Cobb–Douglas functions—any production function that obeys the first law of thermodynamics cannot avoid a strict complementarity between resources on the one hand and capital or labor on the other hand.

Zero marginal physical products of labor and capital, a necessary consequence of including R in any production function that obeys the most basic laws of nature, would destroy neoclassical distribution theory—perhaps too heavy a price to pay for admission that the world, in effect, cannot get along without natural resources! And once we admit that natural processes, as well as labor and capital, add value to the indestructible building blocks, then we must ask who has the right to appropriate nature's contribution? These are not trivial issues! Of course, we can continue to write mathematical functions that contradict physical laws, call them "production" functions, take the partial derivatives of L and K, and still label them marginal products of labor and capital. But then, as Georgescu-Roegen put it, this becomes a "mere paper-and-pencil operation" (PAP was his acronym).

Georgescu's fund-flow model of the production process is superior to the neoclassical production function. It emphasizes that physically what we call "production" is really transformation—of resources into useful products and waste products. Labor and capital are agents of transformation (efficient causes), while resources, low-entropy matter/energy, are "that which is being transformed" (material causes). We can often substitute one efficient cause for another, or one material cause for another, but the relation between efficient and material cause is fundamentally one of complementarity, not substitutability.

If we wish to retain the neoclassical production function then we must at least include natural resource inputs and waste outputs, and must adopt mathematical representations that, unlike the customary multiplicative forms, do not assume that agents of transformation (funds) can substitute for the resources undergoing transformation (flows). Accuracy of analytical representation of reality must replace mathematical tractability as the main criterion of a good model. Once we recognize the reality of inputs from nature then we must inquire about their scarcity and about the ecological processes that regenerate them. Once we recognize the necessity of returning waste outputs to nature then we must inquire about the capacities of ecosystems to absorb those wastes. We will no longer be able to avoid the ecological economist's vision of the economy as an open subsystem of a complex ecosystem that is finite, entropic, non-growing, and materially closed. In effect, neoclassical economists will become ecological economists!

Perhaps the best way to get an answer to Georgescu-Roegen's critique is not to raise it again with the same people that have ignored it for thirty years, but rather to somehow get 10,000 students to ask their economics professors the following questions in class: (1) Do you believe that economic activities must satisfy mass balance? (2) Why is it that neoclassical production functions do not satisfy the condition of mass balance? (3) Do you believe that Georgescu-Roegen's interpretation of production as physical transformation is correct? (4) Do you agree that the economic system is embedded in the larger environmental system, and totally dependent on it as both source and sink for the matter/energy transformed by economic activity? (5) Do you believe that the matter/energy transformations required by economic activity are constrained by the entropy law?

In the aforementioned discussion forum in *Ecological Economics* (1997) these five questions were put to Solow and Stiglitz, along with G-R's resuscitated critique of their neoclassical model of production, as restated above. In their invited replies neither Solow nor Stiglitz even mentioned G-R! For the most part they chose to simply repeat their well-known position rather than to defend that position against the arguments G-R had raised against it. But in closing Solow offered some forthright, if brief, replies to the above questions. The five questions, Solow's replies, and my comment on each are given below.

1. Do you believe that economic activities must satisfy mass balance?
    Solow's answer: "Yes."
    Comment: Agreed.
2. Why is it that neoclassical production functions do not satisfy the condition of mass balance?
    Solow's answer: "Because up until now, and at the level of aggregation, geographic scope and temporal extent considered, mass balance has not been a controlling factor in the growth of industrial economies."
    Comment: Mass balance holds at all levels of aggregation, geographic scope, and temporal extent—so Solow's qualifications seem beside the point. I think what Solow means is that material balance is unimportant because materials themselves are unimportant, which is implied by his use of a production function in which material flows are either absent or somehow substitutable by capital stocks. If material flows themselves are not important then material balances would not be important either. That is why Georgescu-Roegen criticized Solow for analyzing "the Garden of Eden" rather than the real world. The criticism remains unanswered. Does the qualification "up until now" indicate an expectation that the situation is about to change, that the mass balance constraint is gaining relevance?
3. Do you believe that Georgescu-Roegen's interpretation of production as physical transformation is correct?
    Solow's answer: "This is no doubt one aspect of production."
    Comment: Yes, but Solow has treated it as a very unimportant aspect— one that could safely be abstracted from in the analytical representation of production. Georgescu-Roegen criticized him for that—for abstracting from the essential, rather than from the incidental. If production is essentially the transformation of a flow of resource inputs into product outputs, with capital and labor funds serving as agents of transformation, then capital and resources must be more in the nature of complements than substitutes. As Georgescu-Roegen noted, agents of transformation cannot create the materials they transform, nor the materials out of which the agents themselves are made. Agent of transformation and material undergoing transformation are basically complements—they can be substitutes only along the margin of reducing waste of materials-in-process to zero—for example using a press to make particle board out of wood chips and sawdust. But then the press (capital) and the wood chips (resources) are again complements. Solow makes no recognition at all of this fundamental complementarity. Complementarity is pushed further offstage by its more technical definition based on constant output (which rules complementarity

out of existence in a two-factor world). Georgescu-Roegen remains
unanswered.

4. Do you agree that the economic system is embedded in the larger envir-
    onmental system, and totally dependent on it as both source and sink
    for the matter/energy transformed by economic activity?
    Solow's answer: "Certainly, and I welcome any attempts to model the
    dependence in a transparent way, so that it can be incorporated into
    aggregative economics."
    Comment: One should take Solow at his word about what he now wel-
    comes. His recent concern about the greenhouse effect is certainly wel-
    comed by ecological economists.

    However, if one agrees that the macroeconomy is a subsystem
    embedded in an ecosystem that is finite, non-growing, and materially
    closed, then wouldn't one expect the macroeconomy to have an optimal
    scale relative to the total ecosystem—a scale beyond which its growth
    is uneconomic? Why is it that each micro activity has an optimal scale,
    while the aggregate of all microeconomic activities is supposed to grow
    forever, unconstrained by any notion of optimal scale of the macro-
    economy relative to the ecosystem? Ecological economists would
    welcome any attempts by Solow to model the limit to growth resulting
    from optimal scale of the macroeconomy.

5. Do you believe that the matter/energy transformations required by eco-
    nomic activity are constrained by the entropy law?
    Solow's answer: "No doubt everything is subject to the entropy law, but
    this is of no immediate practical importance for modeling what is after
    all a brief instant of time in a small corner of the universe."
    Comment: Solow seems to identify the entropy law only with the ulti-
    mate heat death of the universe. I don't worry much about that either,
    and neither did Georgescu-Roegen, whose critique of Solow was not
    based on such a remote cosmic event. But the entropy law has more
    immediate and relevant implications: that you can't burn the same
    lump of coal twice; that when you do burn it once you get soot, ashes,
    CO_2, and waste heat, as well as useful heat. The entropy law also tells
    us that recycling energy is always a losing proposition, that there are
    limits to the efficiency of conversion of energy from one form to
    another, and that there is a practical limit to materials recycling—all in
    the here and now, not just in the cosmic by and by. Would Solow
    suggest to engineers designing real production recipes that they can
    neglect the second law of thermodynamics because we are concerned
    only with "a brief instant of time in a small corner of the universe"?

    Low-entropy matter/energy is the physical coordinate of usefulness;
    the basic necessity that humans must use up but cannot create, and for

which the human economy is totally dependent on nature's services. Entropy is the qualitative difference that distinguishes useful resources from an equal quantity of useless waste. Solow's statement that entropy is "of no immediate practical importance" to economic life is evidence in support of Georgescu-Roegen's indictment that Solow "must have a very erroneous view of the economic process as a whole." In any event Georgescu-Roegen's criticisms remain unanswered.

These unanswered criticisms bring us back to the question posed in the title—how long can neoclassical economists ignore G-R? The answer, as far as production theory is concerned, seems to be "thirty years and still stonewalling." This is disgraceful, and it is time for those of us who understood Georgescu-Roegen to press his arguments and not allow them to be brushed aside.

NOTE

1. Originally published in Kozo Mayumi and John Gowdy (eds), *Bioeconomics and Sustainability: Essays in Honor of Nicholas Georgescu-Roegen*, Edward Elgar, Cheltenham, UK, 1999, pp. 13–24.

REFERENCES

Ayres, R.U. (1996), "Theories of Economic Growth", INSEAD, September, Fontainebleau, France.

Barnett, Harold and Chandler Morse (1963), *Scarcity and Growth*, Baltimore: Johns Hopkins University Press for RfF.

Blaug, Mark (1985), *Great Economists Since Keynes*, Totawa, NJ: Barnes and Noble.

De Gleria, S. (1995), "Nicholas Georgescu-Roegen: A Mind that Thought Above its Time", *Economia Internazionale*, 13, 3–32.

Ecological Economics (1997), "Forum on Georgescu-Roegen versus Solow/Stiglitz", 22(3), September, 261–306.

Georgescu-Roegen, Nicholas (1975), "Energy and Economic Myths", *Southern Economic Journal*, 41(3), January, 347–81.

Georgescu-Roegen, Nicholas (1979), "Comments on the Papers by Daly and Stiglitz", in V. Kerry Smith (ed.), *Scarcity and Growth Reconsidered*, Baltimore: RfF and Johns Hopkins Press.

Georgescu-Roegen, Nicholas (1992), "Nicholas Georgescu-Roegen about himself", in Michael Szenberg (ed.), *Eminent Economists and their Life Philosophies*, Cambridge: Cambridge University Press, pp. 128–60.

Gowdy, John and Susan Mesner (1998), "The Evolution of Nicholas Georgescu-Roegen's Bioeconomics", *Review of Social Economics*, 56, 136–56.

Maneschi, A. and S. Zamagni (1997), "Nicholas Georgescu-Roegen, 1906–1994", *Economic Journal*, 107(442), May, 695–707.

Nordhaus, William and James Tobin (1972), "Is Growth Obsolete?", in National Bureau of Economic Research, *Economic Growth*, New York: Columbia University Press.

Samuelson, Paul (1965), "Forward" to *Analytical Economics* by N. Georgescu-Roegen, Cambridge, MA: Harvard University Press.

Solow, Robert (1974), "The Economics of Resources or the Resources of Economics", *American Economic Review*, **64**(2), May, pp. 1–14.

Stiglitz, J.E. (1979), "A Neoclassical Analysis of the Economics of Natural Resources", in V. Kerry Smith (ed.), *Scarcity and Growth Reconsidered*, Baltimore: RfF and Johns Hopkins Press.

Victor, P.A. (1991), "Indicators of Sustainable Development: Some Lessons from Capital Theory", *Ecological Economics*, **4**, 191–213.

PART 4

Testimony and Opinion

The articles in this section, and the next two as well, move from concepts and theory to policy—the "political economy" side of ecological economics. Ecological economists do not speak with one voice even on conceptual issues, much less on policy. So I should make it doubly clear that I am speaking for myself here, not for other ecological economists. However, I do try to ground my arguments in ecological economic concepts. I include here an invited testimony before the US Senate on "offshoring," and an invited written testimony to the Russian Duma on resource taxation. These of course must be short and to the point. Also included are two "op-ed" pieces with a similar premium on brevity. The article on involuntary resettlement and the threat power of eminent domain as increasingly important consequences of full-world economics was stimulated by a conference organized by my former World Bank colleague, anthropologist Michael Cernea. Since the World Bank has such a problem with involuntary resettlement I might have included this article in Part 3, but I believe involuntary displacement has become a general problem for the full-world economy, not just for development projects financed by the Bank.

Probably the oddest inclusion in this volume is the speech to OPEC, so I should say a bit about how it came to be. After OPEC meets in Vienna to do their important cartel business, they sometimes follow that meeting with a conference on a topic of more general interest. In September of 2001 that topic was "Towards a Sustainable Energy Future." I accepted an invitation to speak on "sustainable development." The conference took place a few weeks after the terrible events of September 11 in a rather tense atmosphere. I had decided to take a long shot and try to interest OPEC in assuming the global fiduciary role of limiting carbon throughput—the same role that the Kyoto accord was trying but failing to play, thanks largely to the opposition of the US. Kyoto was trying to use the lever of sink controls whereas OPEC could expand its lever of source controls. Whoever controls the source indirectly exerts great control over the sink, and whoever controls the sink exerts control over the rate of use of the source. I confess that my suggestion to OPEC, not my favorite organization, was less than totally sincere. I really preferred the Kyoto alternative, but thought that the prospect of a competing world role for OPEC might be just what the US and other high consuming nations needed to push them to a preemptive agreement in Kyoto. Failing that, then maybe such a move by OPEC would be our best chance to slow global warming, a very serious danger in my opinion. As you might expect, my long shot missed by a mile in interesting OPEC, or anyone else for that matter. Yet my students continue to find the idea pedagogically worthy of autopsy, so I include it.

12. Off-shoring in the context of globalization[1]

Off-shoring is the latest step in the misguided rush toward global economic integration and away from internationalist federation embodied in the United Nations and the Bretton Woods institutions.

Globalization, considered by many to be the inevitable wave of the future, is frequently confused with internationalization, but is in fact something totally different.

Internationalization refers to the increasing importance of international trade, international relations, treaties, protocols, alliances, and so on. *Inter*national, of course, means between or among nations. The basic unit of community and policy remains the nation, even as relations among nations become increasingly necessary and important.

Globalization refers to global economic integration of many formerly national economies into one global economy, mainly by free trade and free capital mobility, but also by easy or uncontrolled migration. It is the effective erasure of national boundaries for economic purposes.

The word "integration" derives from "integer," meaning one, complete, or whole. Integration is the act of combining into one whole. Since there can be only one whole, only one unity with reference to which parts are integrated, it follows that global economic integration logically implies national economic disintegration. By dis-integration I do not mean that the productive plant of each country is annihilated, but rather that its parts are torn out of their national context (dis-integrated), in order to be re-integrated into the new whole, the globalized economy. As the saying goes, to make an omelet you have to break some eggs. The disintegration of the national egg is necessary to integrate the global omelet. It is dishonest to celebrate the latter without acknowledging the former.

No one is arguing for isolationism. Of course the world is highly interdependent, but interdependence is to integration as friendship is to marriage. It is hard enough for nations to be friends, and is utterly foolish to attempt multilateral marriage. A necessary condition for friendship is a healthy respect for differences, for boundaries. All of this points to internationalization, not globalization.

Off-shoring is part of the disintegration of the national economy that is implicit in globalization. We no longer have US capital and US labor cooperating to produce US goods to compete in a world market against, say, Chinese goods produced by Chinese labor and Chinese capital. Instead we have formerly US but now transnational capital moving to China to produce a product with cheap Chinese labor for sale in the US. This is great for a few capitalists, but all capitalists cannot continue to depend on US purchasing power to sell their products without contributing to US purchasing power by employing US labor. Say's law says that in the process of production, factors are paid an amount equal to the value of the product—the incomes generated by production are sufficient to buy the product.[2] There is a circular flow from expenditure to income to expenditure, and so on—depicted in the first chapter of every economics principles textbook. But if factors in China receive the income generated by production of goods sold in the US, then the circular flow is broken, and US incomes will eventually not be sufficient to purchase the new imports plus remaining domestic production. The Chinese income generated by off-shoring will mostly be spent in China, not on US exports, and not on the goods that the off-shoring capitalist is producing in China specifically for the US market. The US ends up with less employment and a larger trade deficit. China ends up with more employment and a trade surplus. That surplus can be used to purchase US assets, whose future earnings will go to China, not the US. It may well be that the gains to China are greater than the losses to the US, but that is certainly not the mutual benefit promised by traditional free trade based on comparative advantage.

If capital is internationally mobile, competition will force it to seek absolute advantage, and one country will lose jobs and income, while another gains. Although there would be an increase in world production, we would no longer necessarily be achieving a better outcome for *each* nation. Specialization and trade according to comparative advantage, as envisioned by free trade, is a clever second-best strategy for the capitalist who, for whatever reason, cannot invest abroad. If he could invest abroad he would simply follow the rule of absolute advantage and never even think about comparative advantage. This is the reality in today's globalized economy, where from the point of view of the capitalist, China and the US are just different regions of the same integrated global economy, not national communities serving their own distinct public interests.

China seems quite capable of looking out for its own national interests. The US, on trade issues at least, seems rather muddled about whether it is even a nation.

NOTES

1. Statement before Senate Democratic Policy Committee, March 5, 2004, Washington, DC.
2. A modern version of Say's law is attributed to Henry Ford who said that he wanted to pay his workers enough so that they could buy his cars. A more modern version is attributed to Sam Walton who is alleged to have said that he wanted to pay his employees so little that they would have to shop at Wal-Mart.

13. Invited testimony to Russian Duma on resource taxation[1]

Date: December 18, 1998
To: Mr. Vyachislav Zvolinsky, and other Honorable Members of the Russian Duma Committee on Natural Resources, SubCommittee on Land and Ecology

Esteemed Representatives:

I am honored to be asked to comment as a part of your deliberations on Valuation of Natural Resources and Tax Reform. Since I have no first-hand knowledge of current realities in Russia I will confine my remarks to some general principles for pricing resources in the service of community, the environment, and a just and sustainable future.

1. While it is true that land and natural resources exist independently of man, and therefore have no cost of production, it does not follow that no price should be charged for their use. The reason is that there is an opportunity cost involved in using a resource for one purpose rather than another, as a result of scarcity of the resource, even if no one produced it. The opportunity cost is the best forgone alternative use. If a price equal to the value of the opportunity cost is not charged to the user, the result will be inefficient allocation and waste of the resource—low-priority uses will be satisfied while high-priority uses are not. Efficiency requires only that the price be paid by the user of these "free gifts of nature"—but for efficiency it does not matter to whom the price is paid. For equity it matters a great deal to whom the price is paid, but not for efficiency.
2. To whom, then, should the price be paid? To the owner, of course. But who is the owner? Ideally ownership of land and resources should be communal since there is no cost of production to justify individual private ownership "by whomever produced it." Each citizen has as much right to the "free gifts of nature" as any other citizen. By capturing the necessary payment for public purposes one serves both efficiency and equity. We minimize the need to take away from people

by taxation the fruits of their own labor and investment. We minimize the ability of a fortunate few private land and resource owners to reap a part of the fruits of the labor and enterprise of others. Land and resource rents (unearned income) are ideal sources of public revenue. In economic theory "rent" is defined as payment in excess of necessary supply price. Since the supply price for land is zero, any payment for land is rent—if we paid no rent the land would not disappear. If the government owns land and resources it can both measure and capture the appropriate rents by auctioning use to those who wish to use it.

3. But what if land and resources are already privatized? For one thing, they might be repurchased by the government. But if that is not feasible, or if one doubts that the competence and honesty of the government is sufficient to handle the auction system, then one could leave ownership in private hands and try to capture the unearned rents for social purposes by taxation. This is the usual case. Taxes should be shifted away from value added (labor and capital) and on to "that to which value is added" (natural resources and land). If we tax away rent, land and natural resources will not disappear. But if we tax wages and profits too heavily then some of the value added to natural resources and land by labor and capital will indeed disappear. The natural resource throughput begins with depletion and, after production and consumption, ends with pollution. Putting the tax at the beginning of the resource flow through the economy (throughput) is better than putting it at the end. A resource tax at the point of depletion induces greater efficiency in production, consumption, and in waste disposal.

4. Not only is land and resource rent the best thing to tax from the point of view of efficiency and equity in a well functioning market, such taxes are also a means for improving the functioning of the market itself by internalizing external costs and benefits. Economic theory says we should tax external costs and subsidize external benefits. Since there are significant external costs from depletion and pollution, taxing this resource flow (even above the level that captures rent) helps to internalize these external costs, in addition to capturing internal rents generated by the market. Since there are significant external benefits from increasing employment and capital accumulation, ceasing to tax (if not actually subsidizing) these socially desirable activities is a further correction of the market's ability to reflect true social benefits accurately. The resource tax at the point of depletion can reflect external costs of depletion and pollution, in addition to capturing rent. Higher resource prices force production technologies to use the resources more efficiently, and also force more frugal and efficient patterns of consumption. Recycling

of wastes is stimulated because the alternative of new extraction is now more expensive. Such recycling reduces pollution as well as depletion. If sufficient revenue had been raised previously by taxing labor and capital, then as we replace labor and capital taxes by resource taxes we encourage (cease to discourage) employment, capital accumulation and enterprise.

5. The above are very basic principles, and lest you think I am being condescending in suggesting them to you, let me assure you that these same principles have not yet been understood by the US Congress, and that I eagerly make these very same suggestions to the government of my own country. The Primakov tax reform bill described in your letter of 16 December seems to be a good step toward applying these principles. I believe that The Netherlands and Sweden are ahead of both the US and Russia in this regard.

With all good wishes for your important deliberations,
Herman E. Daly
Professor

NOTE

1. Invited Statement to Russian Duma, Committee on Natural Resources, SubCommittee on Land and Ecology, December 18, 1998.

14. Involuntary displacement: efficient reallocation or unjust redistribution?[1]

In his little book *The Economy of Love and Fear*, Kenneth Boulding (1973) distinguished three general principles of social organization:

1. the threat principle—you do something good for me or else I will do something bad to you. The motivation is fear.
2. the exchange principle—you do something good for me and in turn I will do something good for you. The motive is self-interest.
3. the integrative principle—I will do something good for you independently of what you do. The motive is love.

All three principles are always necessary and present in varying degrees, but in today's market economy the second—reciprocity—is usually favored.

Involuntary resettlement, by virtue of being involuntary, falls under the rubric of threat rather than exchange, and thereby escapes the domain of market transactions, since the latter are by assumption strictly voluntary. Love, and even fear, are often justifiable principles of social organization, but the justification is not in terms of mutual benefit as with exchange. My point is that involuntary resettlement is overwhelmingly a political, collective matter, not economic in the usual sense of efficient, individualistic, maximizing behavior. Applying to it the tested principles of welfare economics would be the least that could be done to correct some of the inherent and raw inequities built into these forced non-market "transactions," often hidden behind an apparent use of compensation. Yet the economics of development-caused forced displacement and resettlement is one of the least elaborated domains of development economics.

Involuntary resettlement is frequently treated as an externality: "the wellbeing lost by those who are displaced by a project, such as a dam, is an example of an externality, or more strictly, of an external cost."[2] Much better to be counted as an externality than to be fully ignored. I found the Swanson/Pearce paper (presented at the National Academy Workshop,

September 23, 2004) more instructive and insightful, especially the rights-
based approach with the implication that "willingness to accept" should
replace "willingness to pay" as the more relevant principle in deciding compensation. I like this approach much better than Pearce's earlier emphasis
on resettlement as an external cost. Since it is the earlier view, which is still
common among economists, that I want to criticize, I should note that
Pearce himself seems to have moved away from it.

Is involuntary resettlement best viewed as an external cost? An external
cost is an involuntary cost inflicted via non-market interdependence on a
third party as a consequence of a market transaction between two other
parties, usually voluntary. If the dam builder/owner is the first party, and
the electricity users are the second party, then one might well consider the
oustees the third party, for whom the external consequence of the transaction is resettlement, fulfilling the definition of external cost. Although
resettlement is a non-market interdependence like noise or dirty air, it is for
the victim less a traditional nuisance than a tragedy. Resettlement is forced
by government on the oustee in the interest of the project proponents, both
builders and users. It is as if those suffering from air or water pollution were
obliged to relocate so as to avoid the pollution. One might therefore consider the transaction between government and oustee to be primary. The
oustee is not a third party, but one of the two principal parties to another
transaction, an involuntary one. That involuntary transaction may itself
inflict further involuntary costs on third parties, which would then be external costs. But the involuntary surrender of one's property or customary
rights for a sum one did not agree to is more than an external cost. It is a
primary transaction, "an offer you cannot refuse," as the Mafia puts it. In
other words, externalities are glitches in an exchange economy resulting
from non-market interdependence; involuntary resettlement is part of the
threat economy that underlies and backs up the exchange economy. From
the point of view of the oustee it is the difference between being acciden-
tally stepped on and purposefully kicked. Willingness to accept compensation may differ greatly in the two cases.

Involuntary resettlement, at least its first phase, is increasingly referred
to as "displacement," a useful term that highlights a different aspect of
what is happening—namely that something is pushed aside or destroyed as
something else takes its place. What gets destroyed or pushed aside is the
opportunity cost of whatever takes its place. Opportunity cost is the most
basic concept in economics. The fundamental rule of economics is "never
do anything unless it is worth more than its opportunity cost." The concept
of opportunity cost does not necessarily involve an exchange or voluntary
transaction, and is present even when the motive for displacement of one
thing by another is love or fear. All that is necessary for opportunity cost

to exist is that there be scarcity. If there are millions of wild rivers then the opportunity cost of displacing one by a dam is nil—at least as long as no people live there. In the past our world was empty, there were lots of places where no one lived. Now our world is full—people live nearly everywhere, not to mention other species. In my lifetime world population has tripled, and energy and materials use has increased much more. The world is now relatively full of us and our stuff.

As we move from an empty to a full world the box labeled "externalities" has grown very large and important. Indeed, nowadays the very capacity of the earth to support life is treated by neoclassical economists as an "externality." Surely before reaching that point we should rethink and reshape our economic vision so that vital matters are internal to our theory and only trivial issues are external. But so far the priority of the neoclassicals has been to preserve the model by classifying whatever doesn't fit as an "externality." In the empty world one could with some justification say "mere" externality. In the full world externalities are often much more important than what remains internal. Involuntary resettlement is too vital an issue for too many people to be dealt with in such an ad hoc manner.

In the empty world opportunity costs were low and consequently many new projects were worth doing. In the full world opportunity costs are much higher, many more things must be displaced when one thing expands. New projects must exceed a higher default value if they are to be worth doing. To adapt to doing fewer things is not easy for a society addicted to growth. So we tend to do new or more things even when they are worth less than their opportunity cost, just to keep busy and maintain the illusion of growth, while failing to notice when growth has become uneconomic rather than economic.

One way that we maintain this illusion is to underestimate the opportunity cost of displacement by substituting involuntary transactions for voluntary ones. As long as what is being displaced is nature, we have found it easy to understate the opportunity cost because other creatures, like future generations and today's dispossessed, cannot bid against us in the market. Also we are ignorant of many ecological services and consequently value their opportunity cost at zero. While the world was still relatively empty growth displaced mainly nature. Now the world is so full that growth displaces human beings and their activities to an ever-greater extent.

To the extent possible we should sequence our displacements of nature so that low opportunity cost displacements are done first. The opportunity cost of external displacements of nature therefore rises. We then consider the alternative of internally displacing another human activity instead of the ever more valuable natural activity. Efficiency requires that, at the margin, the cost of an internal displacement of other human activity should be equal to the cost of the external displacement of nature. The cost of internal human displacements rises in step with the cost of external displacements as the human economy expands into its containing ecosystem.

Involuntary displacement is of course not limited to developing countries or World Bank projects. In Detroit, Michigan in 1981 the lower middle-class suburb of Poletown was razed, destroying 1400 homes, 140 businesses, and several churches to make room for a General Motors assembly plant.[3] The Michigan Supreme Court ruled that this was a legitimate exercise of eminent domain by the city of Detroit, accepting the argument that job creation and tax receipts rendered the private GM plant a "public use," as required by the state constitution. This Poletown decision, which became an oft-cited precedent in other cases, was recently and unanimously overruled by the Michigan Supreme Court in a similar case. The Court ruled that

> Poletown's "economic benefit" rationale would validate practically any exercise of the power of eminent domain on behalf of a private entity. . . . If one's ownership of private property is forever subject to the government's determination that another private party would put one's land to better use, then the ownership of real property is perpetually threatened by the expansion plans of any large discount retailer, "megastore," or the like.

Note the phrase "threatened by the expansion plans" of some other entity. If property rights become conditional on a court's judgment that someone else might put your property to a more profitable use, then the very foundation of a market exchange economy is undermined, and we are in a threat economy, even if legal under eminent domain. This is not an "externality" of the exchange economy; it is a whole different system based on threat rather than voluntary exchange.

Growth, "expansion plans," become more expensive in a full world as the opportunity cost of displacement rises. Voluntary exchange tends to reflect the rising opportunity cost of displacement. In a property-based market economy, therefore, displacement would become more expensive and less frequent. But we do not really live in a market economy, contrary to much rhetoric. We live in a growth economy, and growth requires displacement. So how do we keep growing in the face of rising opportunity costs of displacement? As noted above, one way is to understate the cost of displacement by taking it out of the exchange economy and putting it in the threat economy. Market prices are abandoned in favor of the calculations of planners, and transactions based on the latter are enforced by threat of official violence. As expansion becomes more and more expensive it becomes "uneconomic growth" and has to be forced on people "for their own good"![4]

The very right of property, without which there can be no exchange, no market prices, becomes conditional on its owner's success in growth maximization!

On June 23, 2005 the US Supreme Court in a 5–4 decision (Kelo v. New London) upheld the use of eminent domain to compel the sale of property from one private entity to another if it increased economic growth and tax revenue.[5] A dissenting opinion from Justice Sandra Day O'Connor stated that now the "specter of condemnation hangs over all property. Nothing is to prevent the State from replacing any Motel 6 with a Ritz-Carlton, any home with a shopping mall, or any farm with a factory." What grows in a growing economy is the reinvested surplus. Since that surplus is mainly owned by the rich it is no surprise that growth primarily benefits the rich, even if some trickles down to the poor.

This is not to say that involuntary displacement is never justified; only that its justification requires more than internalization of external costs. What more is required? As indicated in the quote from the Michigan Supreme Court there must be a conflict between the broad public interest and a narrow private interest that obstructs pursuit of the former. This means that the *distribution* of benefits and costs, not just the total amounts, is critical in deciding whether the forced displacement is justified. The Potential Pareto Criterion, on which much cost–benefit analysis is based, completely abstracts from distribution. On this point there is no disagreement. The centrality of distribution is also evident from the fact that most oustees are the poor; otherwise they would be hard to displace.

One could argue that displacement with compensation is at least an opportunity for redistribution in favor of the poor. This possibility would be strengthened if the resettlement and compensation had to be completed before construction contracts could be made. The easiest way to make sure that the compensation is sufficient is to give the oustee the right of refusal. This basically puts us back under the exchange principle and away from the threat principle. The issue is complicated by lack of property rights, and whether recent settlers have the same claim to compensation as long-term residents. Absolute right of refusal would also run counter to the legitimate use of eminent domain when it truly serves the public interest. The point is that these are issues of distributive justice and should be faced as such without the smokescreen of potential Pareto optimality. Often economists say that we must first be sure that total benefits outweigh total costs in monetary terms before we consider distribution. However, in welfare terms total cost and benefit each depend on how the monetary costs and benefits are distributed, and welfare is the relevant criterion for the public interest, and public interest is the relevant criterion for the exercise of eminent domain. So distribution remains primary.

How might our economic vision be reshaped so that the overflowing box of "externalities" no longer overwhelms the diminishing reality that remains internal to our theory? A suggestion comes from ecological economists who argue that there are three basic parts to the economic problem: *allocation* (apportionment of basic resources to the production of different commodities); *distribution* (apportionment of commodities and resource ownership among different people); and *scale* (the physical size of the human subsystem relative to the total earth ecosystem—how full is the world of us and our stuff). A good allocation is efficient, a good distribution is just, and a good scale is at least sustainable—does not impose depletion and pollution burdens beyond the regenerative and assimilative capacities of the ecosystem. These concepts help to clarify the issue of involuntary displacement. First, as discussed above, an ever-increasing scale will make displacement ever more expensive and involuntary. Second, as noted, just distribution is what involuntary resettlement is all about. It is part of the threat economy, not an externality of the exchange economy. As such it is about just distribution, not efficient allocation. In my view the discussion of involuntary displacement has so far been too much in terms of allocative efficiency and too little in terms of distributive justice, while scale has been entirely off the radar screen. One special aspect of distributive justice is inclusion of the displaced in the distribution of the specific benefits of the investment project. After all, the goal of investment is to make at least some people better off. Why should not the displaced have a right to be among those who actually benefit from the project rather than just be compensated for imposed loss?

NOTES

1. Invited paper, "Economics and Involuntary Displacement", National Academy of Sciences Workshop, September 23, 2004, Washington, DC, organized by Michael M. Cernea.
2. David Pearce, "Methodological Issues in the Economic Analysis for Involuntary Resettlement Operations", in M. Cernea, ed., *The Economics of Involuntary Resettlement*, 1999, p. 51.
3. *Washington Times*, August 11, 2004, "Finding Property Rights in Rubble", by Jacob Sullum.
4. As Robert Goodland has noted, "involuntary resettlement [is] the most widespread and systematic use of force by proponents of economic development projects. The number of people who have been displaced is enormous. Dam projects alone have displaced many tens of millions of people since economic development began in developing countries in the late 1940s and early 1950s. Before being displaced, practically all oustees are poor and voiceless; many are vulnerable ethnic minorities. If involuntary resettlement worked successfully, that is, if it guaranteed that outsees became modestly better off promptly following their move, there might be fewer objections. The tragedy is that the millions of rural people resettled all over the world are almost always further impoverished

because of their sacrifice. There are few, if any, examples where rural resettlement has not intensified poverty.

Economics is predicated on free will, willing seller and willing buyer. If any partner in a transaction is unwilling, economic theory does not apply." (Goodland, 2007, in press)
5. *Washington Post*, June 24, 2005, p. 1, "Justices Affirm Property Seizures", by Charles Lane.

REFERENCES

Boulding, Kenneth (1973), *The Economy of Love and Fear: A Preface to Grants Economics*, Belmont, CA: Wadsworth Publishing Co.

Daly, Herman and Joshua Farley (2004), *Ecological Economics: Principles and Applications*, Washington, DC: Island Press.

Goodland, Robert (2007), "The institutionalized use of force in economic development", in C.L. Soskolne, L. Westra, L.J. Rotze, B. Mackey, W.E. Rees and R. Westra (eds), *Sustaining Life on Earth: Environmental and Human Health through Global Governance*, Lanham, MD: Lexington Books (Rowman and Littlefield Publishers), Chapter 24 (in press).

Pearce, David (1999), "Methodological Issues in the Economic Analysis for Involuntary Resettlement Operations", in M. Cernea (ed.), *The Economics of Involuntary Resettlement*, Washington, DC: The World Bank.

Washington Times (2004), "Finding Property Rights in Rubble", by Jacob Sullum, August 11.

15. Sustainable development and OPEC[1]

INTRODUCTION

In Part I the meaning of sustainable development, along with basic arguments for its desirability and long-term necessity, are considered. In Part II some speculations are offered about how OPEC might take a leading role in developing a global policy and fiduciary institutional framework in the service of sustainable development.

I. THE GOAL OF SUSTAINABLE DEVELOPMENT

Sustainability is not a new idea in economics—it is embedded in the very concept of income. As defined by Sir John Hicks, income is the maximum that can be consumed in a given year without reducing the capacity to produce and consume the same amount next year. By definition income is sustainable consumption. Whatever part of consumption is unsustainable is by definition not income but capital consumption. If income is by definition sustainable, then so is its growth. Why all the fuss about sustainability? Because, contrary to the theoretical definition of income, we are in fact consuming productive capacity and counting it as income in our national accounts.[2] Natural capital lies outside the accounting domain and is being used beyond the natural capacities of the environment to regenerate raw materials and to absorb wastes. Depletion of natural capital and consequent reduction of its life-sustaining services is the meaning of unsustainability.

OPEC countries have certainly been faced with the question of how much of their net receipts from petroleum can legitimately be counted as income in the Hicksian sense, and how much is a draw-down of inventories, or capital consumption, requiring compensating investment in alternative assets. In a sense, the issue of sustainable development is a broadening of this question to include all forms of natural capital—forests, croplands, grasslands, fisheries, mines, wells, atmosphere, water, and so on—not just petroleum. I will not go further into this specific matter of the

156

proper accounting of income from a depletable asset since it has been admirably discussed by my former World Bank colleague, Salah El Serafy, in the references given.

Instead, I will begin by asking—Why has natural capital depletion been ignored for so long? Because the macroeconomy has been envisioned as the Whole rather than a Part. In standard economics nature is just a sector, a part of the macroeconomy—forests, fisheries, agriculture, extractive industries, eco-tourism, and so on. It is not seen as a containing, provisioning, biophysical envelope that sustains the entire macroeconomy. In ecological economics, by contrast, we envision the macroeconomy as an open subsystem of the enveloping ecosystem. The containing ecosystem is finite, non-growing and materially closed. It is open with respect to solar energy, but that flux of energy is itself finite and non-growing. In this view, the physical growth of the economic subsystem (i.e., growth in population and per capita resource use) encroaches on the space and functions of the larger system. Consequently growth of the macroeconomy incurs an opportunity cost (the most important sacrificed natural service) (see Figure 15.1). Opportunity cost of expansion is zero for the Whole, but positive for the Part as it encroaches on the Whole. So if one thinks of the macroeconomy as the Whole, then its expansion is into the Void, encroaching on nothing. There is no opportunity cost of growth in this vision, and the obvious policy is growth forever.

The same practical result is reached even if one considers the economy as a subsystem of the ecosystem, as long as the subsystem is very small relative to the larger system. In this "empty-world vision" (Figure 15.1) the environment is not scarce and the opportunity cost of expansion of the economy would be negligible. But continued growth into a finite and non-growing ecosystem will eventually lead to the "full-world economy" in which the opportunity cost of growth is significant. We are already in such a full-world economy, contrary to the opinion of many economists.

In the ecological economics vision the opportunity cost of encroachment is of two kinds: the emptying of environmental sources (depletion), and the filling up of environmental sinks (pollution). The economic subsystem lives by a metabolic flow, an entropic throughput from and back to the environment. Low entropy resources are taken from the environment (depletion) and eventually are returned to the environment as high entropy wastes (pollution). Just as an animal lives from its environment by its metabolic flow, so the economy lives from the environment by its entropic throughput. As the economic subsystem continues to grow, it grows relative to the total system and eventually would approach the dimensions of the total system. As it does it must approximate ever more closely the characteristics of the total system, namely non-growth—an approximate steady state consisting

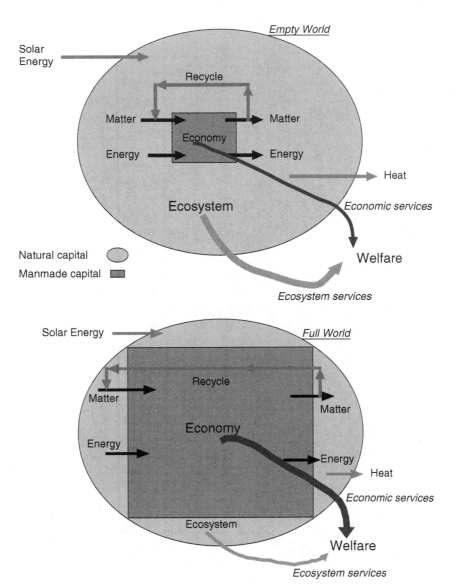

Figure 15.1   A "macro" view of the macroeconomy

of the entire earth maintained by an entropic throughput of solar energy.
The planet earth is non-growing in its physical quantitative dimensions, but
of course it evolves and changes qualitatively. Likewise the economic subsystem, as its scale approaches that of the containing ecosystem, must cease

physical growth, although qualitative evolution continues. The path of progress must shift from quantitative growth to qualitative development, if it is to be sustainable. Sustainable development is, therefore, qualitative improvement without quantitative growth beyond the assimilative and regenerative capacities of the ecosystem.

Growth has moved us from an empty-world economy to a full-world economy. The pattern of scarcity has changed, but the rules of economics remain the same. The rule remains to economize on the limiting factor in the short run, and to invest in increasing its supply in the long run. We have moved from an empty world in which manmade capital was limiting, to a full world in which remaining natural capital is limiting. For example, the fish catch used to be limited by manmade capital (fishing boats), but now it is limited by the fish remaining in the sea (natural capital). We have an excess of fishing boats. Similarly, production from irrigated agriculture is no longer limited by well-drilling or river diversion capacity (manmade capital), but by the size and recharge capacity of aquifers and the flow rates of rivers (natural capital).[3]

The list of examples could be extended, but for now the most relevant example is petroleum. The limiting factor for the throughput of petroleum is no longer the manmade capital of drilling equipment, pipelines, tankers, refineries, and combustion engines, but the natural capital of remaining sources of petroleum in the ground. Perhaps even more limiting is the sink capacity of the atmosphere to absorb the CO_2 resulting from petroleum combustion. Sink capacity is also natural capital. Economic logic says we should economize on and invest in the limiting factor. Economic logic has not changed, but the pattern of scarcity has. More and more it is remaining natural capital that now plays the role of limiting factor. We have been very slow to change our economic policies accordingly and refocus our economizing and investing on natural capital. Instead we have treated natural capital as a free good and accounted its draw-down as income rather than unsustainable capital consumption. To avoid a write-off on the falling value of excess manmade capital that should result from the increasing scarcity of its complementary factor (natural capital), we continue to increase the rate of draw-down of natural capital, hoping for future geological discoveries and technical advances. Hence, US President George W. Bush's energy policy remains that of the Spindletop era in Texas—find more oil, pump it out, and burn it now.

The WTO, the World Bank, and the IMF, while intoning the term "sustainable development" at every opportunity, continue to support the goal of infinite growth for the world, including especially the high consumption societies. They cannot imagine poor countries doing anything other than selling their products to rich countries. How else can they earn the foreign exchange to pay back World Bank and IMF loans? Therefore they think it is vital for rich countries to become ever richer, so they can buy more from the poor. Global trickle-down remains their solution to poverty.

Of course sustainability cannot be our only goal. If it were then we could easily attain it by returning to a hunter-gatherer economy with a low population density and low per capita consumption. The economic goal is to attain sufficient per capita resource consumption for a good life for all the world's people, for a long time. If the product of current per capita resource use and population is so large that it cannot be attained without consuming the earth's capacity to support future life in conditions of sufficiency, then we must reduce per capita resource use, or population, or both. Of course this will be easier to do if we can also improve resource productivity. But improved resource productivity will be slow to happen in a regime of cheap resources. The best way to improve resource efficiency is to make it more necessary by restricting the resource throughput (lowering per capita resource use). This means higher resource prices. Yes, that is a hardship for the poor, and consequently makes serious reduction in income inequality all the more necessary. However, continuing a subsidized price for petroleum means a greater subsidy to the biggest user, which is itself a regressive shift in real income distribution.

Technical improvements in resource efficiency, by themselves, will simply lower demand for resources, resulting in lower prices, which will stimulate further uses. It is fine to have cars that get twice the miles per gallon, but not if it simply means that we travel twice as much and burn the same throughput of petroleum in more, albeit more efficient, cars on more crowded roads. *Efficiency* is more miles per gallon. *Frugality* is using fewer gallons. A policy of "frugality first" stimulates efficiency. A policy of "efficiency first" does not stimulate frugality—indeed it fosters the perception that frugality has become less necessary. With lower resource prices even efficiency becomes less necessary.

The goal of sustainability, then, is not by itself sufficient. We must seek an optimal scale of the macroeconomy relative to its containing and sustaining envelope, the ecosystem. The concept of an optimal scale of the macroeconomy does not exist in current macroeconomics because, as we have seen, the macroeconomy is conceived as the Whole. But in fact the macroeconomy is a Part of a larger Whole, the ecosystem. The physical expansion of the economic subsystem does encroach on the rest of the Whole and does incur an opportunity cost. At some point, perhaps already passed, it is possible that the extra opportunity cost of disrupted environmental services resulting from encroachment will begin to exceed the extra production benefits. In other words we will have reached and passed the optimal scale of the macroeconomy relative to the ecosystem. So-called "economic growth" (growth of the economic subsystem) would then in reality have become uneconomic growth—literally growth that costs us more than it benefits us at the margin. In the prescient words of John Ruskin (*Unto this Last*, 1862), "That which seems to be wealth may in verity be only the gilded index of far-reaching ruin."

Although unknown to macroeconomics, the concept of optimal scale or extent of an activity is the very heart of microeconomics. The "marginal cost equals marginal benefit" rule of optimization has aptly been called the "when to stop rule"—that is, when to stop growth in the activity in question. The common sense logic of microeconomics says that an activity should stop expanding when further expansion begins to cost more than it is worth—to require the sacrifice of alternatives that are more important than the added benefit. But when we turn to macroeconomics, there is no analog to the "when to stop rule." The rule is to grow forever. This is, to put it bluntly, an intellectual disgrace. The only excuse I can think of is the one already discussed—that the macroeconomists' preanalytic vision is that the macroeconomy is the whole, not a part of a larger whole. If there is no opportunity cost of growth there can be no optimal scale, and so uneconomic growth is impossible. But such a vision is contrary to reality and urgently needs correction.

A policy of sustainable development first aims at an optimal scale of the economy relative to the ecosystem. One of the features of an optimal scale is that it is sustainable—that is, the source and sink demands of the resource throughput necessary to sustain that scale are within the regenerative and assimilative capacities of the ecosystem. Second, once the scale of the resource throughput is limited, the distribution of ownership of this newly scarce function must be decided. In the case of petroleum we know specifically who owns the sources in most cases, but not who owns the sinks. This must be decided politically. In third place, after we have a socially defined sustainable scale and a just or at least acceptable distribution of ownership of sources and sinks, then we can allow the market to determine the efficient allocation of resources among competing uses.[4] How might OPEC fit into the emerging vision of sustainable development? Permit me to speculate.

II. SOME SPECULATIONS ON A LEADERSHIP ROLE FOR OPEC IN PROMOTING SUSTAINABLE DEVELOPMENT

Sources of petroleum throughput derive from private or public (national) property; sinks are in an open access regime and treated as a free good.

Therefore, rents are collected on source scarcity, but not on sink scarcity. Different countries or jurisdictions collect scarcity rents in different ways. In the US, for example, Alaska has a social collection and sharing of source rents, institutionalized in the Alaska Permanent Fund whose annual earnings are distributed equally to all citizens of Alaska. Other states in the US allow private ownership of sources and private appropriation of source rents.

New institutions are being designed to take the sink function out of the open access regime and recognize its scarcity (Kyoto). Tradable rights to emit CO_2, requiring first the collective fixing of scale and distribution of total emission rights, are actively being discussed. Ownership of the new scarce asset (emission rights) could be distributed in the first instance to the state, which would then redistribute the asset by gift or auctioned lease.

Ideally sink capacity would be defined as a separate asset with its own market. This would require a big change in institutions. Assuming it were done, the source and sink markets for petroleum throughput, though separate, would be highly interdependent. Sink limits would certainly reduce the demand for the source, and vice versa. The distribution of total scarcity rent on the petroleum throughput between source and sink functions would seem to be determined by the relative scarcity of these two functions, even with separate markets. Alternatively, sink scarcity rent could also be captured by a monopoly on the source side, or source scarcity rent could also be captured by a monopoly on sink side.

To give an analogy, municipal governments, in charging for water, frequently price the source function (water supply) separately from the sink function (sewerage), thus charging different prices for inflow and outflow services related to the same throughput of water. In deciding their water usage consumers take both prices into account. To them it is as if there were one price for water, the sum of the input and output charges. Likewise the petroleum throughput charge would be the sum of the price of a barrel of crude oil input from the source and the price of CO_2 output to the sink from burning a barrel of petroleum. One could consolidate the two charges and levy them at either end, since they are but two ends of the same throughput. This would be a matter of convenience. Since depletion of sources is a much more spatially concentrated activity than pollution of sinks, it would seem that the advantage lies with levying the total source and sink charge at the source end. This is especially so since the sink has traditionally been treated as an open access free good, and changing that requires larger institutional rearrangements than would a sink-based surcharge on the source price. OPEC, given sufficient monopoly power over the source, would be well positioned to function as an efficient collector of sink rents for the world community. Could it also serve as a global fiduciary for ethically distributing those rents in the interests of sustainable development, especially for the poor?

OPEC, assuming it could increase its degree of monopoly of the source, may be in a position to pre-empt the function of the failing Kyoto accord by incorporating sink rents (and even externalities) into prices at the source end of the petroleum throughput. Of course OPEC does not have a monopoly on petroleum, much less on fossil fuels. It does not, even indirectly, control non-petroleum sources of CO_2. So it would be easy to overestimate OPEC's monopoly power, and the scheme suggested here does require an increase in its monopoly power. However, modern mass consumption nations such as the US apparently do not have the discipline to internalize either externalities or scarcity rents into the price of petroleum. Exclusion of developing countries from the Kyoto discipline, while understandable on grounds of historical fairness, undermines the prospects for accomplishing the goal of the treaty, namely limitation of global greenhouse gas emissions to a more sustainable level. OPEC, assuming it had sufficient monopoly power, might be able to provide this discipline for both North and South. The South, as well as the North, would have to face the discipline of higher petroleum prices in the name of efficiency, but would, in the name of fairness receive a disproportionate share of the sink rents. There would be a net flow of sink rents from North to South. The size of those rents would depend on OPEC's degree of monopoly power. The distribution of the rents would be in large part decided by OPEC—a large ethical responsibility which many would be unwilling to cede to OPEC, and which OPEC itself may not want. The obvious alternative to such a global fiduciary authority, however, has already failed. The inability to reach an agreement on international distribution of CO_2 emission rights was the rock on which Kyoto foundered. It is hard to see how such an agreement could be reached, either as a first step toward emissions trading, or as a fixed non-tradable allocation.

It is in OPEC's self-interest to pre-empt the emergence of a separate market for sink capacity, which could surely lower source demand and prices. While this gives OPEC a motivation, it also calls into question the legitimacy of the motivation as pure monopolistic exploitation. A legitimating compromise, as indicated above, would be for OPEC to behave as a self-interested monopolist on the source side, but as a global fiduciary on the sink side—that is, as an efficient collector and ethical distributor of scarcity rents from pricing the sink function. OPEC countries own petroleum deposits, but not the atmosphere. OPEC has a right to its source rents, but no exclusive right to sink rents. However, it may well have the power to charge, and redistribute sink rents as a global fiduciary—exactly what Kyoto wants to do, but lacks the power to do. In addition to effecting this transfer, the expanded role of OPEC as global fiduciary might increase the willingness of other petroleum producers (e.g., Norway) to join OPEC, thus increasing its monopoly power and ability to function as here envisioned. In addition the fiduciary role might provide ethical reasons for OPEC members to adhere to the cartel, when tempted by short-term profit opportunities to cheat.

Actually the existing OPEC Development Fund is already a step in this direction. Expansion of this fund into a global fiduciary institution for collecting and distributing sink rents, as well as the existing source rent contributions generously made by OPEC countries, is what is envisaged in this suggestion.

Just how total rents are determined and divided between source scarcity and sink scarcity is a technical problem that economists have not tackled because they have not framed the problem this way. Economists have focused on capturing source rents through property rights, and then internalizing the external sink costs of pollution through taxes. Only recently has there emerged a theoretical discussion of property rights in atmospheric sink capacity—whether these should be public or private, the extent to which trade in such rights should be allowed, and so on. As an initial rule of thumb we might assume that, since the sink side is now the more limiting function, it should be accorded half or more of the total throughput scarcity rents. In other words, sink rents should be at least as much as source rents. Sink rents would go to an expanded OPEC Development Fund dedicated entirely to global sustainable development in poor countries (especially investments in renewable energy and energy efficiency). Source rents would continue to accrue to the country that owns the deposits, and presumably be devoted to national sustainable development. The focus here is on a new public service function for OPEC of efficiently collecting and ethically distributing sink rents in the interest of global sustainable development. Where Kyoto has failed, OPEC might succeed as a stronger power base on which to build the fiduciary role—a power base that sidesteps the inability of nations to agree on the distribution of CO_2 emission rights among themselves.

Although any exercise of monopoly power is frequently lamented by economists, the early American economist John Ise had a different view in the case of natural resources: "Preposterous as it may seem at first blush, it is probably true that, even if all the timber in the United States, or all the oil, or gas, or anthracite, were owned by an absolute monopoly, entirely free of public control, prices to consumers would be fixed lower than the long-run interests of the public would justify."[5] Ise was referring only to the source function. The emerging scarcity of the sinks adds strength to his view. The reasonableness of Ise's view is enhanced when we remember that for a market to reflect the true price, all interested parties must be allowed to bid. In the case of natural resources the largest interested party, future generations, cannot bid. Neither can our fellow non-human creatures, with whom we also share God's creation, now and in the future, bid in markets to preserve their habitats. Therefore resource prices are almost certainly going to be too low, and anything that would raise the price, including monopoly, can claim some justification. Nor did Ise believe that the resource monopolist had a right to keep the entire rent, even though the rent should be charged in the interest of the future.

The measurement of the two different rents presents conceptual problems. The source rents are in the nature of user cost—the opportunity cost of non-availability in the future of a non-renewable resource used up today. Assuming that atmospheric absorptive capacity is a renewable resource, the sink rent would be the price of the previously free service when the supply of that service is limited to a sustainable level. If we assume separate markets in both source and sink functions we would theoretically have a market price determined for each function. Since the functions are related as the two ends of the same throughput, the source and sink markets would be quite closely interdependent. The separate markets could be competitive or monopolistic, and differing market power would largely determine the division of total throughput rent between the source and sink functions. For example, if, following a Kyoto agreement, the total supply of sink permits were to be determined by a global monopoly, that monopoly would be in a stronger position to capture total throughput rent on petroleum than would a weak cartel that controls the source. OPEC is surely aware of this.

What might the WTO and the World Bank think of such a suggestion? Since these two institutions are well represented at this conference, this question is more than just rhetorical. So far the WTO and the World Bank have been dedicated to the ideology of globalization—free trade, free capital mobility, and maximum cheapness of resources in the interest of GDP growth for the world as a whole, including mass consumption societies. In their view maximum competition among oil-exporting countries resulting in a low price for petroleum is the goal. Trickle down from growth for the rich will, it is hoped, someday reach the poor. I suspect the free-trading globalizers consider themselves morally superior to the OPEC monopolists. But which alternative is worse:

1. price- and standards-lowering competition in the interest of maximizing mass consumption by oil importing countries by minimizing the internalization of environmental and social costs with consequent destruction of the atmosphere, and ruination of local self-reliance by

a cheap-energy transport subsidy to the forces of global economic integration, or

2. monopoly restraints on the global overuse of both a basic resource and a basic life-support service of the environment, with automatic protection of local production and self-reliance provided by higher (full cost) energy and transport prices, and with sink rents redistributed to the poor?

Monopoly restraint results not only in conservation and reduced pollution, but also in a price incentive to develop new petroleum-saving, and sink-enhancing, technologies, as well as renewable energy substitutes. Unfortunately there would also be an incentive to use non-petroleum fossil fuels such as coal which would be a very negative effect from the point of view of controlling CO_2. Independent national legislation limiting emissions from coal may well be a necessary complement.

Ideally most of us would prefer a genuine international agreement to limit fossil fuel throughput, rather than a monopoly-based restriction imposed as a discipline by a minority of countries only on petroleum. But the Western high consumers, especially the US as resoundingly reconfirmed in its recent election, have conclusively demonstrated their inability to accept any restrictions that might reduce their GDP growth rates, even in the likely event that GDP growth has itself become uneconomic, as argued in Part I. The conceptual clarity and moral resources are simply lacking in the leadership of these countries. Perhaps the leadership reflects the citizenry. But perhaps not. The global corporate "growth forever" ideology is pushed by the corporate-owned media, and rehearsed by corporate-financed candidates in quadrennial television-dominated elections.

A lack of moral clarity and leadership in the mass consumption societies does not necessarily imply the presence of these virtues in the OPEC countries. Do there exist sufficient clarity, morality, restraint, and leadership in the OPEC countries to undertake this fiduciary function of being an efficient collector and an ethical distributor of sink scarcity rents? As argued above, there is surely an element of self-interest for OPEC, but to gain general support OPEC would have to take on a fiduciary trusteeship role that would go far beyond its interests as a profit-maximizing cartel. But a strong moral position might be just what OPEC needs to gain the legitimacy necessary to increase and solidify its power as a cartel. Could such a plan, put forward by OPEC, provide a stronger power base for the goals that Kyoto tried and failed to institutionalize? Might the WTO and World Bank recognize that sustainable development is a more basic value than free trade, and lend their support?[6] I do not know. Maybe the whole idea is just a utopian speculation. But given the post-Kyoto state of disarray and the paucity of policy suggestions, I do believe that it is worth initiating a discussion of this possibility. If sustainability is to be more than an empty word we have to evolve mechanisms for constraining throughput flows within environmental source and sink capacities. Petroleum is the logical place to begin. And OPEC is the major institution in a position to influence the global throughput of petroleum.

NOTES

1. Invited paper for the conference, "OPEC and the Global Energy Balance: Towards a Sustainable Energy Future", September 2001, Vienna, Austria.
2. See Salah El Serafy, "The Proper Calculation of Income from Depletable Natural Resources", in *Environmental Accounting for Sustainable Development*, edited by Yusuf J. Ahmad, Salah El Serafy, and Ernst Lutz, Washington, DC: World Bank, 1989; also Salah El Serafy, "The Environment as Capital", in R. Costanza, ed., *Ecological Economics* (The Science and Management of Sustainability), New York: Columbia University Press, 1991; and Salah El Serafy, "Green Accounting and Economic Policy", in *Ecological Economics*, June 1997. For a pioneering general critique of GNP accounting, see Roefie Hueting, *New Scarcity and Economic Growth* (More Welfare through Less Production?), Amsterdam: North Holland Publishing Co., 1980.
3. When factors are complements, the one in short supply is limiting. Manmade capital and natural capital are only substitutable over a very small margin, and are overwhelmingly complements, as evident in the examples given above. Nevertheless, neoclassical economics generally assumes that manmade and natural capital are substitutes. With substitutability there can be no limiting factor.
4. See Herman E. Daly, *Beyond Growth*, Boston: Beacon Press, 1996; and *Steady-State Economics*, Washington, DC: Island Press, 1991, for further discussion of these issues.
5. John Ise, "The Theory of Value as Applied to Natural Resources", *American Economic Review*, June 1925.
6. Such recognition might be stimulated by the plans under discussion by some NGOs to bring suit against the US under the WTO for granting wholesale protection to its domestic producers by refusing to join the Kyoto agreement. The extra cost for internalizing CO_2 emissions paid by Kyoto signatories is equivalent to a discriminatory tax on imports to the US, or a discriminatory subsidy to US producers.

PART 5

Reviews and Critiques

In this section I review two good books and one bad one in an effort to tie the overall discussion to the thoughts of others writing on related subjects. Issues raised in the review of the Ehrlichs' book are further discussed in the essay "Feynman's Unanswered Question." Points raised in reviewing Beck are elaborated in the section on globalization. In the ten years since Beck wrote his book the immigration issue has moved to the front line of political concern in the US, although little seems to have been accomplished toward its solution. The review of Huber serves mainly as a reality check to remind ourselves of the low level at which political discussion of these issues is often carried out. Only by chance will the reader have read any of these books and thus be in a position to judge the fairness of my review. However, in writing book reviews it is usual to assume that the readers of the review will not have read the book, and that, the review itself will help them decide whether to read or avoid it. Given what I said earlier about the excess of publications over readers, I should probably devote more time to reviewing the work of others.

The two inclusions that are not book reviews are rather reviews of particular errors or fallacies that have been prominent in environmental economic literature. There is little to be learned from the errors of ignorant or stupid people. But errors made by intelligent people justly respected by their profession can often teach us important lessons, especially about the blind spots of the profession they represent. As the saying goes, "it ain't what we don't know that hurts us, but what we know for sure that just ain't true."

16.   Can Nineveh repent again?[1]

The subtitle is descriptive of the book's contents; the title is evocative of its forebodings. I will comment on each.

The thrust of the book is to show that the World Scientists' Warning to Humanity—that "Human beings and the natural world are on a collision course"—is correct. The facts indicating the collision are organized around the useful identity introduced by the authors some time ago: Impact = Population × Affluence × Technology, where Affluence is GNP per capita, and Technology is impact per unit of GNP. Much new and old information is clearly and convincingly presented in this framework, interspersed with apt personal recollections.

There is no attempt to present the scientific or economic first principles from which the World Scientists' understanding and consequent warning follows. Instead a wealth of empirical evidence is presented, along with common sense arguments, to show that the Warning is correct.

Earlier the Ehrlichs' textbook with John Holdren, *Ecoscience*, had taken the more basic conceptual approach and equipped the student to follow the scientific arguments himself. I mention this not because I think they should have written a textbook instead, but to publicly lament the fact that *Ecoscience* has long been out of print. Evidently the publishers thought the book had to be "dumbed down" and the authors disagreed. As one who taught undergraduates from the book for several years I can testify that they found it accessible, sometimes with a little help, but then what was I there for? Also, probably the Ehrlichs felt their time was better spent educating the general public up to some minimum rather than helping to dumb down the universities. After all, in a democracy policy cannot rise above the level of understanding of the average citizen, and the Ehrlichs deserve a standing ovation for all they have done to raise that average, as well as for extending the margins of knowledge.

I cannot summarize here what is itself a large summary of facts and issues underlying population policy, immigration, economic growth and its limits, inequality, corporate reform, globalization, and so on. I can report that the discussion is fair and judicious, gracefully written, and without obeisance to the icons of political correctness or too-easy dispassionate consensus.

Policy recommendations mostly involve getting prices right in the many senses of that term: parents should bear most of the cost of having children;

growth-inducing subsidies, especially in agriculture, should be eliminated; consumers should each bear the full social and environmental cost of their consumption, and so on. Support for a consumption tax is especially welcome, but I would have been happier if, instead of a mild critique, they had rejected the value added tax in favor of a tax on throughput—that is, tax "that to which value is added," the metabolic flow from source to sink, not the value added to that flow by labor and capital which is really income. Also welcome were suggestions for limiting the power of corporations— their size and their phony status as persons under the bill of rights. The authors recognize that more is required than the many good policies they identify—"Nothing less is needed than a rapid ethical evolution toward readjusting our relationship with nature so that the preservation of biodiversity becomes akin to a religious duty" (p. 270). "Preservation of biodiversity" may sound like an innocent technical term, but as the Ehrlichs show, it really means limiting the scale of the human occupation of our finite globe. Neoclassical economists have so far either aggressively ignored this limit or, in effect, treated it as a religious matter by deifying technology as savior.

The last point leads me to the evocative and enigmatic title. "One with Nineveh" comes from Rudyard Kipling's 1897 poem "Recessional," most of which is prominently reprinted at the beginning of the book, with the remaining stanzas supplied in the endnotes. I had not read the poem since freshman English, and found it even more moving now than I did then. But why did the authors choose it for their title and epigraph? Is it just a literary hook to snag English majors, or a credo foreshadowing the book's message? I think the latter, but it is not easy to spell out the reasons, which may be why the authors left it to the reader. Speculation is irresistible.

A "recessional" is the closing hymn sung as the choir exits the sanctuary. Did Kipling mean that in 1897 Western Civilization's worship service had already ended, and that in the future the danger would be that we forget what is worthy of worship—hence the refrain "lest we forget"? Kipling's poem is a hymn, in fact a prayer, since every stanza addresses God in an attitude of contrition and supplication. Far from a celebration of imperialism, something often reasonably enough attributed to Kipling, this poem is a prayer of repentance for the national sins of imperialism. Could the connection be that civilization's imperial conquest of the natural world (as well as the related US economic imperialism also noted in the book) requires the same kind of repentance that Kipling called for from Imperial Great Britain?

Reference to Nineveh also brings to mind (more so in 1897) the biblical story of the reluctant prophet Jonah. Jonah preaches God's message to the

Ninevites, "repent or be smitten," and is both surprised and peeved when the Ninevites (temporarily?) repent and are forgiven.

Now many of us, including the Ehrlichs, have, like Jonah, been preaching to the modern Nineveh in which we live. Our message is similar, "change your basic outlook and behavior or suffer the consequences; that is, repent or be smitten." Unlike the ancients, our modern Ninevites retort:

> There is nothing to repent. Guilt is a Judeo-Christian hang-up, or perhaps just a chemical imbalance. Even if one felt like repenting, to whom would we offer repentance? Who is going to smite us if we don't repent? You say the unintended collective consequences of our own actions will smite us? We are too smart for that old Greek trap of Judgment by hubris! Look at how our economists have proved by rigorous mathematics, over and over again, that the free market converts private greed into public beneficence; look at our technology, look at systems theory and chaos theory . . . Here, Jonah, have a Prozac and chill out.

If we liken our scientific arguments and evidence to a lever that we prophets want to use to move the world, and further argument and evidence to an extension of the lever, then we still need a fulcrum, a fixed point of value or right purpose against which to pivot the lever of science, or else the world will not be moved. Extending the lever does not create a fulcrum. I suspect that the lure and appeal of Kipling's poem is that he is praying for such a fixed point on which to rest the unwieldy scientific lever, the "reeking tube and iron shard" in which "the heathen heart puts her trust."

Physicist Richard Feynman raised the same question in a 1963 lecture (*The Meaning of it All*):

> the great accumulation of understanding as to how the physical world behaves only convinces one that this behavior has a kind of meaninglessness about it . . . ["All valiant dust that builds on dust," in Kipling's words] . . . The source of inspiration today, the source of strength and comfort in any religion, is closely knit with the metaphysical aspects. That is, the inspiration comes from working for God, from obeying His will. . . . So when a belief in God is uncertain, this particular method of obtaining inspiration fails. I don't know the answer to the problem, the problem of maintaining the real value of religion as a source of strength and courage to most men while at the same time not requiring an absolute faith in the metaphysical system.

I don't know the answer either—how to conjure inspiration, purpose, and ethical behavior from a materialist metaphysics ending in meaninglessness. Whether the authors' choice of epigraph and title was intended to evoke these deep issues, I don't know, but for me they did. In any case I am grateful to Paul and Anne Ehrlich for the sanity, clarity, and goodness they continue to bring to the world. Maybe Nineveh will repent again.

NOTE

1. For *BioScience*, Vol. 54, No. 10 (October 2004), pp. 956–7, review of Paul and Anne Ehrlich, *One With Nineveh* (Politics, Consumption, and the Human Future), Island Press, Washington, DC, 2004, 447 pages, $27, hardback, ISBN 1-55963-879-6.

17. Beck's *Case Against Immigration*[1]

There is a big difference between being "anti-immigrant" and "anti-immigration." Immigrants are people, and immigration is a national policy. Beck is not an "immigrant basher." He manages to love the immigrant while hating the national policy of easy immigration. The US policy of immigration at current levels of about one million per year, with eligibility based mainly on kinship, is in his view a very bad policy. He argues that the number of immigrants should be cut back to pre-1965 traditional levels of around or below 200,000 annually. This amount suffices to meet the legitimate reasons for immigration. In this he is in agreement with the Congressional commission on immigration chaired by the late Democratic Congresswoman from Texas, Barbara Jordan, and with a large majority of the American people, if one is to believe the polls, which in this case I do. How we came to have an immigration policy that serves the cheap-labor appetite of the large corporations, and is counter to the will of the great majority of Americans is a fascinating and disturbing history well told by Beck.

Although the book is about the US it is of general interest since all countries have immigration policies, and some may be tempted to repeat US mistakes. There are some illuminating international comparisons, especially with New Zealand.

Mainly Beck focuses on legal immigration, taking it for granted that illegal immigration should be stopped. It is outrageous that the federal government does such a poor job of enforcing immigration laws. This is a breach of faith not only with citizens who democratically enacted those laws, but also with legal immigrants who have obeyed our laws, and who do not like to see "queue-jumpers" so kindly tolerated. But again, the cheap-labor interests are particularly fond of illegal immigrants because they have no legal rights and must put up with low wages and poor working conditions. The corporate view is that controlling the border is "not practical."

Beck explains how easy immigration has mainly hurt Blacks, the descendants of slavery (involuntary immigration), and how it makes a mockery of affirmative action. Beck is sympathetic to affirmative action as an indemnification to the heirs of slavery, but quite logically asks why it should be extended to other "minorities" whose ancestors were never slaves—at least not in the US. To further complicate matters these other "minorities," including many immigrant groups, understandably feel no historical responsibility for slavery in America, and consequently no special obligation to the descendants of slavery. The result is increasing conflict between Blacks and some immigrant groups.

In 1896 Booker T. Washington already saw through the cheap-labor policy of easy immigration. He urged the employment of American Blacks first, instead of pushing them to the end of the line behind increasing numbers of European, Asian, and Latin immigrants. The use, both past and present, of immigration policy to keep labor cheap in the interests of corporations and to the detriment of the US working class, especially Blacks, is convincingly argued by Beck. It is not a simple conspiracy story, but one of confused interests and conflicting values. Nevertheless there has been a conscious willingness on the part of employers to exploit the situation even though they did not totally create it.

The cheap-labor-by-immigration policy is being extended from manual labor to skilled labor. Computer programmers, doctors, engineers, and so on are seeing their salaries competed down by the importation of workers with critical skills needed to meet alleged labor shortages and "keep America competitive in the world economy." Some 140,000 immigrants per year are added to reduce the "skill shortage," plus another 65,000 temporary permits, good for six years. If companies were not allowed to import cheap engineers and computer technicians then we would have to train our own people to do these jobs, and in the process get them off welfare and help them attain a good livelihood. But of course it is cheaper in the short run for corporations to import skilled foreigners than to train our own people. Also the increased supply of labor from immigration lowers the wage of all workers, nationals as well as new immigrants, and thereby increases profits. The consequence is the abandonment and alienation of our working class, and a disincentive to American youth to prepare themselves for technical jobs that pay less and less. This situation is "justified" by the corporations in the name of comparative advantage. Global competition forces short-run cost cutting. Some also claim that we are incapable of producing highly trained people at home. That claim is belied by the fact that many of the foreign scientists and technicians hired under the critical skills allowance got their training in US universities. The sorry role of US universities in the exploitation of cheap foreign graduate student labor, especially in engineering and physics, does not escape Beck's notice or criticism.

To all the scare talk about "labor shortage" Beck replies, quoting economist Vernon Briggs, that he is delighted by a labor shortage—it is just what we all should want, since in a capitalist economy that is what leads to higher wages and better living standards for the working class, some 80 percent of the population. And Beck might have added that anyone who can speak of a labor shortage while real wages are falling deserves to flunk Econ 101.

Immigration of course increases population growth, and consequently has all the environmental costs associated with increasing population. Immigrants to the US have had higher fertility than native Americans, and, taking that into account, Beck calculates that between 1970 and 1995 immigrants plus their descendants contributed 30 million to the US population. The social and environmental effects of absorbing that extra 30 million in our schools, communities, and in the work force of particular industries, is told in rich and specific detail. Particularly interesting is the case study of the meat packing industry and how the availability of cheap immigrant labor, beginning in the early 1980s, resulted in low wages, unsafe working conditions, and a decline in community responsibility.

One further connection needs emphasis, and that is the link between immigration and the other major elements of globalization, namely free trade and free capital mobility. Beck does not really discuss the link, but does call attention to it in the final pages of the book, quoting a report by the *Washington Post* on an attempt in Congress to slightly reduce immigration in 1995. The senior policy director of the National Association of Manufacturers was quoted as saying "If they [US corporations] can't get the [foreign] people they want, they will move overseas." Exactly so. If we limit the immigration of labor without limiting the emigration of capital then the problem will not be solved—mobile capital will move to the cheap labor if the cheap labor can no longer come to where the capital is. Indeed, it is the mobility of capital that is the dominant force in globalization today, but its power is reinforced by easy immigration.

Beck has provided a great service in raising the moral and analytical level of the immigration debate, while also providing a solid factual base and an illuminating historical perspective. His book is highly recommended.

NOTE

1. Review, *Ecological Economics*, November, 1997 of Roy Beck, *The Case Against Immigration* (The Moral, Economic, Social, and Environmental Reasons for Reducing US Immigration Back to Traditional Levels), New York: W.W. Norton, 1996, 287 pages.

18.   Hardly green[1]

In *Hard Green*, author Peter Huber, lawyer and PhD engineer with the Manhattan Institute, concludes a paragraph about the efficiency of the free market in handling trash with the sentence, "In times of desperate famine, starving African children pick through human excrement in search of undi- gested kernels of corn." I have been engaged in the less tragic, though wholly analogous task of trying to find some kernels of intellectual nourishment in Huber's book. I did find a few and will share them later. But I confess that they were hard to extract, given the repetitive harangue and overstatement that Huber prefers to systematic argument and documentation.

But then, this is not a scholarly book. It is a political tract aimed at the coming election. The political message is that Al Gore-style environmen- talism is bad, and Teddy Roosevelt-style environmentalism is good. Of course Roosevelt will not be running against Gore, but George W. Bush might find a use for Huber's hard green banner. Environmentalists liked Gore's book, *Earth in the Balance*, and to the extent they think that Gore still remembers it, will be inclined to vote for him rather than for "Dubya." But Huber's hope seems to be that if the Republican mantle of Roosevelt's conservationism can be cleaned up, then Dubya could wear it to the ball and dance with the environmentalists without alienating the growth- pushing roughriders who brought him and expect to take him home.

Huber's plan of argument is to "Expose the soft green fallacy. Reverse soft green policy. Rediscover Theodore Roosevelt. Reaffirm the conserva- tionist ethic. Save the environment from the environmentalists." Critical to Huber's case is the big difference he sees between Roosevelt and Gore on the environment. Roosevelt is "hard," macho, high-tech green, concerned with the macro, visible environment of mountains, forests, geysers, big game, big dams, and nuclear power plants. Gore is a "soft," sissy, low-tech green, a nervous Nellie worried about the micro environment, invisible things like molecules, and intangibles like complex systems and ecological fragilities. The macro environment can be separated by boundaries and governed by hard green property rights and markets, invariably "free" markets, which lead to unlimited wealth and are immune to resource shortages or polluted spaces. The micro environment of migrating molecules and complex inter- dependencies that the soft greens emphasize does not respect property rights, and therefore efforts to deal with them lead to central planning and communism, under the intellectual leadership of Huber's bête noire, the soft-technology guru and alleged market-hating central planner, Amory Lovins.

Huber borrowed the hard–soft imagery from Lovins (author of *Soft Energy Paths: Toward a Durable Peace*) as a way of emphasizing their differences, but without specifically engaging Lovins's arguments. Lovins, in fact, is a strong proponent of markets and the profit motive. He believes that resource-efficient technologies already exist and more are being developed rapidly by the market—the same market that has turned thumbs down on nuclear power in spite of the enormous government subsidies and regulative apparatus that Huber glosses over in discussing his favorite hard green technology. Lovins sees big, dangerous, subsidized nuclear power as inconsistent with Jeffersonian democracy, while end-use efficiency improvements are smaller, cheaper, decentralizing, and more conducive to democracy. A more systematic critique of Lovins's arguments would have been helpful.

What has led Gore and the soft greens astray, Huber believes, is the "sandpile metaphor," which Huber explains: "You can see it in an egg timer. The sand trickles down to form a pile, the pile grows, its sides grow steeper, until finally they exceed some critical slope, and there is a sudden avalanche. Each additional grain produces almost no visible effect until the last one kicks off a massive slide." The problem with "sandpiles unlimited," Huber points out, is that "Lots of complex things aren't sandpiles. When honey descends drop by drop onto a plate, guess what? The collapse never comes, it all stays slow and smooth, and you can stop the gooey spread whenever you like . . . If you believe [James] Lovelock, the biosphere itself is honey, not sand." This for sure raises an interesting question—in what aspects does the world behave like sand and in what aspects like honey? For Huber it is mostly honey, but again I would have been grateful for a more systematic defense of that belief.

The most interesting thing about hard green Huber is that for him the natural environment is entirely unnecessary. For example,

> Cut down the last redwood for chopsticks, harpoon the last blue whale for sushi, and the additional mouths fed will nourish additional human brains, which will soon invent ways to replace blubber with olestra and pine with plastic. Humanity can survive just fine in a planet-covering crypt of concrete and computers . . . There is not the slightest scientific reason to suppose that such a world must collapse under its own weight or that it will be any less stable than the one we now inhabit.

Huber's only reason for caring about the environment is aesthetic—if we think it is pretty we should keep some, but strictly because we like it, not because we need it. All we need is knowledge, and that is unlimited. Even though I think it is Gnostic nonsense that we do not need the environment and can live on knowledge, it is certainly not nonsense that we might also want to protect the environment for purely non-utilitarian reasons. That is one of the kernels I promised to share. If Huber can convince his fellow free marketeers to take more land completely out of the economy as parks and nature reserves, and to look kindly upon and contribute to The Nature Conservancy for privately buying up land to retire it from economic use, then I will be happy to join in, whether this is labeled soft or hard. Huber did not suggest any particular lands or specific acreages to remove from the economy, nor how the opportunity costs of removal should be shared, and he may well think that Teddy Roosevelt already did enough. But he did not say that, so I remain hopeful.

Another kernel of interest is Huber's oft-repeated distinction between efficiency and frugality, and the point that achieving efficiency does not guarantee frugality. We gain efficiency by inventing cars that get more miles per gallon. But we then travel more miles in more cars and end up using more gasoline. Frugality requires that we use less gasoline. For precisely this reason I have always thought that the policy instrument should be frugality, leading to restrictions on the quantity of aggregate resource flow, trusting the market to then make the best adaptation by inducing innovation and efficiently allocating the limited resource total. I am pretty sure that Huber would not go along with any limitation on resource flows (he even rejects shifting the tax base from goods to bads) because he does not think that resources are ultimately scarce—he says there are no environmental limits to growth. In the absence of scarcity one wonders why Huber cares about either frugality or efficiency in the first place, and why he emphasizes the distinction. But it is a useful distinction and, to his credit, in later chapters he frequently contradicts his earlier overstatements. For example, early on Malthus is wrong on every count and "Malthusian limits will never arrive." Later Malthus has become "half right." At that rate Huber will be a Malthusian in his next book.

Since Huber's only reason for hard green environmentalism, as opposed to no environmentalism at all, is aesthetics, one might expect to find some serious discussion of aesthetics. Perhaps a theory of aesthetics, or at least a catalog of things Huber thinks are pretty. The only clue he gives us is that, "Whales and redwoods are magnificent. Smallpox and tapeworms are vile." I'd be happy if our free market economy found it profitable to deplete the supply of both smallpox and tapeworms, but unfortunately it prefers to exploit whales and redwoods, contrary to my aesthetic judgments, and Huber's. Is beauty purely in the subjective eye of the beholder, or does it have an objective relation to truth and goodness? I love landscapes, but

I also think buildings and even offshore drilling rigs can be beautiful. Is a Central Bureau of Aesthetics going to replace the Bureau of Central Planning? Or is something automatically beautiful by virtue of the fact that some moron bought it? If the latter, then we are back to economistic relativism and "aesthetic" becomes an empty word.

Combing the book for some normative principles does not yield much. Huber offers a normative critique of Garrett Hardin's "lifeboat ethics," and correctly puts his finger on the critical assumption that we can have accurate knowledge of consequences in the future, sometimes the distant future. But in harshly dismissing Hardin as one who assumes what he does not know in order to support misanthropic judgments, Huber is being disingenuous as well as ungenerous. Huber himself is cocksure that there are no limits to carrying capacity. Just like Hardin, Huber assumes precise knowledge of future carrying capacity: that it is precisely infinite. Thus, Huber dismisses Hardin's consequentialist ethics by virtue of his own extreme technological optimism—future technology will eliminate all negative consequences of any act. That leaves only positive consequences and the inherent rightness of the act as ethical criteria. It is just too facile for technological optimists to take this high road to ethical purity.

It is odd that Huber gives so little discussion of aesthetics when it is so central to his overall case. But even more central is the market, and it too gets scant analysis. There is some grudging discussion of externalities, and a welcome recognition (despite his earlier claims) that the market cannot constrain its own expansion into the biosphere and needs an external limit. But markets also require competition to be efficient, which suggests the need for many small buyers and sellers—small enough so that no single participant can affect the price. In a time of massive mergers and corporate giantism you would expect that ardent followers of Adam Smith would be calling for trust busting—especially if they are also admirers of Theodore Roosevelt! Not a word on the subject from Huber. Ronald Coase in his classic article on the theory of the firm said that firms are islands of central planning in a sea of market relationships. As the islands of planning grow and the market sea dries up between them, more and more allocative decisions are made by corporate central planning and less by the market. Unlike Adam Smith and Teddy Roosevelt, our free market friend does not worry about monopoly power—or distributive inequality of any kind. Perhaps he thinks technology will cure that too! But the free market will not.

In spite of fundamental differences, I do agree with Huber on a number of things: that communism is bad, that central planning is inefficient, that the Unabomber is bad, that well-defined property rights and markets can be a big help in environmental-economic policy, and that some greens, like some growth enthusiasts, are extreme in their views. I knew all this long before reading Huber. But I am older than the average reader and have been teaching economics for a long time. Huber is writing for the general public, especially conservative, young, technically trained Republicans. He may well teach them some important lessons, once he gains their confidence by excoriating the godless, Malthusian, communistic, soft greens. What I personally learned from reading Huber is that the ancient Christian heresy of Gnosticism (salvation by esoteric knowledge that allows transcendence of matter) is still a perversion to be reckoned with. The salvific knowledge is now less spiritual and more technical, but the heresy of human transcendence of the material Creation by esoteric knowledge is the foundation of Huber's book, and that, unfortunately, will appeal to many readers.

NOTE

1. Reviewed in *American Prospect*, April 24, 2000, *Hard Green: Saving the Environment from the Environmentalists* (A Conservative Manifesto) by Peter Huber, Basic Books.

19. The return of Lauderdale's paradox[1]

In giving up one unit of a good in exchange for another, a rational individual will sacrifice the least important, or marginal, use value of the good given up, and gain the marginal use value of the additional unit of the good acquired. The exchange value of one good relative to another, price, is determined by marginal use value. For things that are not normally exchanged in markets, but which are implicitly traded off against each other as a necessary consequence of the expansion of humanity's niche in the biosphere, we try to calculate the marginal utilities of natural capital as "shadow prices." If we are to avoid uneconomic growth we must be sure that the value of the natural capital services sacrificed as a result of human expansion is not greater than the value of the services gained from the expanded manmade capital. This logically requires some comparison of the value of natural capital services with the value of manmade capital services. We measure value as value-in-exchange (marginal utility) not as value-in-use (total utility). Prices reflect marginal use value, not total use value. All economists who have pondered the diamonds–water paradox, including the authors of the study under discussion, are aware that margins, while useful means for maximizing totals, are nevertheless very treacherous means for evaluating totals. Yet we rely on marginal valuation because that is the way the market works and we want to come up with measures that are comparable to our usual economic measure of value.

The purpose of the authors of "Pricing the Planet" is quite reasonable, and not, contrary to some wags, to sell, or rather rent, the earth to extraterrestrials. Nor do I consider their exercise in any way blasphemous, akin to putting a price on God. The pricing effort is, in the interest of better stewardship, to put relative values on various aspects of creation, not on the Creator. Philosophical naturalists usually deny the existence of a Creator, but then often invest nature (no longer a creation, but an accident) with the reverence they genuinely and deeply feel, but for which they no longer have an appropriate reference. Theists are fond of saying "we worship the Creator, not the creation"—and if really inspired they go on to add that "caring for creation is a necessary part of worshipping the Creator." In making these observations I do not presume to speak for the authors of the study under discussion whose religious views are unknown to me, but just to record my own reason for not joining those critics who take high offense at the very idea of pricing nature.

At the micro level of evaluating specific natural capital services on a small scale, we are in the proper realm of paying attention to margins for the sake of maximizing totals, and are not concerned with evaluating totals or aggregates. At the macro level, however, we are forced to face the contradictions involved in using margins to evaluate totals and aggregates. This issue was brought home to me by the comment of a reporter who called me to ask about the significance of "Pricing the Planet." The reporter commented that, since natural capital was now estimated to be worth some 33 trillion dollars, "we are a lot richer than we thought, and must think carefully about what should we do with the extra wealth." Of course this is a totally perverse understanding of the meaning of the study, but it is important to recognize that an intelligent person drew essentially the opposite conclusion from what the study showed, and from what the authors intended to convey. The reporter's confusion is an example of Lauderdale's paradox.

James Maitland, Earl of Lauderdale (Lauderdale, 1819), a classical economist writing in 1819, distinguished between "public wealth" and "private riches." Public wealth "consists of all that man desires that is useful or delightful to him." Private riches consist of "all that man desires that is useful or delightful to him, which exists in a degree of scarcity." Scarcity is necessary for an item to have exchange value. Use value is sufficient for something to be classed as public wealth, but not as private riches. The latter requires exchange value as well. Lauderdale called attention to the paradox that private riches could expand while public wealth declined simply because formerly abundant things with great use value but no exchange value became scarce, and thereby acquired exchange value and were henceforth counted as riches. Although scarcity is a necessary condition for a thing to have exchange value, Lauderdale felt that "the common sense of mankind would revolt at a proposal for augmenting wealth by creating a scarcity of any good generally useful and necessary to man." Of course the authors of the *Nature* article were making no such proposal, but, contrary to Lauderdale's expectation, the common sense of the reporter was not sufficient to rebel at the thought that increasing scarcity of natural capital really increased public wealth. No doubt the reporter identified public wealth with the sum of private riches.

In the Garden of Eden (no scarcity of natural capital) private riches in terms of natural capital would be zero because marginal utility of natural capital would be zero. But public wealth in the form of natural capital (total utility) would be at its maximum. As the Garden of Eden gets crowded due to population growth and economic growth, previously free goods become scarce and get a price greater than zero. We therefore observe an increase in private riches and perversely celebrate, while not noticing the decline in public wealth. Lauderdale's paradox seems to be the price we pay for measuring wealth in terms of exchange value. In Lauderdale's "empty world" of 1819 the paradox was just a vexing theoretical anomaly, but in our "full world" of 1997 it is a concrete and practical problem.

In the light of the above, I think that the best way to interpret the aggregate number in the *Nature* study, and a way in harmony with the authors' intentions, is to think of the measured scarcity value of natural capital services (33 trillion dollars) as an indirect index of the extent of past sacrifice of natural capital, and thus of the scarcity of remaining natural capital. Think of it as an index of how far we have moved away from the baseline of the "Garden of Eden" when the marginal utility of natural capital was zero, and its total utility at a maximum for that "empty world" state. The higher the measured scarcity value of remaining natural capital the farther away we are from some historical base period or "Garden of Eden" or "empty world" in which private riches in the form of natural capital were zero and public wealth in that form was a maximum. The higher that measured value, the more we should resist further conversion of natural into manmade capital. The figure of 33 trillion dollars screams at us to save what natural capital is left. There are evident physical consequences of excessive human expansion that scream the same message without need of explicit valuation. But for those who only hear dollars, let us scream now and then in dollars! It is a crude and inaccurate measure, but I think it is more than just "a bad underestimate of infinity." For decision making, valuing natural services at infinity is not a great advance over valuing them at zero. The aggregate figure is less reliable than measures of particular ecosystem service values, but, at least in the interpretation I suggested, responds to the macroeconomic need to have some measure of the cost of aggregate growth.

My own view is that the argument for restraining the excessive conversion of natural capital into manmade capital is better made by recognizing the fundamental complementarity between the two, and the fact that the complementary factor in short supply (increasingly natural capital) is the limiting factor. Standard economic theory as well as common sense urges us to economize on the limiting factor. But standard economic theory is so dedicated to the idea of substitution that it can hardly say the word "complementarity" any longer, and without complementarity there can be no limiting factor. The authors might reply that one would expect the price of the limiting factor to be high, and that their findings could be thought of as an empirical confirmation of the complementarity thesis. Perhaps so.

Of course there remain technical questions about the best way to measure exchange value of non-marketed goods and services even while accepting the broad interpretation given above. Although the authors have not solved these technical and philosophical problems whose roots go back to classical economics, they are to be commended for trying, and especially for the shining example of good conduct they set for the rest of the scientific community in actively seeking public criticism and suggestions for improving their work.

NOTE

1. *Ecological Economics*, Vol. 25, 1998, pp. 21–3.

REFERENCE

Lauderdale (1819), *An Inquiry into the Nature and Origin of Public Wealth and into the Means and Causes of its Increase*, 2nd edn, Edinburgh: Constable, p. 57.

20. When smart people make dumb mistakes[1]

Errors made by ignorant or stupid people, even when corrected, usually do not enlighten us very much. However, errors made by very intelligent and highly educated people often reveal a flaw in the state of the art of thinking on a subject, and therefore can be highly enlightening. I would like to consider one such enlightening error. It has been made by at least three leading economists, people who are at the top of our profession and deservedly command the respect of all economists:

1. In *Science* magazine's report (September 14, 1991, p. 1206) of a National Academy of Science study on climate change and greenhouse adaptation, Yale economist William Nordhaus is quoted as saying:

   > Agriculture, the part of the economy that is sensitive to climate change, accounts for just 3% of national output. That means there is no way to get a very large effect on the US economy.

2. In his 1995 book, *Small is Stupid*, Oxford economist Wilfred Beckerman (p. 91) also tells us that greenhouse-gas induced climate change is no worry because it affects only agriculture and agriculture is only 3 percent of GNP. Beckerman elaborates, "even if net output of agriculture fell by 50% by the end of the next century this is only a 1.5% cut in GNP."

3. In the November/December 1997 issue of *Foreign Affairs* (p. 9), former president of the American Economic Association (and subsequent 2005 Nobel Laureate in economics), Thomas C. Schelling, elaborates a bit more:

   > In the developed world hardly any component of the national income is affected by climate. Agriculture is practically the only sector of the economy affected by climate and it contributes only a small percentage—three percent in the United States—of national income. If agricultural productivity were drastically reduced by climate change, the cost of living would rise by one or two percent, and at a time when per capita income will likely have doubled.

It is not true that agriculture is the only climate-sensitive sector of the economy—just ask the insurance firms (and the citizens of New Orleans after Katrina!). But that is not the error that most concerns me. The error that concerns me here is to treat the importance of agriculture as if it were measured by its percentage of GNP. Surely these distinguished economists know all about the diamonds–water paradox, the law of diminishing marginal utility, consumer surplus, and the fact that exchange value (price) reflects marginal use value, not total use value. They know that GNP is measured in units of exchange value. They surely know that other economists have long referred to agriculture as *primary* production, and understand the reason for that designation. Presumably they also know that the demand for food in the aggregate (agricultural output) is famously inelastic. With this in mind it should be evident that in the event of a climate-induced famine the price of food would skyrocket and the percentage of GNP going to agriculture, which is not a constant of nature, could easily rise from 3 percent to 90 percent. No doubt adaptation would be possible, since in the past agriculture did account for 90 percent of national product and we (many fewer of us) survived. Clearly the percentage of the gross national product derived from agriculture is a measure of the importance only of *marginal* (very small) changes in agricultural output—certainly not Beckerman's "50% fall," or Schelling's "drastic reduction," or Nordhaus' unqualified "no way."

The assumption required by the "3 percent argument" therefore is that climate change will have only a marginal *physical* effect on agricultural output. The mere 3 percent of agriculture in GNP adds no evidence or reason for complacency beyond the bald and dubious assumption that any climate change will be obligingly marginal in its effect on agricultural output—too small to affect the price of agricultural goods, even in the face of inelastic demand. One way of looking at the error is therefore that it represents an elementary failure to distinguish marginal from inframarginal change.

Another related dimension of the error is that it treats all parts of GNP as substitutable, not only on the margin, but on the average and on the whole. If GNP declines by 3 percent due to disruption of agriculture that will presumably be no problem if GNP simultaneously increases by 3 percent due to growth in information technologies. A dollar's worth of anything is assumed to be indifferently substitutable for a dollar's worth of anything else. The same for a hundred billion dollars' worth. Although money is indeed fungible, real GNP is not. We measure GNP in monetary units, but GNP is certainly not money. A dollar is a piece of paper or a bookkeeping entry; a dollar's worth of food is a physical quantity of something necessary to support life. The fungibility of dollars does not imply the fungibility of food and, say, information services. Unless we first have enough food we just will not be interested in information services. If I am hungry I want a meal, not a recipe. Maybe that is why economists traditionally have called agriculture "primary" and services "tertiary."

True, agriculture accounts for only 3 percent of GNP, but it is precisely the specific 3 percent on which the other 97 percent is based! It is not an indifferently fungible 3 percent. The foundation of a building may be only 3 percent of its height, but that does not mean that we can subtract the foundation if we only add 3 percent to the top of the building. Economists who confuse fungibility of money with fungibility of real wealth proclaim publicly that they don't care if we produce computer chips or potato chips, as long as the dollar value is the same. While that may be roughly true for small changes at the margin, it is completely false applied to large changes, to averages, or to totals.

But it is still hard to understand how such distinguished economists could make such an elementary mistake. In all three cases the bad argument was part of a larger defense of economic growth. Could it be that, because the argument led to the "right" conclusion, it was exempted from the discipline of passing the test of elementary economics? The "right conclusion" is that economic growth is the solution to all our problems, including climate change, and that the solution cannot possibly induce the problem. Is the test of an argument that it leads to the right conclusion? Not really, but if we are totally committed to the conclusion (economic growth as measured by GNP is always good), then naturally we will be suspicious of any arguments that undermine that conclusion. And we may also look too kindly and indulgently on arguments that support the undoubted conclusion. I am not at all sure that this explains the error. But I am sure that the error cannot be attributed to ignorance or stupidity, and this is the only remaining explanation I can think of. As far as I know, none of the three distinguished economists has recanted the error though they have had roughly a decade to do so.

NOTE

1. *Ecological Economics*, Vol. 34, No. 1 (July 2000), pp. 1–3.

PART 6

Globalization

If by "globalization" one means world-wide communication via the Internet and cell phones, cultural exchange, scientific collaboration, international treaties regulating trade and environment, and so on, then it is all to the good. But that is not what the World Bank, the IMF, and the WTO mean by globalization. They mean the erasure of national boundaries for economic purposes. Specifically they mean free trade, free capital mobility, and increasingly free migration—where "free" refers to deregulated economic flows across national borders. The vision of world community shifts from that of a federation of independent national economies loosely connected by trade, to that of a single integrated global economy. Formerly national economies become mere nodes in a tightly interrelated global market for capital and labor, as well as for goods and services. These markets are no longer regulated by national governments, and not yet regulated by that hypothetical future world government imagined by some. The charter for the Bretton Woods institutions set up at the end of World War II was to pursue the federated model of trade among national economies in so far as it mutually benefited the cooperating nations, not to integrate these national economies into a single global market. If the IMF–WB–WTO are no longer serving the interests of their member nations as per their charter, then whose interests are they serving? The interests of the integrated "global economy" we are told. But what concrete reality lies behind that grand abstraction? Not real individual workers, peasants, small businessmen, or local communities, but rather giant fictitious persons, the transnational corporations.

Globalization has already come up several times in this collection. Yet the issue is of such pervasive importance, and so many people are so confused about it, that much more needs to be said. A major confusion to be dealt with in this section is that of many economists who persist in believing that David Ricardo's comparative advantage argument for free trade settled the question once and for all in favor of globalization. This boner might have been included as another dumb mistake often made by smart people discussed in the previous section, but it fits better in the globalization context.

21. Globalization versus internationalization, and four reasons why internationalization is better[1]

I. INTRODUCTION

My lecture has three parts: first I distinguish two concepts often confused, namely internationalization versus globalization. Second, I consider four negative consequences of globalization that to my mind constitute four good reasons for rejecting globalization, and accepting internationalization as the model to follow. Third, I consider the two most common objections to the case I have made against globalization (or for internationalization), and offer a refutation of each.

II. AN IMPORTANT DISTINCTION

The newspapers and TV say that if you oppose globalization you must be an "isolationist" or even worse a "xenophobe." Nonsense. The relevant alternative to globalization is internationalization, which is neither isolationist nor xenophobic. The media don't know the difference, so let us define the terms clearly:

Internationalization refers to the increasing importance of relations between nations: international trade, international treaties, alliances, protocols, and so on. The basic unit of community and policy remains the nation, even as relations among nations, and among individuals in different nations, become increasingly necessary and important.

Globalization refers to global economic integration of many formerly national economies into one global economy, by free trade, especially by free capital mobility, and also, as a distant but increasingly important third, by easy or uncontrolled migration. *Globalization is the effective erasure of national boundaries for economic purposes.* National boundaries become totally porous with respect to goods and capital, and increasingly porous with respect to people, viewed in this context as cheap labor, or in some cases cheap human capital.

In sum, globalization is the economic integration of the globe. But exactly what is "integration"? The word derives from "integer," meaning one, complete, or whole. Integration means much more than "interdependence"—it is the act of combining separate albeit related units into a single whole. Interdependence is to integration as friendship is to marriage. Since there can be only one whole, only one unity with reference to which parts are integrated, it follows that global economic integration logically implies national economic *dis*integration—parts are torn out of their national context (dis-integrated), in order to be reintegrated into the new whole, the globalized economy. As the saying goes, to make an omelet you have to break some eggs. The disintegration of the national egg is necessary to integrate the global omelet. This obvious logic, as well as the cost of disintegration, is frequently met with denial.

Denial aside, all that I have just said was expressed with admirable clarity, honesty, and brevity by Renato Ruggiero, former director-general of WTO: "We are no longer writing the rules of interaction among separate national economies. We are writing the constitution of a single global economy." This is a clear affirmation of globalization and rejection of internationalization as just defined. It is also a radical subversion of the Bretton Woods Charter. Internationalization is what the Bretton Woods Institutions were designed for, not globalization.

After the April 2000 disruption of its meetings in Washington, DC, the World Bank sponsored an Internet discussion on globalization. The closest they came to offering a definition of the subject under discussion was the following: "the most common core sense of economic globalization . . . surely refers to the observation that in recent years a quickly rising share of economic activity in the world seems to be taking place between people who live in different countries (rather than in the same country)." Mr. James Wolfensohn, then president of the World Bank, told the audience at the Aspen Institute's Conference, that "Globalization is a practical methodology for empowering the poor to improve their lives." The latter is a wish, not a definition, and the former says nothing about the central defining characteristic—the deregulation of exchanges across national boundaries.

Does economic integration imply or entail political and cultural integration? I suspect it does over the long run, but I honestly do not know which would be worse—an economically integrated world with, or without, political integration. Everyone recognizes the desirability of community for the world as a whole—but we have two very different models of world community: (1) a federated community of real national historical communities (internationalization), versus (2) a cosmopolitan direct membership in a single abstract global community (globalization). The "global community" so-called is simply an open-access commons, like the high seas, in which unfettered individualism among fictitious "persons," giant transnational corporations, has free reign.

III. FOUR NEGATIVE CONSEQUENCES OF GLOBALIZATION

1. Standards-Lowering Competition

Globalization undercuts the ability of nations to internalize environmental and social costs into prices. Economic integration under free market conditions promotes *standards-lowering competition* (a race to the bottom). The country that does the poorest job of internalizing all social and environmental costs of production into its prices gets a competitive advantage in international trade. More of world production shifts to countries that do the poorest job of counting costs—a sure recipe for reducing the efficiency of global production. As uncounted, externalized costs increase, the positive correlation between GDP growth and welfare disappears, or even becomes negative. We no longer know if growth is economic or uneconomic.

Another dimension of the race to the bottom is the increasing inequality in the distribution of income in high-wage countries, such as the US, fostered by globalization. In the US there has been an implicit social contract established to ameliorate industrial strife between labor and capital. Specifically, a just distribution of income between labor and capital has been taken to be one that is more equal within the US than it is for the world as a whole. Global integration of markets necessarily abrogates that social contract. US wages will fall drastically because labor is relatively much more abundant globally than nationally. It also means that returns to capital in the US will increase because capital is relatively more scarce globally than nationally. Theoretically, one might argue that wages would be bid up in the rest of the world. But the relative numbers make this a bit like saying that, theoretically, when I jump off a ladder gravity not only pulls me to the earth, but also moves the earth toward me.

2. Sacrifice of Competititive Structure of National Market

Fostering global competitive advantage is used as an excuse for *tolerance of corporate mergers and monopoly in national markets* (we now depend on international trade as a substitute for domestic trust busting to maintain competition). We must allow "our" firms to be big to compete globally. It is ironic that this is done in the name of deregulation and the free market. Chicago School economist and Nobel laureate Ronald Coase in his classic article on the Theory of the Firm, said "Firms are islands of central planning in a sea of market relationships." The islands of central planning become larger and larger relative to the remaining sea of market relationships as a result of corporate mergers. More and more resources are allocated by within-firm central planning, and less by between-firm market relationships. And this is hailed as a victory for markets! It is no such thing. It is a victory for corporations relative to national governments that are no longer strong enough to regulate corporate capital and maintain competitive markets in the public interest. Of the 100 largest economic organizations 52 are corporations (by sales) and 48 are nations (by GDP). One-third of the commerce that crosses national boundaries does not cross a corporate boundary; that is, is an intra-firm non-market transfer. The distribution of income within these centrally planned corporations has become much more concentrated. The ratio of salary of the Chief Executive Officer to the average employee has passed 400 on its way to infinity—what else can we expect when the chief central planners set their own salaries! Need I mention Enron?

3. Excessive National Specialization

Free trade and free capital mobility *increase pressures for specialization* according to competitive (absolute) advantage. Therefore the range of choice of ways to earn a livelihood becomes greatly narrowed. In Uruguay, for example, everyone would have to be either a shepherd or a cowboy in conformity with the dictates of competitive advantage in the global market. Everything else should be imported in exchange for beef, mutton, wool, and leather. Any Uruguayan who wants to play in a symphony orchestra or be an airline pilot should emigrate. After specialization nations are no longer free not to trade—yet freedom not to trade is essential if trade is to remain voluntary—a precondition for trade to be mutually beneficial!

Most people derive as much satisfaction from how they earn their income as from how they spend it. Narrowing that range of choice is a welfare loss uncounted by trade theorists. Globalization assumes either that emigration and immigration are costless, or that narrowing the range of occupational choice within a nation is costless. Both assumptions are false.

While the range of choice in *earning* one's income is ignored by trade theorists, the range of choice in *spending* one's income receives exaggerated emphasis. For example, the US imports Danish butter cookies and Denmark imports US butter cookies. The cookies cross each other somewhere over the

North Atlantic. Although the gains from trading such similar commodities cannot be great, trade theorists insist that the welfare of cookie connoisseurs is increased by expanding the range of consumer choice to the limit.

Perhaps, but could not those gains be had more cheaply by simply trading recipes? One might think so, but *recipes* (trade related intellectual property rights) are the one thing that free traders really want to protect.

4. Further Enclosure of the Knowledge Commons in the Name of Trade-Related Intellectual Property Rights

Of all things knowledge is that which should be most freely shared, because in sharing it is multiplied rather than divided. Yet, our trade theorists have rejected Thomas Jefferson's dictum that "Knowledge is the common property of mankind" in exchange for a muddled doctrine of "trade-related intellectual property rights" (TRIPS) by which they are willing to grant private corporations monopoly ownership of the very basis of life itself—patents to seeds (including the patent-protecting, life-denying terminator gene) and to knowledge of basic genetic structures.

The argument offered to support this grab, this enclosure of the knowledge commons, is that, unless we provide the economic incentive of monopoly ownership for a significant period of time, little new knowledge and innovation will be forthcoming. Yet, as far as I know, James Watson and Francis Crick, who discovered the structure of DNA, do not share in the patent royalties reaped by the second rate gene-jockeys who are profiting from their monumental discovery. Nor of course did Gregor Mendel get any royalties—but then he was a monk motivated by mere curiosity about how Creation works—a politically incorrect attitude these days! The globalizers seem to have forgotten a basic economic principle—that public goods, which are inherently non-rival and non-excludable, cannot be efficiently allocated by the market.

The idea behind TRIPS is not free trade, but rather the threat of trade restrictions as a sanction against any country that, along with Thomas Jefferson, considers knowledge to be the common property of mankind.

This is not to say that we should abolish all intellectual property rights—that would create more problems than it would solve. But we should certainly begin restricting the domain and length of patent monopolies rather than increasing them so rapidly and recklessly. And we should become much more willing to share knowledge. Freely shared knowledge increases the productivity of all labor, capital, and resources. It also removes an implicit tax on the production of new knowledge. *International development aid should consist far more of freely shared knowledge, and far less of foreign investment and interest-bearing loans.*

In support of this policy recommendation let me offer my favorite quote from John Maynard Keynes, one of the founders of the recently subverted Bretton Woods Institutions:

> I sympathize therefore, with those who would minimize, rather than those who would maximize, economic entanglement between nations. Ideas, knowledge, art, hospitality, travel—these are the things which should of their nature be international. But let goods be homespun whenever it is reasonably and conveniently possible; and, above all, let finance be primarily national.

IV. TWO COMMON OBJECTIONS RECOGNIZED AND REFUTED

Having now offered four good reasons against globalization (for internationalization) it remains to confront the two most common objections that are sure to be raised. The first is that the comparative advantage argument of David Ricardo proved once and for all that free trade, and by extension free capital mobility, is mutually beneficial, so any contrary conclusion must be wrong. The second is that whatever the problems with globalization the extra growth it stimulates is worth it. Let us deal with each briefly.

1. Comparative Advantage "Proves" that Global Integration is Beneficial

Since I am an economist, and really do revere David Ricardo, the great champion of classical free trade, I think it is important to point out that if he were alive now, he would *not* support a policy of free trade and global integration as it is understood today.

The reason is simple: Ricardo was very careful to base his comparative advantage argument for free trade on the explicit assumption that capital was immobile between nations. Capital, as well as labor, stayed at home, only goods were traded internationally. It was the fact that capital could not, in this model, cross national boundaries, that led directly to replacement of absolute advantage by comparative advantage. Capital follows absolute advantage as far as it can within national boundaries. But since by assumption it cannot pursue absolute advantage across national boundaries, it has recourse to the next best strategy, which is to reallocate itself within the nation according to the principle of comparative advantage. Comparative advantage is an argument for internationalization, not for globalization.

For example, if Portugal produces both wine and cloth cheaper than does England, then capital would love to leave England and follow absolute advantage to Portugal where it would produce both wine and cloth. But by assumption it cannot. The next best thing is to specialize domestically in the production of cloth and trade it for Portuguese wine. This is because England's disadvantage relative to Portugal in cloth production is less than its disadvantage relative to Portugal in wine production. England has a comparative advantage in cloth, Portugal a comparative advantage in wine. Ricardo showed that each country would be better off specializing in the product in which it had a comparative advantage and trading it for the other, regardless of absolute advantage. Free trade between the countries, and competition within each country, would lead to this mutually beneficial result.

Economists have been giving Ricardo a standing ovation for this demonstration ever since 1817. So wild has been the enthusiasm for the conclusion that some economists forgot the assumption upon which the argument leading to that conclusion was based; namely, internationally immobile capital (and labor). Whatever the case in Ricardo's time, in our day it would be hard to imagine anything more contrary to fact than the assumption that capital is immobile internationally. It is vastly more mobile than goods. Mobile capital follows absolute advantage, both wine and cloth would be produced in Portugal, and England, producing nothing, would surely be worse off.[2]

The argument for globalization based on comparative advantage is therefore embarrassed by a false premise. When starting from a false premise, one would have a better chance of hitting a correct conclusion if one's logic were also faulty! But unfortunately for the globalizers Ricardo's logic is not faulty.

To use the conclusion of an argument that was premised on capital *immobility*, to support an argument in favor of capital *mobility*, is too illogical for words. To get away with something that illogical you have to hide it under a lot of intimidating, but half-baked mathematics. It also helps in misunderstanding an argument if one's salary and position depend on not understanding it.

2. Growth Will Compensate

Some globalists will admit that the problems just outlined are real, but that whatever costs they may entail are more than compensated by the welfare increase from GNP growth brought about by free trade and global integration. While it may be true that free trade increases GNP growth (debatable but I will accept it for now), the other link in the chain of argument, that GNP growth increases welfare, is devoid of empirical support in the US since 1947.

It is very likely that we have entered an era in which growth is increasing environmental and social costs faster than it is increasing production benefits. We measure the latter but not the former, so we can't be sure. Growth that increases costs by more than it increases benefits is *uneconomic* growth, and should be called that. But Gross National Product can never register uneconomic growth because nothing is ever subtracted. It is much too gross.

Although economists did not devise GNP to be a direct measure of welfare, nevertheless welfare is assumed to be positively and closely correlated with GNP. Therefore if free trade promotes growth in GNP, it is assumed that it also promotes growth in welfare. But the link between GNP and welfare has become very questionable, and with it the argument for deregulated international trade and capital flows, and indeed for all other growth-promoting policies.

Evidence for doubting the correlation between GNP and welfare in the United States is taken from two sources.

First Nordhaus and Tobin (1972) asked, "Is Growth Obsolete?" as a measure of welfare and hence as a proper guiding objective of policy. To answer their question they developed a direct index of welfare, called Measured Economic Welfare (MEW) and tested its correlation with GNP over the period 1929–65. They found that for the period as a whole GNP and MEW were indeed positively correlated—for every six units of increase in GNP there was, on average, a four unit increase in MEW. Economists breathed a sigh of relief, forgot about MEW, and concentrated on GNP.

Some twenty years later John Cobb, Clifford Cobb, and I (1989) revisited the issue and began development of our Index of Sustainable Economic Welfare (ISEW) with a review of the Nordhaus and Tobin MEW. We discovered that if one takes only the latter half of the period (i.e., the eighteen years from 1947 to 1965) the correlation between GNP and MEW *falls* dramatically. In this most recent period—surely the more relevant for projections into the future—a six unit increase in GNP yielded on average only a one unit increase in MEW. This suggests that GNP growth at this stage of United States history may be a quite inefficient way of improving economic welfare—certainly less efficient than in the past.

Our first inclination was to extend the MEW beyond 1965. That proved difficult, and also revealed to us many shortcomings in the MEW. The ISEW was then developed to replace MEW, since the latter omitted any correction for environmental costs, did not correct for distributional changes, and included leisure, which dominated the MEW and introduced many arbitrary valuation decisions. The ISEW, like the MEW, though less so, was positively correlated with GNP up to a point beyond which the correlation turned slightly negative.

Measures of welfare are difficult and subject to many arbitrary judgments, so sweeping conclusions should be resisted. However, it seems fair to say that for the United States since 1947, the empirical evidence that GNP growth has increased welfare is *very* weak. Consequently any impact on welfare via free trade's contribution to GNP growth would also be very weak. In other words, the "great benefit," for which we are urged to sacrifice community standards and industrial peace, turns out on closer inspection not to exist.[3]

This conclusion has been strongly supported by the independent research of economists and psychologists to measure "self-evaluated happiness." The basic finding of these studies is that beyond some threshold, already passed in the US, further growth in income has little if any effect on self-reported happiness. One's income *relative* to others continues to be related to happiness, but not one's absolute income. Growth, while it can increase absolute incomes, is powerless to increase everyone's relative income, and it is relative income that, beyond the threshold, influences happiness! Growth, like an arms race, becomes self-canceling in terms of happiness.

One might object that although growth in rich countries might be "uneconomic," growth in poor countries where GDP consists largely of food, clothing, and shelter, is still very likely to be "economic." There is much truth in this, even though poor countries too are quite capable of deluding themselves by counting natural capital consumption as income. But, more to the point, the current policy of the IMF, WTO and WB is *not* for the rich to decrease uneconomic growth while the poor increase economic growth. Rather the vision of globalization is for the rich to grow rapidly in order to provide markets in which the poor can sell their exports. It is thought that the only option poor countries have is to export to the rich, and to do that they have to accept foreign investment from corporations who know how to produce the high-quality stuff that the rich want. The last thing poor countries are expected to do is to produce anything for their own people—those things are supposed to be imported.

The whole global economy must grow for this policy to work, because unless the rich countries grow rapidly they will not have the surplus to invest in poor countries or buy their exports. As a *New York Times* columnist put it, "the only thing giving the world's poorest nations any hope at all" is "continued global economic growth led by import-happy Americans whose purchases help put food on the table from Bolivia to Bangladesh."[4] Although by our overconsumption we intend only our own benefit, nevertheless we are led, as if by an "invisible mouth," to benefit the world's poor! (Apologies to Adam Smith.)

In an economically integrated world, one with free trade and free capital mobility, it is difficult to separate growth for poor countries from growth for rich countries, since national boundaries become economically meaningless. Only by adopting internationalization rather than globalization can we say that growth should continue in some countries (the poor) but not in others (the rich). But the globalizing trio, the IMF, WTO, and WB cannot say this. They can only advocate continual global growth in GDP. The concept of uneconomic growth anywhere just does not compute in their vision of the world, which is the same world as that of the neoclassical economist.

V. SUMMARY

I have distinguished globalization from internationalization; offered four reasons for preferring internationalization and rejecting globalization; and have anticipated and refuted two common objections to my overall argument.

No doubt there are other objections that I have not anticipated. There always are!

NOTES

1. Address at Southwestern University, Georgetown, Texas, February 21, 2002.
2. But wait, say some defenders of free trade. Shareholders in England would be better off since their investments would be more profitable employing cheaper Portuguese labor, and their gains might offset labor's losses. Not likely. Losses to labor would be the English wage, EW, times the number of jobs lost, N, giving (EW)N for total loss. The gain to English shareholders would be EW minus PW (Portuguese wage), times number of jobs N, or (EW − PW)N. For losses to equal gains then (EW)N = (EW − PW)N, which can only be true if PW = 0. For any Portuguese wage greater than zero (!) England is a net loser, even balancing monetary interests of few shareholders against that of many laborers. (I am grateful to Mark Lutz for pointing this out.)
3. Neither the MEW nor ISEW considered the effect of individual country GNP growth on the *global* environment, and consequently on welfare at geographic levels other than the nation. Nor was there any deduction for harmful products, such as tobacco or alcohol. Nor did we try to correct for diminishing marginal utility of total income (only for changes in distribution between rich and poor). Such considerations, we suspect, would further weaken the correlation between GNP and welfare. Also, GNP, MEW, and ISEW all begin with Personal Consumption. Since all three measures have in common their largest single category there is a significant autocorrelation bias, which makes the poor correlations of ISEW and MEW with GNP all the more dramatic.
4. *New York Times*, August 5, 2001, Section 3, p. 4, "In Genoa's Noise, a Trumpet for Capitalism", by Daniel Akst.

22. Population, migration, and globalization[1]

The trend toward globalization (free trade, free capital mobility), is not usually associated with migration or demography. If globalization were to be accomplished by free mobility of people, then demographers would certainly be paying attention. However, since globalization is being driven primarily by "free migration" of goods and capital, with labor a distant third in terms of mobility, it has often escaped notice that the economic consequences of this free flow of goods and capital are equivalent to those that would obtain under a free flow of labor. They are also driven by the same demographic and economic forces that would determine labor migration, if labor were free to migrate.

The economic tendency resulting from competition is to equalize wages and social standards across countries. But instead of cheap labor moving to where the capital is, and bidding wages down, capital moves to where the cheap labor is, and bids wages up—or would do so if only there were not a nearly unlimited supply of cheap labor, a Malthusian situation that still prevails in much of the world. Yet wages in the capital-sending country are bid down as much as if the newly employed laborers in the low-wage country had actually immigrated to the high-wage country. The determinant of wages in the low-wage country is not labor "productivity," nor anything else on the demand side of the labor market. It is entirely on the supply side—an excess and rapidly growing supply of labor at near-subsistence wages. This demographic condition—a very numerous and still rapidly growing underclass in the third world—is one for which demographers have many explanations, beginning with Malthus.

Globalization, considered by many to be the inevitable wave of the future, is frequently confused with internationalization, but is in fact something totally different. Internationalization refers to the increasing importance of international trade, international relations, treaties, alliances, and so on. Inter-national, of course, means between or among nations. The basic unit remains the nation, even as relations among nations become increasingly necessary and important. Globalization refers to the global economic integration of many formerly national economies into one global economy, mainly by free trade and free capital mobility, but also by somewhat easier or uncontrolled migration. It is the effective erasure of national boundaries for economic purposes. What was international becomes interregional.

The word "integration" derives from "integer," meaning one, complete, or whole. Integration is the act of combining into one whole. Since there can be only one whole, it follows that global economic integration logically implies national economic disintegration. As the saying goes, to make an omelet you have to break some eggs. The *dis*-integration of the national egg is necessary to integrate the global omelet. It is dishonest to celebrate the benefits of global integration without counting the consequent costs of national disintegration.

FORGOTTEN ROOT

Those costs are significant. It is not for nothing that the population explosion in the third world has only recently affected wages in the industrial world. Populous colonial India was not allowed by the British to compete in global markets with its cheap labor, nor did the Chinese Communists seek to compete in world markets under the isolation policies of Chairman Mao. It is only in the last 30 years that the World Bank has become converted to the now "incontestible" orthodoxy of export-led development based on foreign investment as the key part of structural adjustment. But although "free trade" is the new mantra, it is critical to notice that free trade now means something very different from what it meant in the early nineteenth century, when English economist David Ricardo gave it the enduring blessing of his comparative advantage argument.[2]

In the classical nineteenth-century vision of Ricardo and Adam Smith, the national community embraced both national labor and national capital. These classes cooperated (albeit with conflict) to produce national goods, which then competed in international markets against the goods of other nations produced by their own national capital/labor teams. This was internationalization, as defined above.

However, in the globally integrated world of the twenty-first century, both capital and goods are free to move internationally—and capital, or at least money, can be shifted electronically with almost no effort at all. But free capital mobility totally undercuts Ricardo's comparative advantage argument for free trade in goods, because that argument is explicitly and essentially premised on capital (and other factors) being immobile between nations. Under the new globalization regime, capital tends simply to flow to wherever costs are lowest—that is, to pursue absolute advantage.

Nevertheless, the conventional wisdom seems to be that if free trade in goods is beneficial, then free trade in capital must be even more beneficial.

However, you cannot use the conclusion of an argument to deny one of its premises! In any event, it no longer makes sense to think of national teams of labor and capital in the globalized economy. There are competing global capitalists, and national laborers thrown into global competition by mobile capital.

Back, finally, to the costs mentioned above. What are the consequences of globalization for national community? Here in the United States, we have seen the abrogation of a basic social agreement between labor and capital over how to divide up the value that they jointly add to raw materials (as well as the value of the raw materials themselves, i.e., nature's often-uncounted value added). That agreement has been reached nationally, not internationally, much less globally. It was not reached by economic theory, but through generations of national debate, elections, strikes, lockouts, court decisions, and violent conflicts. That agreement (that US distribution of income between labor and capital should be more equal than that for the world as a whole), on which national community and industrial peace depend, is being repudiated in the interests of global integration. That is a very poor trade, even if you call it "free trade."

STRESSES AND STRAINS

At a deeper level, what if globalization began to entail the overt encouragement of free migration? Even some free trade advocates might recoil from the radical cosmopolitanism of such a policy. Perhaps they can see that it would lead to massive relocation of people between world regions of vastly differing wealth, creating a tragedy of the open access commons. The strain on local communities, both the sending and the receiving, would be enormous. In the face of unlimited migration, how could any national community maintain a minimum wage, a welfare program, subsidized medical care, or a public school system? How could a nation punish its criminals and tax evaders if citizens were totally free to emigrate? Indeed, one wonders, would it not be much cheaper to encourage emigration of a country's poor, sick, or criminals, rather than run welfare programs, charity hospitals, and prisons? (Fidel Castro took precisely this course of action in opening Cuba's jails in 1980. His policy encouraged migration of prisoners and others that became part of the wave of "marielito" immigrants to the United States.)

Further, one might reasonably wonder how a country could reap the benefit of educational investments made in its own citizens if those citizens are totally free to emigrate. Would nations continue to make such investments in the face of free migration and a continuing "brain drain"? Would a country make investments in education if it experienced massive immigration pressures, which would dilute the educational resources of the nation? Would any country any longer try to limit its birth rate, since youths who migrate abroad and send back remittances can be a good investment, a fact that might increase the birth rate? (With unfettered migration, a country could never control its numbers anyway, so why even talk about the controversial issue of birth control?)

To some this skepticism will sound like a nationalistic negation of world community. It is not. It is the view that world community should be viewed as a "community of communities," a federation of national communities rather than a cosmopolitan world government lacking any historical roots in real communities. A "world with no boundaries" makes a sentimental song lyric, but community and policy cannot exist without boundaries. For mainstream—neoclassical—economists, only the individual is real; community is just a misleading name for an aggregate of individuals. From that perspective, national communities impose "distorting" interferences upon the individualistic free market, and their disintegration is not a cost but something to be welcomed. To the contrary, I would argue, this aspect of globalization is just another way in which capitalism undermines the very conditions it requires in order to function.

Few would deny that some migration is a very good thing—but this discussion concerns free migration, where "free" means deregulated, uncontrolled, unlimited, as in "free" trade, or "free" capital mobility, or "free" reproduction. One must also be intensely mindful that immigrants are people, frequently disadvantaged people. It is a terrible thing to be "anti-immigrant." Immigration, however, is a policy, not a person, and one can be "anti-immigration," or more accurately "pro-immigration limits" without in the least being anti-immigrant. The global cosmopolitans think that it is immoral to make any policy distinction between citizen and non-citizen, and therefore many favor free migration. They also suggest that free migration is the shortest route to their vision of the summum bonum, equality of wages worldwide. Their point is fair enough; there is some logic in their position—so long as they are willing to see wages equalized at a low level. But those who support free migration as the shortest route to equality of wages worldwide are silent on the increasing inequality between wages and property incomes, and could only with great difficulty try to contend with problems of an open-access commons, the destruction of local community, and other issues raised above.

A more workable moral guide is the recognition that, as a member of a national community, one's obligation to non-citizens is to do them no harm, while one's obligation to fellow citizens is first to do no harm and then try to do positive good. The many dire consequences of globalization (besides those mentioned above)—over-specialization in a few volatile export commodities (petroleum, timber, minerals, and other extractive goods with little value added locally, for instance), crushing debt burdens, exchange rate risks and speculative currency destabilization, foreign corporate control of national markets, unnecessary monopolization of "trade-related intellectual property rights" (typically patents on prescription drugs), and not least, easy immigration in the interests of lower wages and cheaper exports—amply show that the "do no harm" criterion is still far from being met.

Some feel that US economic policies have harmed third-world citizens, and that easy immigration to the US is a justified form of restitution. I have considerable sympathy with the view that US policies (precisely those of globalization) have harmed third-world citizens, but for reasons already stated, no sympathy with the idea that easy immigration is a fair or reasonable restitution. For restitution I would prefer a series of small grants (not large interest-bearing loans), accompanied by free transfer of knowledge and technology.

FREE TRADE'S HIDDEN SHACKLES

Free trade, specialization, and global integration mean that nations are no longer free not to trade. Yet freedom not to trade is surely necessary if trade is to remain voluntary, a precondition of its mutual benefit. To avoid war, nations must both consume less and become more self-sufficient. But free traders say we should become less self-sufficient and more globally integrated as part of the overriding quest to consume ever more. We must lift the laboring masses (which now include the formerly high-wage workers) up from their subsistence wages. This can only be done by massive growth, we are told. But can the environment sustain so much growth? It cannot. And how will whatever growth dividend there is ever get to the poor; that is, how can wages increase given the nearly unlimited supply of labor? If wages do not increase then what reason is there to expect a fall in the birth rate of the laboring class via the "demographic transition"? How could we ever expect to have high wages in any country that becomes globally integrated with a globe having a vast oversupply of labor? Why, in a globally integrated world, would any nation have an incentive to reduce its birth rate?

Global economic integration and growth, far from bringing a halt to population growth, will be the means by which the consequences of over-population in the third world are generalized to the world as a whole. They will be the means whereby the practice of constraining births in some countries will be eliminated by a demographic version of the "race to the bottom," rather than spread by demonstration of its benefits. In the scramble to attract capital and jobs, there will be a standards-lowering competition to keep wages low and to reduce any social, safety, and environmental standards that raise costs.

Some are seduced by the idea of "solving" the South's population problem and the North's labor shortage problem simultaneously—by migration. However, the North's labor shortage is entirely a function of below-equilibrium wages. The shortage could be instantly removed by an increase in wages that equated domestic supply and demand—simply by allowing the market to work. But the cheap-labor lobby, in the United States at least, thinks we must import workers in order to keep wages from rising and thereby reducing profits and export competitiveness. Of course this also keeps 80 percent of our citizens from sharing in the increased prosperity through higher wages. But never mind! They will still benefit, because importing workers is the key to saving Social Security—which, we are told, will collapse without growth in the cohort of working-age people provided by immigration. And when the large cohort of worker-immigrants retires? Well, we will just repeat the process.

The real solution to the Social Security imbalance is to raise the age of retirement and lower the benefits. The real solution to the South's problem is for those countries to lower their birth rates and to put their working-age population to use at home producing necessities for the home market. And the reply to the half-truth that the United States is really more overpopulated than India because each American consumes so much more than each Indian, is that the United States needs mainly to lower its per capita consumption (and secondarily its population growth), while India and China need primarily to lower their population growth, and are in no position to lower per capita consumption, except for the elite. Serious efforts to reduce birth rates in these countries are sometimes condemned, because, with the advent of ultrasound technology that can discern the gender of the fetus, the cultural preference for males has led to selective abortion of females. The problem here, however, is not birth control per se, nor ultrasound technology, but rather the immoral preference for males and indifference to the social costs of a gender imbalance a generation hence.

Demographers and economists have understandably become reluctant to prescribe birth control to other countries. If a country historically "chooses" many people, low wages, and high inequality over fewer people, higher wages, and less inequality, who is to say that is wrong? Let all make their own choices, since it is they who will have to live with the consequences.

But while that may be a defensible position under internationalization, it is not defensible under globalization. The whole point of an integrated world is that these consequences, both costs of overpopulation and benefits of population control, are externalized to all nations. The costs and benefits of overpopulation under globalization are distributed by class more than by nation. Labor bears the cost of reduced wage income; capital enjoys the benefit of reduced wage costs. Malthusian and Marxian considerations both seem to foster inequality. The old conflict between Marx and Malthus, always more ideological than logical, has now for practical purposes been further diminished. After all, both always held that wages tend toward subsistence under capitalism. Marx would probably see globalization as one more capitalist strategy to lower wages. Malthus might agree, while arguing that it is the fact of overpopulation that allows the capitalist's strategy to work in the first place. Presumably Marx would accept that, but insist that the overpopulation is only relative to capitalist institutions, not to any limits of nature's bounty, and would not exist under socialism. Malthus would disagree, along with the post-Mao Chinese communists. I confess that my sympathies lean more toward Malthus, and that I lament the recent tendency of the environmental movement to court "political correctness" by soft pedaling issues of population, migration, and globalization.

NOTES

1. *Ecological Economics*, special issue on immigration, Vol. 59, 2006, pp. 187–90.
2. Because of differences in climate, natural resources, education levels, wealth (capital) endowments, and many other factors, countries differ in the efficiency with which they can make various goods. A country has an *absolute advantage* over its trading partners if it can produce a good at lower absolute cost than they can. It has a *comparative advantage* if it can produce the same good more cheaply *relative to other goods it produces* than its trading partners, regardless of absolute costs.

PART 7

Philosophy and Policy

I teach in a graduate School of Public Policy. It is not difficult to suggest policies that would work if people accepted them. Some have been suggested in previous pages. The big difficulty always raised by my students is, "yes, but people will never accept that. Congress will never pass the needed legislation." Then the question that follows is "how do we make people do . . . whatever it is that the policy requires." Invariably some aspects of policies in the public interest go against some people's private interests. There is little faith among today's students that the common good is strong enough, or even real enough, to ever prevail over private interests.

One reason for this view is that the economic theory they have been taught is radically individualistic—only the atomistic individual is real, and the idea of community as anything other than a mere aggregate of individuals is considered metaphysical mystery mongering. John Cobb and I wrote a book (*For the Common Good*, 1989, 1994) in which we argued that homo economicus is in reality not an atomistic individual but a person in community. An individual person is in truth constituted by his relations in community. My identity is made up of internal relations in community. Who am I? I am son of . . ., brother of . . ., friend of . . ., citizen of . . ., student of. . . . Shorn of all these relations in community there is not much left of me. These relations are internal to who I am, not merely relations that connect "me" externally to another atomistic individual. Consequently my welfare as a person depends very much on the quality of all the relations in community by which I am constituted—far more than on the quantities of anything I consume as an individual, once subsistence is met.

The importance of the common good is rooted in the way we are—we *are* persons in community, not isolated individuals. Yet economic theory is based on this extreme individualist abstraction, and the more we follow it the more we are led to remake ourselves in the image of this abstract lie. This is one way to respond to the students' skepticism.

Another way is to ask what are the presuppositions for studying or engaging in policy—any kind of policy? What must you believe if policy is to make sense? Students and teachers in a School of Public Policy really need to be able to answer this question, but we are not the only ones. To anticipate the discussion that follows I will briefly state what I think are two presuppositions: non-determinism and non-nihilism. If there is only one possible future (determinism) then we hardly need policy. And even if there are several realistic futures, but we are unable to say that one is any better than another (nihilism) then again we hardly need policy. I think that the assumptions of determinism and nihilism have wormed their way into our cultural presuppositions and eaten away the pillars on which policy rests. It is not so much that we affirm determinism and nihilism, although some do, especially neo-Darwinists, but that we think they just might be right, and that inconsistency lurking in the back of our minds renders policy half-hearted if not feckless.

The first two chapters spell out the above. The third was written for a Festschrift honoring the pioneering contribution of the Dutch economist, Roefie Hueting. It connects several technical aspects of economic theory and policy to the deeper philosophical questions raised in the two preceding chapters.

23. Policy, possibility, and purpose[1]

I. INTRODUCTION

Policy presupposes knowledge of two kinds: of possibility and of purpose; of means and of ends. Possibility reflects how the world works. In addition to keeping us from wasting time and treasure on impossibilities, this kind of knowledge gives us information about tradeoffs among real alternatives. Purpose reflects desirability, our ranking of ends, our criteria for distinguishing better from worse states of the world. It does not help much to know how the world works if we cannot distinguish better from worse states of the world. Nor is it useful to pursue a better state of the world that happens to be impossible. Without both kinds of knowledge policy discussion is meaningless.

The plan of this chapter is to raise two basic questions, suggest a broad answer to each, and consider objections to each answer. First, in the realm of possibility the question is, of what does our ultimate means consist? Is there a common denominator of possibility or usefulness that we can only use up and not produce, for which we are totally dependent on the natural environment? Second, what ultimately is the end or purpose in whose service we should employ these means? The question of purpose is the more difficult and will receive most emphasis. But the means question is considered first both for completeness of context, and because, surprisingly, religious attitudes arise here as well. Finally, I offer some thoughts on how contradictory premises at the basis of modern thought about possibility and purpose have enfeebled policy.

II. MEANS AND POSSIBILITY

Ultimate means, the common denominator of all usefulness, consist of low entropy matter-energy. Low-entropy matter-energy is the physical coordinate of usefulness; the basic necessity that humans must use up but cannot create, and for which the human economy is totally dependent on nature's services. Entropy is the qualitative difference that distinguishes useful resources from an equal quantity of useless waste. We do not use up matter and energy per se (first law of thermodynamics), but we do irrevocably use up the quality of usefulness as we transform matter and energy to achieve our purposes (second law of thermodynamics). All technological transformations require a before and after, a gradient or metabolic flow from concentrated source to dispersed sink, from high to low temperature.[2] The capacity for entropic transformations of matter-energy to be useful is reduced both by the depletion of finite sources and by the pollution of finite sinks. If there were no entropic gradient between source and sink the environment would be incapable of serving our purposes or even sustaining our lives. Technical knowledge helps us to use low entropy more efficiently—it does not allow us to eliminate or reverse the metabolic flow.

Matter can of course be recycled from sink back to source by using more energy (and more material implements). Energy can only be recycled by expending more energy to carry out the recycle than the amount recycled, so it is never economic to recycle energy—regardless of prices. Recycling also requires material implements for collection, concentration, and transportation. The entropic dissipation of these material instruments requires still more recycling. Nature's biogeochemical cycles powered by the sun can recycle matter to a high degree, some think 100 percent. But this only underlines our dependence on nature's services, since in the human economy we have no source equivalent to the sun, and our finite sinks fill up because we are incapable of 100 percent recycling.

There is a strong tendency to deny our dependence on nature for the basic capacity to effect our purposes in the world. Among the more explicit denials is that from George Gilder:[3]

> Gone is the view of a thermodynamic world economy, dominated by "natural resources" being turned to entropy and waste by human extraction and use . . . The key fact of knowledge is that it is anti-entropic: it accumulates and compounds as it is used . . . Conquering the microcosm, the mind transcends every entropic trap and overthrows matter itself.

According to *The Economist* (March 25, 2000, p. 73), George Gilder is "America's foremost technology prophet" whose recommendation can cause the share price of a company to increase by 50 percent the next day. If Gilder is really that influential then the current stock market boom, like most perpetual motion machines, is based on a denial of the second law of thermodynamics! To cast further doubt on Gilder's Gnostic prophecy one need only recall the aphorisms of Nobel chemist, Frederick Soddy, "No phosphorous, no thought," and of Loren Eisley, "The human mind . . . burns by the power of a leaf." And as Kenneth Boulding pointed out, knowledge has to be imprinted on physical structures in the form of improbable arrangements before it is effective in the economy. And only low entropy matter-energy is capable of receiving and holding for significant time periods the improbable imprint of human knowledge. Furthermore, as important as knowledge is, it is misleading to say it grows by compounding accumulation. New dollars from compound interest paid into a bank account are not offset by any decline in the principal. Yet new knowledge often renders old knowledge obsolete. Do scientific theories of phlogiston and the ether still count as knowledge? As E.J. Mishan noted, technological knowledge often unrolls the carpet of increased choice before us by the foot, while simultaneously rolling it up behind us by the yard. Yes, knowledge develops and improves, but it does not grow exponentially like money compounding in the bank. Furthermore, new knowledge need not always reveal new possibilities for growth; it can also reveal new limitations. The new knowledge of the fire-resisting properties of asbestos increased its usefulness; subsequent new knowledge of its carcinogenic properties reduced its usefulness. New knowledge can cut both ways. Finally, and most obviously, knowledge has to be actively learned and taught every generation—it cannot be passively bequeathed like an accumulating stock portfolio. When society invests little in the intergenerational transfer of knowledge, some of it is lost and its distribution becomes more concentrated, contributing to the growing inequality in the distribution of income.

The common view among economists and many others is that waste is just a resource we have not yet learned to use, that nature supplies only the indestructible building blocks of elemental atoms, and all the rest either is or can be done by humans. What counts to economists is value added by human labor and capital—that to which value is added is thought to be totally passive stuff, not even worthy of the name natural resources as evidenced by Gilder's putting the term in quotation marks. Natural processes, in this view, do not add value to the elemental building blocks—and even if they did, manmade capital can substitute for such natural services.

The brute fact remains, however, that we cannot burn the same lump of coal twice (sources are depleted), and that the resulting ashes and heat scattered into nature's sinks really are polluting wastes and not just matter-energy of equally useful potential, if only we knew how to use it. Eroded topsoil washed to the sea, and chlorofluorocarbons in the ozone layer, are also polluting wastes on a human time scale, not just "resources out of place." No one denies the enormous importance of knowledge. But this denigration of the importance of the physical world, and exclusive emphasis on the salvific efficacy of knowledge is a modern version of Gnosticism. It is religiously motivated by a denial of our creaturehood as part of the material world, by the belief that we have, or soon will have, transcended the world of material creation and entered an unlimited realm of esoteric knowledge, albeit technical now rather than spiritual. Hence even in the discussion of means we encounter alternative religious premises, including most prominently an ancient Christian heresy.

III. ENDS AND DESIRABILITY

It was argued above that there is such a thing as ultimate means, and that it is the entropic transformation of matter-energy. Is there such a thing as an ultimate end, and if so, what is it? Like Aristotle, I think there are good reasons to believe that there must be an ultimate end, but it is far more difficult to say just what it is. In fact it will be argued that, while we must be dogmatic about the existence of the ultimate end, we must be very tolerant about our differing perceptions of it.

In an age of pluralism the first objection to the idea of ultimate end is that it is singular. Do we not have many "ultimate ends"? Clearly we have many ends, but just as clearly they conflict and we must choose among them. Furthermore, syntactically "ultimate" requires the singular. We rank ends. We prioritize. In setting priorities, in ranking things, something— only one thing—has to go in first place. That is our practical approxima- tion to the ultimate end. What goes in second place is determined by how close it came to first place, and so on. Ethics is the problem of ranking plural ends or values. The ranking criterion, the holder of first place, is the ultimate end (or its operational approximation), which grounds our under- standing of objective value—better and worse as real states of the world, not just subjective opinions.

I do not claim that the ethical ranking of plural ends is necessarily done abstractly, a priori. Often the struggle with concrete problems and policy dilemmas forces decisions, and the discipline of the concrete decision helps us to implicitly rank ends whose ordering would have been too obscure in the abstract. Sometimes we have regrets and discover that our ranking really was not in accordance with a subsequently improved understanding of the ultimate end.

My point is that we must have a dogmatic belief in objective value, an objective hierarchy of ends ordered with reference to some concept of the ultimate end, however dimly we may perceive the latter. This sounds rather absolutist and intolerant to modern devotees of pluralism, but in fact it is the very basis for tolerance. If you and I disagree regarding our hierarchy of values, and we believe that objective value does not exist, then there is nothing for either of us to appeal to in an effort to persuade the other. It is simply your subjective values versus mine. I can vigorously assert my pref- erences and try to intimidate you into going along, but you will soon get wise to that. We are left to resort to physical combat or political manipulation, with no possibility of truly reasoning together in search of a clearer shared vision of objective value, because by assumption the latter does not exist. We each know our own subjective preferences better than the other, so no clarification is needed. If the source of value is in my own subjective preferences, then I don't really care about yours, except as they may serve as means to satisfying my own. Tolerance becomes a sham, a mere strategy of manipulation, with no real openness to persuasion.[4]

In spite of this simple rationale the concept of objective value is rejected by the modern intelligentsia. Often it is explicitly rejected. Sometimes it is rejected implicitly by affirming determinism—if there are no real alternatives to choose among, then there is no need for a criterion by which to choose, so objective value becomes a fifth wheel, even though not explicitly rejected. Yet those who reject the concept of objective value have to have some alternative philosophy of value. I will argue that the incoherence of the alternatives provides indirect but strong additional support for the idea of objective value. There are, I believe, four basic alternative positions, outlined below.

1. *The perennial Judeo-Christian worldview* as discussed above—real alternatives from which to choose by reference to an objective criterion of value.
2. *Criterionless choice*—alternatives are real options, but there is no objective criterion for choosing among them.
3. *Providential determinism*—there are no real options, but there is an objective criterion of value by which to choose, if we had a choice. Fortunately providence has chosen for us according to the objective criterion, which we would not be wise or good enough to have followed on our own.
4. *Criterionless determinism*—there are no real alternatives to choose from, and even if there were there is no objective criterion of value by which to choose. All is random variation and natural selection as claimed by the neo-Darwinists.[5]

For policy to make sense we must have real alternative possibilities before us and a criterion for choosing among them. Position (4), neo-Darwinism, fails on both counts—choice is an illusion and even if we had real options we have no criterion for choosing among them. Natural selection does it for us, even though it may, for presumed survival reasons, delude us with the illusion of choice. Position (3), providential determinism, tells us that objective value exists and we are tied to it by providence. Fortunately for us we have no freedom because if we did we would likely choose wrongly. Position (2), criterionless choice, extols our existential freedom and the reality of alternatives, but denies that we have any criterion by which to choose one thing over another except arbitrary individual preferences. Position (1) affirms both the reality of our options, and the objectivity of the criterion by which we should choose among them. Only in (1) do we have both the real alternatives and the objective criterion required for responsible rational choice—for policy to make sense. It follows therefore that people engaged in policy, yet holding to positions (2), (3), or (4) are in the grip of a severe and debilitating inconsistency.

Real options and objective value (1) constitute the Judeo-Christian religious premises upon which most of our laws and customs depend. They are the foundation of past legislation and our current laws as well as the rationale for any future policy. Yet many intellectuals[6] today reject the traditional position (1) in favor of neo-Darwinism (4). Do they, as consistent criterionless determinists, forgo all advocacy of policy? Most do not. How then do they resolve the logical contradictions of their position? They do not! Witness Wendell Berry's[7] legitimate consternation at the insouciant self-contradiction he found in Edward O. Wilson's book, *Consilience*:

> A theoretical materialism as strictly principled as Mr. Wilson's is inescapably deterministic. We and our works and acts, he holds, are determined by our genes, which are determined by the laws of biology, which are determined ultimately by the laws of physics. He sees that this directly contradicts the idea of free will, which even as a scientist he seems unwilling to give up, and which as a conservationist he cannot afford to give up. He deals with this dilemma oddly and inconsistently.
>
> First, he says that we have, and need, "the illusion of free will," which, he says further, is "biologically adaptive." I have read his sentences several times, hoping to find that I have misunderstood them, but I am afraid that I understand them. He is saying that there is an evolutionary advantage in illusion. The proposition that our ancestors survived because they were foolish enough to believe an illusion is certainly optimistic, but it does not seem very probable. And what are we to think of a materialism that can be used to validate an illusion? Mr. Wilson nevertheless insists upon his point; in another place he speaks of "self-deception" as granting to our species the "adaptive edge."
>
> Later, in discussing the need for conservation, Mr. Wilson affirms the Enlightenment belief that we can "choose wisely." How a wise choice can be made on the basis of an illusory freedom of the will is impossible to conceive, and Mr. Wilson wisely chooses not to try to conceive it. (p. 26)

Instead of dealing with contradiction some scientists levitate above it and ex cathedra denounce their critics as fundamentalist religious nuts. This is not to deny the existence of real fundamentalist religious nuts, but even if all these nuts disappeared the problem stated here would remain. The real conflict between traditional religions and neo-Darwinism is that of criterionless determinism, not the evolutionary kinship of mankind with the rest of creation. Repeated replays of Wilberforce vs Huxley, and Darrow vs Bryan, however entertaining, do not meet the issue. People who assert (a) that choice is an illusion, and (b) that even if it were not illusory, the criteria by which one chooses are arbitrary—such people owe it to all concerned to remain silent about policy. In fact their participation in policy dialogue should be subject to "estoppel"—a legal injunction to restrain a witness from contradicting his own testimony.[8]

Although the contrast is most stark between the neo-Darwinists and traditional religion, the providential determinists and the criterionless choosers should also keep silent about policy. So a word about each is in order.

Providential determinism is partially rooted in the doctrine of predestination. We hear little about theological predestination today, but the idea that forces bigger than ourselves control our lives is very much with us. The faith that the inevitable advance of science, economic growth, and globalization will save us in spite of ourselves is alive and well. Technology can be trusted because it is an instrument of providence. Nobel laureate chemist R.A. Millikan,[9] disagreed with the warnings about the danger of nuclear energy given by fellow Nobel chemist Frederick Soddy, and told his readers that they could "sleep in peace with the consciousness that the Creator has put some foolproof elements into his handiwork, and that man is powerless to do it any titanic physical damage." Providence has placed toddling mankind in a playpen full of soft and colorful things that have no sharp edges or poisons, and that are tolerant of our technological probings. The dangerous choices have already been made for us by a wiser power and we can concentrate on safely developing our motor skills and technical inventions. Yes, we may bump our heads now and then, but we need not worry about what Millikan called "hobgoblins and bugaboos that crowd in on the mind of ignorance"—such as fears about atomic energy. In hindsight it is easy to see that Soddy was the true prophet and that Millikan was whistling in the dark. But Millikan's trust in the providential goodness and irresistible power of technology, as well as his Gnostic faith in knowledge itself, is still with us. Millikan too should have remained silent, not just because he turned out to be wrong, but because there was never a real issue for him—just a hobgoblin which would disappear in the providential daylight of scientific progress.

Criterionless choice is thought by existentialists to be a heroic stance. Witness the famous concluding statement by biologist Jacques Monod (*Chance and Necessity*, 1972):

> The ancient covenant is in pieces; man knows at last that he is alone in the universe's unfeeling immensity, out of which he emerged only by chance. His destiny is nowhere spelled out, nor is his duty. The kingdom above or the darkness below: it is for him to choose.

Unfeeling chance, no destiny, no duty—but man must choose. Choose what? The "kingdom above or the darkness below" we are told. But where did such value-laden language come from? It sounds suspiciously like the ancient covenant which Monod has just told us is in pieces. It certainly does not fit the context of random unfeeling immensity. But neither does it fit the neo-Darwinist denial of both real options and an objective criterion of value by which to choose. Monod, in spite of his neo-Darwinist views, affirms freedom to choose. But criterionless choice is a rather meaningless choice, like flipping a coin, which at least is consistent with our presumed random origin. Existentialists, however much they seem to enjoy the personal angst of criterionless choice, are ill-equipped to make public policy. They too owe it to the rest of us to remain silent in public policy debates.

To summarize: the argument has been made that the Judeo-Christian belief in both objective value and real alternatives is a necessary condition for public policy to make any sense, as well as necessary for the virtue of tolerance. Additional indirect support for this position has been adduced by looking at the modern alternatives to it and pointing out their logical incoherence.

IV. WHITEHEAD'S "LURKING INCONSISTENCY"

If this is a correct view of the situation then it should not be so surprising that our current public policies are feeble, halfhearted, and ineffective. Policy thought is enfeebled by what Alfred North Whitehead called the "lurking inconsistency." An example is provided by one of our leading political scientists, L.K. Caldwell, a pioneer in environmental policy. Caldwell asks in the title of a recent address, "Is Humanity Destined to Self-Destruct?"[10]

I'd like to consider a shorter question, "Is Humanity Destined?" To be destined means to be "determined beforehand, preordained to an inevitable outcome." Whether the inevitable outcome is ecological destruction or salvation is a further question that arouses our curiosity, but, as long as either outcome is our destiny, no policy recommendations would be called for. Does Caldwell believe that humanity is destined, and is he merely curious about which outcome is preordained? He seems to me ambivalent—but let him speak for himself:

> At our present state of knowledge, it still seems rational, with some reservations, to believe that social choice is possible. . . . But we do not know the extent to which meaningful choice is really possible. Human society may be driven by innate forces that, in effect, determine our destiny. Choice may be an illusion. The fate of Homo sapiens may be destined by evolutionary "necessity" overriding all

hypothetical rational choice. But until forced by evidence to this conclusion, it seems reasonable to assume that humans possess or may acquire the capacities to make the choices necessary to a sustainable future.

Elsewhere in the article Caldwell uses the conditional phrases, "If choice rather than necessity is an option available to humanity . . .," and, "To the extent that humans choose their future . . . ." Such usage indicates that for Caldwell the idea that "Choice may be an illusion" is a very real possibility. Yet he does offer some policy proposals, which would be a silly thing to do if he really believed that choice is an illusion. From this and the last sentence quoted above, I will take it that his ambivalence is biased toward the view that humanity is not destined, and will confine myself to some thoughts about the consequences of a half-hearted belief that choice might be real. I believe this ambivalence is characteristic not just of Caldwell, but of most of us. Caldwell just expressed more clearly and honestly what is in the minds of many.

Caldwell, and most of the modern intelligentsia, halfway believe that Monod's nihilism is justified (Caldwell quoted the famous statement from Monod just discussed). But they want a bit more proof. So they say, let us assume that choice and purpose are real and act on them until the evidence proves us wrong. Only then will we give up on purpose and policy, and devote ourselves to simply analyzing and describing the inevitable process of self-destruction. But I wonder what "evidence" could possibly mean in a world in which choice were truly an illusion? If choice is an illusion then is not the idea of choosing according to evidence also an illusion? If evidence guides one's choice to conclude that choice an illusion, then has one not contradicted one's conclusion in the process of reaching it?

Such incoherence is an outcome of Whitehead's "lurking inconsistency," a contradiction among the most basic premises of the modern worldview. As Whitehead put it:

> A scientific realism, based on mechanism, is conjoined with an unwavering belief in the world of men and of the higher animals as being composed of self-determining organisms. This radical inconsistency at the basis of modern thought accounts for much that is half-hearted and wavering in our civilization . . . It enfeebles [thought], by reason of the inconsistency lurking in the background . . . For instance, the enterprises produced by the individualistic energy of the European peoples presuppose physical actions directed to final causes. But the science which is employed in their development is based on a philosophy which asserts that physical causation is supreme, and which disjoins the physical cause from the final end. It is not popular to dwell on the absolute contradiction here involved.[11]

In other words, our scientific understanding of nature is based on mechanism and efficient causation, with no room for teleology or final causation.

Yet we ourselves, and higher animals in general, directly experience purpose, and within limits, act in a self-determining manner. We respond to the persuasive lure of final causes (purposes), as well as to the push and pull of mechanical, efficient causes. If we are part of nature then so is purpose; if purpose is not part of nature then neither, in large part, are we.

The purposeful nature of environmental policy is in total contradiction with the purposeless nature of biological science, at least the current neo-Darwinian orthodoxy. Biology is unable to embrace purpose and cannot be relied on by itself to conserve the biosphere, since that is surely a purpose. So conservation must be asserted as a purpose that comes from elsewhere, even if it makes use of biological science as a means. The problem comes in the word "elsewhere," because neo-Darwinists do not accept "elsewhere," insisting that all is nature, nature is mechanism, and that what we call purpose is an illusion. This belief, even if it is only half believed, lurking as a possibility in the back of the mind of those who may not explicitly affirm materialism, is nevertheless logically, emotionally, and politically enfeebling. Just as Whitehead recognized, the lurking inconsistency enfeebles thought and action by leading us to consider our direct conscious experience of purpose and choice as somehow less real than an abstract theory of materialist determinism that denies our concrete experience—the "fallacy of misplaced concreteness."

As noted, purpose or final cause must, in the view of materialism, be an "epiphenomenon"—an illusion which itself was selected because of a presumed reproductive advantage that it chanced to confer on those under its influence. It is odd that the illusion of purpose should be thought to confer a selective advantage while purpose itself is held to be non-causative. First we are asked to believe that our ancestors survived thanks to actions based on the illusion of purpose. Second we are told that purpose itself is non causative. What then, are we to believe that only *illusory* purposes are causative and adaptive? And is it not a contradiction that materialism should depend so heavily and selectively on illusions? Can an illusion remain effective once exposed? The policy implication of the mechanistic dogma that purpose is not causative is laissez faire beyond the most libertarian economist's wildest model. The only "policy" consistent with this view is, "let it happen as it will anyway."

Teleology has its limits, of course, and from the Enlightenment onward it is evident that mechanism has constituted an enormously successful research paradigm for science in general, including biology. Although mechanism has lost its hold on physics, it remains dominant in biology. The temptation to elevate a successful research paradigm to the level of a complete worldview is perhaps irresistible. But mechanism too has its limits. To deny (or even to doubt) the reality of our most immediate and universal experience (that of purpose) because it doesn't fit the research paradigm is radically anti-empirical. To refuse to recognize the socially devastating logical consequences that result from the denial of purpose is profoundly anti-rational. Yet environmentally minded economists and political scientists take their cues from biologists and ecologists who, as adherents to the standard neo-Darwinist worldview, are heirs to its blindness as well as its insights.

Fortunately the personal behavior of biologists often transcends the philosophical foundations of their science, and they advocate policies to conserve biodiversity. Naturally the public asks the biologists what purpose would be served by saving an obscure threatened species at the cost of other species, or at the cost of inconvenience to human beings? Since most leading biologists claim not to believe in purposes, ends, or final causes, this is not an easy question for them to answer. They reveal the inconsistency that Whitehead saw lurking in the background by the feeble fecklessness and wavering half-heartedness of their answers. They tell us about biodiversity, and ecosystem stability and resilience, and about a presumed instinct of biophilia that we, who systematically drive other species to extinction, are nevertheless supposed to have encoded in our genes. But the biologists are too half-hearted to affirm any of these descriptive concepts as an abiding purpose, and thereby question the fundamental assumption of neo-Darwinism. For example, biophilia could be appealed to as a virtue, a persuasive value rather than a wishfully imagined part of the deterministic genetic code. But that would be to admit purpose. Instead the neo-Darwinists try to find some overlooked mechanistic cause that will make us do what we think we ought to do, but can't logically advocate without thereby acknowledging the reality of purpose.

Absent purpose, the biologists' appeals to the public are both logically and emotionally feeble. Is it too much to ask the neo-Darwinist to speculate about the possibility that the survival value of neo-Darwinism itself has become negative for the species that really believes it? Could this be a lethal consequence of the lurking inconsistency? By undermining the very belief in purpose the lurking inconsistency fosters a world in which choice becomes, if not an illusion, certainly a neglected possibility.

The economic determinism of Marx has now collapsed both intellectually and politically. The psycho/sexual determinism of Freud is increasingly considered pseudo science of the worst kind. The remaining member of the nineteenth-century trinity of determinism, Darwin, is still riding high. However, the neo-Darwinist evolutionary determinism of chance and necessity with its total rejection of purpose and design, is undergoing serious reconsideration in many quarters, even though somewhat underground.[12]

As I write this, the news media are full of the story of Kansas having rejected the teaching of evolution in public schools. I hope it is clear that one may point to problems with neo-Darwinism without in the least advocating the excision of evolution from school curricula. By all means teach it, both its strengths and weaknesses. But can we please include a reference to Whitehead's lurking inconsistency as well? Seventy-five years later Whitehead's observation remains true: "It is not popular to dwell on the absolute contradiction here involved." We pay a price for suppressing contradictions, however unpopular they may be. That price, in this instance, is feebleness of purpose and half-heartedness of policy—at a time when clarity of purpose and strength of commitment are critical.

NOTES

1. *Worldviews* (September 2002).
2. For a scholarly development of this theme the reader is referred to Nicholas Georgescu-Roegen, *The Entropy Law and the Economic Process*, Harvard University Press, Cambridge, MA, 1971.
3. *Microcosm: The Quantum Revolution in Economics and Technology*, Simon and Schuster, New York, 1989, p. 378. Similar views are expressed by the late Julian Simon in *The Ultimate Resource*, Princeton University Press, Princeton, NJ, 1981. Recently Peter Huber has continued the tradition in *Hard Green: Saving the Environment from the Environmentalists*, Basic Books, New York, 2000.
4. For a fuller exposition of this argument see C.S. Lewis, *The Abolition of Man*, Macmillan Publishing Co., New York, 1947.
5. The term "neo-Darwinist" refers most narrowly to the union of Darwin's theory of evolution and modern genetics, a union that characterizes mainstream biology. More broadly, in nearly all expositions, the underlying philosophy of neo-Darwinism is reductionistic materialism, which I include in my usage of the term. I recognize, however, that some biologists who unite Darwin with genetics do not accept the worldview of reductionistic materialism. I hope that someday they will be a majority, but for now the correlation between reductionistic materialism and neo-Darwinism is so high that I believe the more inclusive usage would be more misleading than the narrower usage here adopted.
6. For example, Francis Crick, E.O. Wilson, Stephen Jay Gould, Carl Sagan, Daniel Dennett, Richard Dawkins, Douglas Futuyama, . . .
7. Wendell Berry, *Life is a Miracle* (An Essay Against Modern Superstition), Counterpoint Press, Washington, DC, 2000.
8. Estoppel = "a bar or impediment preventing a party from asserting a fact or claim inconsistent with a position that the the party previously took, either by conduct or words, esp. where a representation has been relied or acted upon by others." (*Random House Dictionary of the English Language.*)
9. R.A. Millikan, 1930, "The Alleged Sins of Science", *Scribner's Magazine*, Vol. 827, pp. 119–30.
10. Lynton Keith Caldwell, "Is Humanity Destined to Self-Destruct?," plenary lecture delivered at the Eighteenth Annual Meeting of the Association for Politics and the Life Sciences, September 4, 1998, Boston. Quotes are from the printed revised version, in *Politics and the Life Sciences*, September 1999, Vol. 18, No. 2.
11. *Science and the Modern World*, 1925, p. 76, Free Press, New York.
12. For a critique of neo-Darwinist orthodoxy, see Michael Behe, *Darwin's Black Box*, The Free Press, New York, 1996; and Phillip M. Johnson, *Reason in the Balance*, InterVarsity

Press, Downer's Grove, IL, 1995. For an orthodox biologist's reply to Behe, Johnson and others, see Kenneth R. Miller, *Finding Darwin's God* (A Scientist's Search for Common Ground Between God and Evolution), Harper Collins, New York, 1999. Miller is refreshingly critical of the atheistic evangelism of his more famous colleagues, such as E.O. Wilson, Stephen Jay Gould, Richard Dawkins, and the philosopher Daniel Dennett. Miller points out the self-reference fallacy committed with such abandon by Wilson and others (pp. 284–5) who argue that religious beliefs are merely survival mechanisms selected by evolution. By the same reasoning so is rational thought, including the present thought that rational thought is a mere survival mechanism. Miller's critique of Behe's thesis (that design strains credulity less than randomness) is interesting, but to me a bit facile. Miller gets rid of Behe's "irreducible complexity" argument by substituting what might be called the "fortuitous multiple coincidence" argument (components of a complex organ are independently selected for separate functions that no longer exist and had nothing to do with the function that the complex organ assumed, once assembled). I am hard pressed to say which story seems a priori more improbable and therefore more suggestive of either design or just-so speculation. John F. Haught has given us a cogent Whiteheadian synthesis in *God After Darwin* (A Theology of Evolution), Westview Press, Boulder, CO, 2000. Haught argues that too much focus on design (as in the works of Behe and Johnson) is as neglectful of Biblical faith (its emphasis on freedom) as too much emphasis on contingency and random. Evolution is the un-coerced response of Creation to God's lure from the future, the promise inherent in the Creator's self-limiting love, by which we are endowed with freedom. Haught, like Teilhard and Whitehead, strives to be respectful of good science while rejecting materialist metaphysics. But, like Teilhard and Whitehead, Haught is also likely to be dismissed by the neo-Darwinists. Haught criticizes Johnson for implying that neo-Darwinism is in principle indistinguishable from atheistic materialism, however much the two seem to be associated in practice. Johnson replies in *The Wedge of Truth* (Splitting the Foundations of Naturalism) (2000) that the neo-Darwinists built their church on scientific determinism and must fall with it, even though some other theory need not abandon all of neo-Darwinism—just its philosophical base. From a different angle Wendell Berry (*Life is a Miracle: An Essay Against Modern Superstition*) (2000) has taken E.O. Wilson's *Consilience* as a representative specific statement of materialist reductionism and subjected it to an autopsy, after first mercifully killing it with a lethal injection of commonsense. No doubt Wilson will rise from the dead in a future book. In any event the philosophical discussion of neo-Darwinism is a very welcome end to the critical free ride that the neo-Darwinists' have too long enjoyed.

24. Feynman's unanswered question[1]

INTRODUCTION

In a series of lectures given in 1963, and only recently published, physicist Richard P. Feynman raised what he called a central question to which he said he did not have the answer. Thirty years later that same question arose in a conference on science and religion, and once again remained unanswered. Probably the question has been raised by others on other occasions as well, and perhaps even answered. If so the answer has not yet reached me, and so I raise the question again. In beginning his discussion of science and religion Feynman noted that:

> even the greatest forces and abilities don't seem to carry with them any clear instructions on how to use them. As an example, the great accumulation of understanding as to how the physical world behaves only convinces one that this behavior has a kind of meaninglessness about it. The sciences do not directly teach good and bad.

Most people seek enlightenment on good and bad from religion in the broad sense. Feynman distinguishes three aspects of religion—the metaphysical, the ethical, and the inspirational. By the last he means a ground for conviction that one's actions are not meaningless—"if you are working for God and obeying God's will, you are in some way connected to the universe, your actions have meaning in the greater world, and that is an inspiring aspect."

However, Feynman continues a few pages later:

> That brings me to a central question that I would like to ask you all, because I have no idea of the answer. The source of inspiration today, the source of strength and comfort in any religion, is closely knit with the metaphysical aspects. That is, the inspiration comes from working for God, from obeying His will, and so on. Now an emotional tie expressed in this manner, the strong feeling that you are doing right, is weakened when the slightest amount of doubt is expressed as to the existence of God. So when a belief in God is uncertain, this particular method of obtaining inspiration fails. I don't know the answer to the problem, the problem of maintaining the real value of religion as a source of strength and courage to most men while at the same time not requiring an absolute faith in the metaphysical system.

Feynman said this in 1963.[2] Today the question is sharper and more obvious—how to maintain inspiration to provide the strength to do good in the face, not of a slight doubt as to the existence of God, but in the face of aggressive assertions by the high intelligentsia that the very idea of God is an infantile superstition.

Of course many today claim that ethics does not require a theistic or even a religious basis—it can, they say, be explained scientifically. But Feynman rejected this, noting that scientific understanding of nature's behavior simply increases one's sense of meaninglessness. Furthermore, he argues that ethics by itself, merely knowing good and bad, from wherever this knowledge is derived, is powerless to produce action without inspiration, the third element of religion. We are then back to the dilemma that the more we understand the behavior of nature, the more meaningless it seems, and consequently the harder it is to find inspiration to serve any goal at all.

A MORAL COMPASS IN AN INERT WORLD?

The logic of Feynman's question was played out in a meeting on science and religion some thirty years later. Some prominent scientists, turned part-time prophets calling for environmental repentance, asked themselves this same question. They noted that science has the techniques, but is unable to ignite sufficient inspiration or moral fervor to induce the public to accept and finance policies that apply these techniques to even so basic a goal as conserving the capacity of the earth to support life. They thought that it would be worth a try to appeal to religion to supply the missing inspiration as a basis for policy. This resulted, in May of 1992, in the "Joint Appeal by Science and Religion on the Environment," led by the eminent scientists Edward O. Wilson, the late Stephen Jay Gould, and the late Carl Sagan, along with a few religious leaders, and hosted by then Senator Al Gore. The three scientists are quite well known for their affirmations of scientific materialism and consequent renunciations of any religious interpretation of the cosmos, as well as for their highly informed and genuine concern about the environment. Their rationale for courting the religious community was that while science had the understanding on which to act, it lacked the moral fire to inspire action by others (and perhaps itself). In a frequently used metaphor, religion was asked to supply the moral compass, to show the direction, and science would supply the vehicle to get there.

I was a participant in the conference, and was vaguely troubled at the time by what seemed to me a somewhat less than honest appeal by the scientists to a somewhat puzzled group of religious leaders. A year or so later

I read a book by theologian John F. Haught, who had also been present, and discovered that he had precisely articulated my uneasiness.

Haught wondered aloud:

> whether it is completely honest for them [the scientists] to drink in this case so lustily from the stream of moral fervor that flows from what they have consistently taken to be the inappropriate and even false consciousness of religious believers . . . the well-intended effort by the skeptics to co-opt the moral enthusiasm of the religious for the sake of ecology is especially puzzling, in view of the fact that it is only because believers take their religious symbols and ideas to be disclosive of the truth of reality that they are aroused to moral passion in the first place. If devotees thought that their religions were not representative of the way things really are, then the religions would be ethically impotent.

He further wondered:

> It is hard to imagine how any thorough transformation of the habits of humans will occur without a corporate human confidence in the ultimate worthwhileness of our moral endeavors. And without a deep trust in reality itself, ecological morality will, I am afraid, ultimately languish and die. Such trust . . . must be grounded in a conviction that the universe carries a meaning, or that it is the unfolding of a "promise." A commonly held sense that the cosmos is a significant process, that it unfolds something analogous to what we humans call "purpose," is, I think, an essential prerequisite of sustained global and intergenerational commitment to the earth's well-being.

Haught's point, of course, is that Sagan, Wilson, and Gould proclaim the cosmology of scientific materialism, which considers the cosmos an absurd accident, and life within it to be no more than another accident ultimately reducible to matter in motion. In their view there is no such thing as value in any objective sense, or purpose, beyond short-term survival and reproduction which are purely instinctual, and thus ultimately mechanical. Calling for a moral compass in such a world is as absurd as calling for a magnetic compass in a world in which you proclaim that there is no such thing as magnetic north. A sensitive compass needle is worthless if there is no external lure toward which it is pulled. A morally sensitive person in a world in which there is no lure of objective value to pull and persuade this sensitized person toward itself, is equally worthless.

In Feynman's earlier formulation religion loses its power to inspire when the truth of its metaphysics is denied, or even doubted. If science tells us nothing about good and evil, and if it pictures the universe as basically meaningless, and denies the existence of God, then what is the ground for inspiration to do anything, to serve any purpose (which could only be an illusion anyway)? In the conference this void of purpose was papered over by sentimental references to "our children," and to "other species." But if we are purposeless accidents then so are they, and the dilemma is not solved by pushing it one generation forward, or one species to the side. The meaninglessness refers to all of Creation, a term which, from these scientists' perspective, should be replaced by "Accidentdom" or "Randomdom."

Feynman's question, sharpened by Haught, is still awaiting an answer. At least it deserves to be taken seriously, even if we can't answer it—especially if we can't answer it!

METAPHYSICAL IMPATIENCE

It is worth considering Feynman's question anew because it underlies the culture war over the issue of intelligent design versus neo-Darwinism. Much of this debate is simply noise and knee-jerk reaction from both sides. Let us try to cut away some irrelevancies. First, there are the biblical literalists who do a disservice to both science and the Bible. Let's forget them. Beyond that we must ask just what is meant by "evolution" in each case. Some deny the considerable evidence for microevolution (natural selection for differing characteristics within a species, including such things as development of resistance to antibiotics in bacterial populations). This has been confirmed by repeated observation, and those who deny microevolution can also be ignored. Macroevolution is an extrapolation of the same mechanism observed in microevolution (random mutation and natural selection) to explain the development of all species from a presumed single ancestor over a very long period of time. This cannot be directly observed or repeated in a laboratory and is an extrapolation, a conjecture. Is it a reasonable conjecture? Certainly. Is there evidence for it? Yes. Are there gaps in the evidence and logical glitches in the theory? Yes. Scientists themselves debate these when they think creationists are not listening.

The intelligent design folks, however, have been listening attentively, and while they may not have understood everything they heard, they have understood enough to raise some questions within the framework of science. The main question, at the level of macroevolution, is the one that Darwin himself proposed as the key to refuting his theory, namely: "If it could be demonstrated that any complex organ existed which could not possibly have been formed by numerous, successive, slight modifications, my theory would absolutely break down." The critics claim that this is indeed the case not only for much-discussed complex organs such as the eye—they consider existing Darwinian explanations unconvincing—but also for many molecular machines at the sub-cellular level. These recently discovered micro machines at the most basic level of life exhibit, they say, "irreducible complexity," that is, every part must be present before the machine can perform its function. Within microbiology, they claim, even attempts to explain the origin of such irreducible complexity by Darwinian "numerous, successive, and slight" modifications are largely absent from the literature. The logical glitch is that natural selection selects by how well a system functions (to perform a task that increases reproductive success). If the system cannot function at all until it has been completed by the numerous, successive, slight modifications, then how could natural selection preserve successive random modifications that by themselves confer no advantage, until the system is completed? The modifications would have to be more simultaneous than successive, large rather than slight, or few rather than numerous. The gap in the evidence that critics point to is mainly the relative absence in the fossil record of gradual change, and the presence of the Cambrian explosion in number of species. These are questions that, except for the microbiology dimension, have been around for a long time. All the more reason to expect that by now, say the critics, we would have better answers to them.

Instead of forthrightly answering such questions of micro- and macroevolution, as best they can, many neo-Darwinists have reacted defensively and insecurely by attacking the motives of their critics, and even claiming that consideration of their questions in the curriculum would undermine science itself, and even weaken US scientific pre-eminence and competitive advantage in the global economy! It is probably true that the motivation of many in the intelligent design camp is ultimately to reopen a metaphysical space for God in modern intellectual discourse. But it is an elementary rule of logic that the correctness of an argument, or relevance of a question, does not depend on the motivations of the persons raising it. Science generally abhors ad hominem refutations, and should not make an exception in this case. Both sides seem to suffer from a certain metaphysical impatience (to employ Haught's useful term) in the face of uncertainty and mystery.

Sometimes "evolution" is stretched beyond the descent of all species from a common ancestor to the origin of that first living ancestor from what is invariably called the "primal soup." Many scientists, including Sir Francis Crick, think that there simply has not been enough time since the earth's beginning for any random physical process to create life from inanimate matter, let alone differentiate it into so many forms. Crick prefers the hypothesis of "panspermia"—that the primordial ancestor arrived on earth from space in some unexplained cosmic ejaculation. Some scientists dislike this apparent retreat from randomness and postulate that although the random origin of life in our single world is infinitely improbable, it so happens that our world is just one of infinitely many other (unobservable) worlds, and is obviously the one in which the improbable event actually happened. Surely the people who want evolution to be referred to as a "fact, not a theory" in the textbooks should at least exclude this whimsy from their meaning of "evolution."

The "infinitely many worlds" hypothesis shows the extreme a priori devotion of some scientists and philosophers to randomness as universal cause. It is also employed against the "anthropic principle," which holds that the extremely balanced fine-tuning of many physical constants necessary for life to exist is infinitely improbable in an accidental universe. Some conclude that our single universe is therefore not accidental; others that there "must" be infinitely many accidental universes! Interestingly, physicists seem willing to discuss and debate the anthropic principle in a relatively civil manner, in spite of its creationist implications.

SURVIVAL VALUE?

In addition to the distinctions between micro- and macroevolution, and the cosmic evolution of the living from the non-living, there is another set of ambiguities inherent in the way we use the word "evolution." Specifically, what range of human experience is thought to be explained by random mutation and natural selection? The stories of the giraffe's long neck, and of our opposable thumb, and so on, are generalized by some to an explanation of everything, including morality, religion, reason, and self-awareness. If reason itself is merely the product of randomness (no matter over how long a time period), then why should we trust it? Remember, mutations are considered random, as are changes in the environment to which natural selection adapts. If morality is likewise reducible to the random, then why obey it? Good and evil are reduced to survival value, and even survival is just something that happens or doesn't, not a purpose or a good thing.

To reply that we trust reason and obey morality because evolution has programmed us that way as evidenced by our survival so far, fails in several respects. First, it is inherently circular or tautological—if irrationality had resulted in survival then presumably we would follow it, and logic and mathematics would be incoherent if they existed at all. If mathematics has survival value, it is probably because it is independently true. Its truth is not likely a function of its presumed survival value. Further, once we understand evolution we are in a position to control it, to decide at least to some extent what genetic combinations henceforth will be eligible to play in the (rigged) survival lottery. In order to decide the direction in which to influence evolution, we need an external criterion for goodness (one other than survival). Otherwise evolution is still controlling us through a happy illusion. Finally, in a world that is the product only of random events, survival (or extinction) of our species is just another random event. Is it not self-contradictory to have policies in favor of one "random" event (survival) over another (extinction)?

Charles Darwin expresses his own "horrid doubt" at the recognition of the circularity of the argument that we trust reason and obey morality because evolution programmed us that way. To a correspondent he writes:

> Nevertheless you have expressed my inward conviction, though far more vividly and clearly than I could have done, that the Universe is not the result of chance. But then with me the horrid doubt always arises whether the convictions of man's mind, which has been developed from the mind of the lower animals, are of any value or at all trustworthy. Would any one trust in the convictions of a monkey's mind, if there are any convictions in such a mind?

This is a curious statement. Darwin asserts an inward conviction that the Universe is not the result of chance. But he then disparages his own troublesome conviction as untrustworthy, having developed from a "monkey's mind." Yet he seems not to discount his own theory for that reason, although it must have the same mental ancestry as his other convictions.

It has been said before that a theory that explains everything ends up explaining nothing. Pushed to its logical limit randomness explains away explanation itself. Scientists have shown a remarkable incapacity for recognizing the nihilistic implications of their materialism when it is extrapolated from a working hypothesis to a metaphysical world view. Feynman, and no doubt many others, are exceptions. But the public mainly hears the evangelical atheism of Sagan, Gould, and Wilson, aided by Richard Dawkins, Daniel Dennett, and others. The public, whether vaguely or clearly, senses the nihilistic consequences of these ideas and sensibly reacts against them. Unfortunately, the public often shoots at the wrong target, denying that microevolution is a fact, or that macroevolution is a fruitful working hypothesis. Feynman's question helps us to identify the right target—namely the apotheosis of a good working hypothesis about the origin of species from a presumed common ancestor, to a complete materialist world view having no room for the most important parts of human experience, namely freedom, purpose, good, and evil. Unfortunately, the more successful the working hypothesis in its limited domain, the greater its imperialist ambitions.

American writer, philosopher, and farmer Wendell Berry clarifies this overreach in the following comment on biologist Edward O. Wilson's book, *Consilience*:

> A theoretical materialism as strictly principled as Mr. Wilson's is inescapably deterministic. We and our works and acts, he holds, are determined by our genes,

which are determined by the laws of biology, which are determined ultimately by the laws of physics. He sees that this directly contradicts the idea of free will, which even as a scientist he seems unwilling to give up, and which as a conservationist he cannot afford to give up. He deals with this dilemma oddly and inconsistently.

First, he says that we have, and need, "the illusion of free will," which, he says further, is "biologically adaptive." I have read his sentences several times, hoping to find that I have misunderstood them, but I am afraid that I understand them. He is saying that there is an evolutionary advantage in illusion. The proposition that our ancestors survived because they were foolish enough to believe an illusion is certainly optimistic, but it does not seem very probable. And what are we to think of a materialism that can be used to validate an illusion? Mr. Wilson nevertheless insists upon his point; in another place he speaks of "self-deception" as granting to our species the "adaptive edge."

Later, in discussing the need for conservation, Mr. Wilson affirms the Enlightenment belief that we can "choose wisely." How a wise choice can be made on the basis of an illusory freedom of the will is impossible to conceive, and Mr. Wilson wisely chooses not to try to conceive it.

Also, if a particular illusion has survival value, then would not recognizing and seeing through the illusion diminish our odds of surviving? Can an illusion be effective once exposed? Contrary to Wilson, might it turn out that the survival value of the neo-Darwinist world view is negative for the species that really believes it?

It may seem contradictory to complain of science's excessive reliance on randomness, and at the same time of its determinism. The point is that in neither case is there room for purpose as an independent cause in the real world. Neither deterministic nor stochastic models of the world allow purpose to exert any independent influence on events—in that sense it is all determinism, whether law-like or random.

MISPLACED CONCRETENESS

The British logician and philosopher Alfred North Whitehead identified an error characteristic of modern thought that he called the "fallacy of misplaced concreteness." This fallacy consists in taking our abstractions as more real than the concrete experiences that our abstractions seek to explain. We all have the experience of purpose and freedom. This experience is well known and direct, unmediated by the sometimes deceptive senses, and apparently universal. Whitehead's radical empiricism says we should take that experience itself as the more well-known thing in terms of which we try to explain less well-known things. If I, the part of the universe I know best, experience freedom and purpose, then freedom and purpose are at least not absent from the part of the universe consisting of me.

Instead we seem to start with less well known things—abstractions like random mutation and natural selection—and use them to explain away our direct experience of freedom, purpose, good and evil, as illusory. This is anti-empirical. Abstraction is powerful, and we cannot think without it. All the more reason, says Whitehead, to be conscious of its limits. And the more reason yet to be conscious of the danger of moral and intellectual decay inherent in preaching a misplaced metaphysic of purposelessness that aborts the very possibility of policy.

We cannot all be as brilliant as Richard Feynman or as clear-headed as Wendell Berry, but if both sides in the evolution culture war would reflect deeply on the questions these thinkers have raised, maybe a bit of their honesty, humility, and metaphysical patience will rub off on us, opening the way to both reconciliation and coherent policy. And if it turns out that the conflict is too deep to be reconciled, then at least we will have a better understanding of what we are fighting about.

NOTES

1. *Philosophy & Public Quarterly*, Vol. 26, No. 1/2 (Winter/Spring, 2006).
2. Feynman's question was also implicit in the famous closing statement of Stephen Weinberg's 1977 book, *The First Three Minutes*: "The more the universe seems comprehensible, the more it also seems pointless" (New York: Basic Books, 1977).

REFERENCES

Berry, Wendell (2000), *Life is a Miracle: An Essay Against Modern Superstition*, Washington, DC: Counterpoint.
Darwin, Charles (1988), *Origin of Species by Means of Natural Selection*, 6th edn, New York: New York University Press.
Feynman, Richard P. (2005), *The Meaning of It All: Thoughts of a Citizen-Scientist*, New York: Basic Books.
Haught, John F. (1993), *The Promise of Nature: Ecology and Cosmic Purpose*, Mahwah, NJ: Paulist Press.
Life and Letters of Charles Darwin (1986), "Religion", in Francis Darwin (ed.), Vol. I, Ch. VIII, New York: D. Appleton & Co., pp. 274–86.
Whitehead, Alfred North (1967), *Science and the Modern World*, New York: The Free Press, first published 1925.

25. Roefie Hueting's perpendicular "demand curve" and the issue of objective value[1]

I. INTRODUCTION

A logical difficulty encountered in the technical problem of correcting national income for the loss of natural functions has led Roefie Hueting into a fundamental conflict not only with orthodox economics, but also, surprisingly, with the dominant assumption of Western culture since the Enlightenment. That assumption of our modern culture is the rejection of teleology, of final causation or purpose, as a real and undeniable part of the world in which we live. I do not think that Roefie Hueting was seeking such a conflict—on the contrary I think it makes him uneasy. But Hueting is relentlessly logical and honest—characteristics that often lead one to situations of conflict. Furthermore, all of us are involved in that conflict whether we are aware of it or not. It is not just Hueting's problem. My task in this chapter is to explain more fully and give reasons for what I have just asserted. To do that I should begin with some words about the technical problem that has led to the philosophical confrontation.

II. THE TECHNICAL PROBLEM

The loss of natural functions, the "New Scarcity" that Hueting (1974, 1980) has been a pioneer in identifying, explaining, and measuring, has traditionally not been recognized in national income accounting. Loss of environmental function has been an unmeasured reduction in both productive capacity and direct welfare. To account for this loss in true national income it is necessary to value natural functions in order to subtract the loss. This requires prices for natural functions, which in turn requires supply and demand curves. Hueting's supply function is the marginal cost curve of restoration of the natural function. His difficulty arises with the demand curve which is unknown because markets for many natural functions do not exist, and even if they did most interested parties (e.g., future generations,

237

other species) are not allowed to bid in the market. The logic of income accounting requires the subtraction of the value of sacrificed ecological functions. But sacrificed functions cannot be valued in the same way as other goods and services because the demand curve cannot be defined— that is, cannot be defined in the same way as other demand curves, namely in terms of individual preferences expressible in markets. Hueting's resolution is a perpendicular "demand curve," an expression of objective value, not individual preferences (Hueting, 1991). The objective value is sustainability. This entails a rejection of the dogma that individual subjective preferences are the sole source of value, and introduces collective objective value as an additional source.

Roefie Hueting has been led by the logic of practical problem solving into a rather basic conflict with the dogma that all value arises from private subjective preferences. He needs a perpendicular demand curve at a level of environmental exploitation that is sustainable in order to determine prices proper for the calculation of sustainable national income. Income is by definition (Hicks, 1948), an amount of output such that its production during this year does not impair our capacity to produce the same amount next year. In other words, productive capacity must be maintained intact, there must be no net consumption of capital, either manmade or natural capital. Since we currently consume natural capital without deducting it, our calculation of national income is erroneous both by the quantity of natural capital consumed and by the price distortions caused by the drawdown of that natural capital. The condition of ecological sustainability has to be imposed in some way before one can calculate national income that is true to the very concept of income as sustainable production. So Roefie Hueting is led by standard economic logic to his imposition of a perpendicular demand curve at a sustainable level of exploitation of natural functions. It is not a gratuitous desire on his part to impose his personal preferences on the rest of the world. It is the honest national income accountant's professional duty to measure true income, not some amalgam of capital drawdown and production. Hueting appeals to the Brundtland Commission and other political bodies who have advocated sustainability as a social goal, in at least partial justification for his treating sustainability as an objective value.

He might also appeal more explicitly to the very concept of income. Strictly speaking the term "sustainable income" is a redundancy because income is by definition sustainable. The very concept embodies the implicit purpose of prudential behavior, of avoiding unplanned impoverishment by inadvertent consumption of productive capacity. National income is not a "value-free" fact—it is a concept built around a prudential purpose. Its definition is not decided by aggregating individual preferences. If we did not have the purpose of avoiding capital consumption and consequent impoverishment (and, yes, of increasing wealth) there would be little reason to calculate national income in the first place. But practice has strayed far from theory, both because the purposive element in the concept has been forgotten, and the "new scarcity" has been overlooked or denied. Consequently, what we currently call national income is decidedly unsustainable, necessitating the awkward pleonasm "sustainable national income" for the corrected figure, in order to again convey the original meaning of income.

III.   SOME CONFLICTS IN ECONOMIC PHILOSOPHY

To understand valuation we must pay some attention to the valuer—the valuing agent or self that is presupposed by valuation. Economists take this valuer to be the human individual. The market weights and aggregates individual valuations. Individual values, usually called preferences by economists, are taken to be subjective in the sense that, if they were objective, individuals could agree on them and enact them collectively. It is assumed that there is no objective value or standard for judging preferences. Values are by assumption reducible to subjective individual preferences. By motivating individual choices these subjective preferences become causative in the real world through the market. But they are not causative through collective action because they are assumed to lack the degree of objectivity necessary for the agreement presupposed by collective action.

Since the marginalist revolution economics has accepted a subjectivist theory of value—that value is rooted in utility conceived as the satisfaction of individual preferences. Diminishing marginal utility underlies the demand curve, which in combination with supply (based on increasing marginal costs) determines prices. Earlier in the history of economic thought value had been considered objective in the sense of being rooted in "real costs," especially labor cost. Today some ecologists believe in an energy cost theory of value, so objective cost theories of value have not completely died out. Among economists, however, cost means "opportunity cost," the best alternative benefit forgone. Thus the ultimate root of cost is the same as that of benefit—subjective preference, whether enjoyed or forgone. I am not objecting to opportunity cost, or to marginal utility. My use of the term "objective value" in this chapter refers not to costs but to preferences—the notion of objectively good preferences. This notion has been rejected by economists who hold that preferences are purely personal and subjective. Moreover, any appeal to the concept of objective value in this sense is thought to be merely the veiled imposition of the speaker's personal preferences on everyone else. Indeed this must follow from the dogmatic assumption that the only locus of value is subjective individual preference. If this is true then any claim on behalf of objective value can only be, at best confusion, and at worst an attempt to "undemocratically" promote one's own preferences at the expense of others. Of course if the value of democracy too is simply a personal preference rather than an objective value, then it is hard to see why it should be privileged over non-democratic pursuit of one's own preferences. But for now my point is simply that the non-existence of objective value is an assumption, not a conclusion of rational argument or empirical investigation. It may have started out as a methodological assumption, but today it functions as an ontological axiom.

Hueting's perpendicular demand curve represents an objective concept of sustainability in two senses: first that a sustainable level of aggregate resource use is objectively definable ecologically and subject to at least crude measurement; second, that sustainability so defined is itself an objective value whose authority over private preferences should be accepted by individuals and expressed by their democratic representatives. Surprisingly, even the objectivity of sustainability in the first sense seems controversial, and Roefie Hueting and Lucas Reijnders (1998) had to write an article countering the notion that the very concept of ecological sustainability is subjective. My concern here is with objectivity in the second sense—that sustainability, in addition to being objectively definable (at least as definable as the concept of "money"), is a good thing—an objective value worthy of being a goal of public policy. If the objective value of sustainability conflicts with private subjective preferences, then too bad for private subjective preferences. As offensive as this last statement is to economists, most would accept that preferences for murder and robbery should be ruled out, presumably because they conflict with objective value. But they remain reluctant to rule out "revealed preferences" for unsustainable levels of consumption, because they do not recognize sustainability as an objective value.

Others, including myself, have been led to the same conflict as Hueting, but from a somewhat different starting point. If, instead of measuring national income in a way that reflects sustainability, one is trying to design a policy for actually attaining sustainability in a market economy, one encounters the same problem. For example, the policy of tradable permits for depletion or pollution requires as a first step that total quantity extracted or emitted be limited to an amount that is sustainable. In this case it is the supply function that becomes a perpendicular at the chosen total quantity. Supply is decided socially by reference to the objective value of sustainability, and demand is left to the market. But demand is only allowed to determine the price that rations the fixed total quantity that has been set socially. Demand, subjective individual preference, is not allowed to influence quantity—it only determines the rationing price, subject to the total quantity that is set by the objective value of sustainability.

It is interesting that one approach leads to a perpendicular demand curve, and the other to a perpendicular supply curve. This difference in analytical representation deserves further reflection and explanation, but for present purposes I want to emphasize that both analytical adaptations represent the introduction of objective value, and therefore both conflict with the fundamental dogma that all value arises from subjective individual preferences.

Is it possible to go too far in granting monopoly rights to subjective individual preferences in the determination of value? Recently I had a conversation with a young professor of environmental economics that brought home to me the force of the preference dogma. He confided to me that personally he had a strong preference for sustainability, but since he doubted that sustainability was derivable from the individual preferences of the population, he could not justify devoting time and effort as a professional economist to furthering the idea. I was shocked by what he said. However, if all value really is reducible to subjective preference then his position is not unreasonable—except one wonders why he is so diffident about asserting his own preferences, unless he just happens to have a personal preference for diffidence rather than assertiveness.

Of course the same logic applies to all social goals—full employment, a just distribution of income, avoidance of inflation, and indeed also the promotion of aggregate economic growth. By definition social goals cannot be derived from individual preferences, so more and more they are thought by young economists, who reflect the current university teaching, not to exist. Goals like full employment and distributive justice were recognized in an era in which the dogma of individual preference was not so well established, and they continue to command respect thanks to historical inertia and to our enormous capacity to believe contradictory things. But more and more I suspect that they will fall into the same orthodox disrepute as sustainability as we continue to try to live by the dogma of subjective personal preference, and its corollary, the denial of objective value. I believe that sustainability is an objective public value whose legitimacy does not derive from private subjective preferences any more than does democracy or justice. We do not submit the institution of democracy itself to a popular vote, nor do we allow free market participants to sell themselves into slavery even if that is their preference.

IV. OBJECTIVE VALUE AND TOTALITARIANISM

While I believe that logic and honesty have driven Hueting to his perpendicular, I also believe that he is personally very uncomfortable with it, for a
number of reasons. Not the least of these reasons is that he is a child of
World War II. As a witness to the atrocities of Nazism, Imperialism, and
Communism, Hueting is very sensitive to the evils that can result from
totalitarian regimes that are only too willing to trample individuals in the
name of collective and presumably objective values. Hueting worries that
departure from the dogma of individual preferences would lead to a slip-
pery slope that could end again in totalitarianism. One can certainly understand his concern. While I respect this fear, and the life experience that
underlies it, I want nevertheless to suggest that it is the preference dogma
that is today the broader path to totalitarianism, and that only a commitment to objective value can save us from it.

The argument has already been made by C.S. Lewis (1944) and I need
only try to summarize it. A good place to begin is Lewis's statement, so
shocking to modern prejudices, that, "A dogmatic belief in objective value
is necessary to the very idea of a rule which is not tyranny or an obedience
which is not slavery."

Nothing could be more contrary to the dogma of subjective preference.
Yet Lewis's logic is both simple and compelling. If you and I disagree in our
purposes or preferences, and neither of us believes in objective value, then
there is nothing that either of us can appeal to in an effort to persuade the
other. I can only restate and clarify my preferences, and you can only do the
same. I hope that once you clearly understand my preferences you will agree
with them, and you hope the same. But that usually does not happen. Our
different preferences or purposes have no authority beyond the strength of
personal conviction with which we hold them. Once our differences have
been made unmistakably clear the only resolution is coercion, either by
physical force or psychological manipulation. Only if we accept the reality
of objective value whose authority trumps our personal preferences is
there any possibility of reasoning together and of being genuinely open to
persuasion.

We may not agree in our perceptions of objective value either, but as long
as we are trying to discern more clearly a reality whose existence we both
recognize, there is reason for at least a modicum of patience, tolerance, and
good will. But why should I be tolerant of your subjective preferences
which have no more authority than mine, indeed none at all to me since
I am by assumption guided only by my own preferences. If I happen to be
the stronger or the cleverer I will have my way. It makes no sense to appeal
to my "moral sensitivity" unless we believe that there is something real to

which we should be sensitive. A "moral compass" implies the existence of objective value, a true magnetic north to lure the sensitive needle toward itself. If our individual moral compass needles point in different directions we can try to sensitize them by reasoning together, but we must sensitize them to objective magnetic north, not to our own subjective preferences. If we believe there is no magnetic north, then we should find an alternative use for our compass—such as throwing it at the cat.

V. THE BIG PHILOSOPHICAL ISSUE

In what follows I want to reconsider critically a major feature of our culture that provides the larger context for the economist's preference dogma: the separation of the world of private subjective preferences that make no truth claims and are therefore not cross-examined—from the world of purposeless efficient causation in which truth claims are both made and cross-examined (Newbigin, 1986). To put it paradoxically, how can it be that the only things that are supposed to have value in public discourse are "value-free" facts?

Why has this assumption that all value is rooted in individual preferences become a basic dogma in economics? I suspect because it is coherent with, and likely derivative from, a larger cultural assumption that excludes purpose from science. If objective value exists then its attainment obviously constitutes a purpose, and the hallmark of modern science is the exclusion of final causation and the focus only on efficient causation. Purpose and value have been confined to the private subjective world of individual experience in which one person's experience or preference is as good as another's. In the public world of facts upon which agreement is expected and truth claims are made, efficient causation reigns, and purpose is not allowed. Our age is often called "pluralistic"—but we are pluralistic only in the private realm of values and purposes. In the public realm of fact, pluralism would be considered irresponsible indifference to the truth.

Of course purpose continues to exist in the private subjective world of individuals and is presumed by economists to be causative in the public world, as noted earlier. Even this degree of causative efficacy via purpose as individual preference is an embarrassment to many scientists who, consistent with the overall banishment of teleology from science, dismiss our conscious experience of individual purpose as an epiphenomenon, an illusion. Economists usually do not go this far, but they do try to confine purpose to the private subjective world of individuals and devote their efforts to explaining mechanistically how these individual actions, motivated by private preferences, give rise to public consequences, to definite

prices and allocations under different market structures. This market allocation is usually taken as implicitly good, in the same way that democracy
is considered good, although such goodness is impossible to demonstrate
on the basis of personal subjective preferences with no appeal to objective
value. Some people like markets and some do not, some people have a preference for democracy and others do not—just as some people like apples
better than oranges. If one insists on deriving all value from the private
sphere of individual preferences, and to deny any notion of publicly objective value, then one must accept the consequences, however nihilistic.

The problem is that economists, and with them modern culture, do not
believe in objective value. Modern culture believes passionately in objective
facts in the public world of efficient causation from which purpose has been
expunged, and allows purpose to exist only in the private world of subjective experience in which no truth claims are allowed. One person's purposes
are as good as another's; but one person's facts have to stand up to public
scrutiny. An attitude that, as just noted, would be considered irresponsible
indifference to truth in the public realm of facts is considered humble tolerance in the realm of purpose. This is because, in our plausibility structure, purpose is considered less real than fact. Therefore discussing purpose
is less serious than discussing fact—we can afford to be "tolerant" about
subjective matters, like dreams, that don't really matter. Besides, if we start
taking objective value seriously we may end up with religious wars like we
had before the Enlightenment. If purpose is, as many scientists claim, just
an illusion, or if, as economists claim, one person's purposes are as good as
another's, then it would indeed make sense not to pay too much attention
to purpose, and that benign neglect would contribute to peace and tran-
quility. Furthermore, the elimination of final causation from the study of
nature has been enormously fruitful in physics, chemistry, and even biology.
Why not apply the same philosophy to the study of everything, of all that
is, including economics? This indeed is the current program. The problem
is that this program is leading us to conceptual absurdity, political paraly-
sis, and ecological catastrophe—because it is founded on an inconsistency.

VI.   WHITEHEAD'S "LURKING INCONSISTENCY"

Alfred North Whitehead (1925) recognized this cultural contradiction back
in 1925, and referred to it as the "lurking inconsistency":

> A scientific realism, based on mechanism, is conjoined with an unwavering
> belief in the world of men and of the higher animals as being composed of self-
> determining organisms. This radical inconsistency at the basis of modern

thought accounts for much that is half-hearted and wavering in our civilization . . . It enfeebles [thought], by reason of the inconsistency lurking in the
background . . . For instance, the enterprises produced by the individualistic
energy of the European peoples presuppose physical actions directed to final
causes. But the science which is employed in their development is based on a philosophy which asserts that physical causation is supreme, and which disjoins the
physical cause from the final end.

Whitehead went on to observe that, "It is not popular to dwell on the
absolute contradiction here involved."

Biologist Charles Birch (1990), a keen student of Whitehead, has written
an insightful book entitled *On Purpose*, in which he begins to come to grips
with Whitehead's lurking, radical inconsistency, which Birch restates as
follows: "The central symbol of ecological thinking in this book is purpose.
It has become the central problem for contemporary thought because of
the mismatch in modernism between how we think of ourselves and how
we think and act in relation to the rest of the world." Economics involves
both thinking about ourselves and thinking and acting in relation to the
rest of the world, the environment—thus neatly straddling the two poles of
the lurking inconsistency.

In the emerging transdiscipline of ecological economics many of us,
including sometimes Roefie Hueting, have spent the last decade criticizing
economists for their neglect of the embededness of the economy in the
larger ecosystem, and for their (our) ignorance of ecology in general. It has
been the economist who needed correction and the ecologist who supplied
it. I think this was, and still is, entirely necessary. However, as we try to
develop policy on the basis of that theoretical understanding, it seems that
ecologists are not only becoming less helpful, but also something of an
obstacle. Why is this? I think Whitehead gives us the clue in the quotation
above.

The enfeeblement of modern thought, noted by Whitehead, is evident
today in the environmental movement, especially as it is promoted by biologists and ecologists, at least by their most visible representatives. Their
science and philosophy is mechanistic. No final causes or purposes are per-
mitted into their neo-Darwinian world of efficient causation by random
mutation and natural selection. This mechanical process, over long time
periods, is held to explain not only the evolution of all living things from
a common ancestor, but also, in some versions, the emergence of the
common ancestor itself from the "primordial chemical soup." For human
beings in particular, random mutation and natural selection are thought to
determine not only such characteristics as eye color and height, but also
intelligence, consciousness, morality, and capacity for rational thought.
Powerful though it is, the neo-Darwinist explanation nevertheless faces

severe difficulties even in the realm of mechanism. But leave those aside. My point is that it is obviously inconsistent to declare the world void of purpose, and then exempt one's self from that declaration by urging some policy in pursuit of—guess what?—a purpose! The manipulator (policy maker) credits himself with the very capacity for purposeful action in pursuit of objective value that he denies to the manipulated (the rest of the world). Herein lies the broad path to totalitarianism, alluded to earlier.

VII.   PURPOSE AND VALUE

We, and perhaps higher animals in general, directly experience purpose, and within limits, act in a self-determining manner guided or lured by purpose. If we are part of nature then so is purpose; if purpose is not part of nature then neither, in large part, are we. However, the immediate reality of final cause and purpose that we all directly experience, must, in the mechanist's view, be an "epiphenomenon"—an illusion which itself was selected because of the reproductive advantage that it chanced to confer on those under its influence. The policy implication of the dogma that purpose is not causative in the world is laissez faire beyond the most libertarian economist's wildest model. The only "policy" consistent with this view is, "let it happen as it will anyway." It is odd that the illusion of purpose should be thought to confer a selective advantage while purpose itself is considered non-causative—but that is the neo-Darwinist's problem. Economists do not go so far as to declare purposes illusory, but, as we have seen, they attain nearly the same result by confining them to the realm of private subjectivity exempt from the discipline to which public claims of objective truth are submitted. If one person's preferences are as good as another's, and preference is the ultimate source of value, then there is really nothing for us to talk about. There remains, however, a great deal for us to fight about.

But economists do vigorously affirm at least one public purpose, one apparently objective value. That purpose is of course aggregate growth in GDP. It is thought to be derivable from individual preferences by the (invalid) argument that more and more preference satisfaction by more and more individuals must necessarily result from aggregate growth in GDP. But the "New Scarcity" (remember the subtitle—"more welfare through less production") means that GDP growth has unmeasured costs which might be growing faster than the measured benefits (usually taken as GDP itself). So the inference is unwarranted. However, even an unworthy and unwarranted purpose, such as GDP growth forever, will dominate the absence of purpose. Economists, for all their (our) shallowness and ignorance of the natural world, will continue to dominate ecologists in the policy forum simply because they affirm a purpose while the ecologists do not—and logically cannot as long as they remain faithful neo-Darwinists.

The relevance of the lurking inconsistency to the new subdiscipline of "conservation biology" should be evident—conservation is, after all, a policy in the service of a purpose. What are we trying to conserve? Biodiversity? Habitat? Why are they valuable, and which parts of the biota are more valuable? Although economists do not know how to value biodiversity, it seems that biologists are even more clueless, having purged their science of the very concept of value because it is tainted with teleology. But the very existence of conservation biology means that some biologists want to affirm purpose at least implicitly. According to economists, preferences are the ultimate standard of value and expression of purpose. Witness economists' attempts to value species by asking consumers how much they would be willing to pay to save a threatened species, or how much they would accept in compensation for the species' disappearance. The fact that the two methods of this "contingent valuation" give different answers only adds comic relief to the underlying tragedy which is the reduction of value to taste.

VIII. MORE NEO-DARWINIST FALLOUT

Biologists have taken extreme pains for many years to rid their science of any trace of teleology. As Whitehead (1925) remarked:

> Many a scientist has patiently designed experiments for the purpose of substantiating his belief that animal operations are motivated by no purposes. He has perhaps spent his spare time writing articles to prove that human beings are as other animals so that purpose is a category irrelevant for the explanation of their bodily activities, his own activities included. Scientists animated by the purpose of proving that they are purposeless constitute an interesting subject for study.

Teleology has its limits, of course, and it is evident that mechanism has constituted an enormously successful research paradigm for biology (if for the moment we allow the biologist the implicit purpose whose achievement defines their success). The temptation to elevate a successful research paradigm to the level of a complete worldview is perhaps irresistible. But mechanism too has its limits. To deny the reality of our most immediate and universal experience (purpose) because it does not fit the mechanistic paradigm is radically anti-empirical. To refuse to recognize the devastating logical contradictions that result from the denial of purpose is profoundly anti-rational. That people already unembarrassed by the fact that their major intellectual purpose is the denial of the reality of purpose itself, should now want to concern themselves deeply with the relative valuation of accidental pieces of their random world is incoherence compounded. If there is objective value then its attainment becomes a public purpose. Even if value is subjective it remains causative for individuals who act on it as a private purpose. Neo-Darwinists who do not accept the reality of purpose in either sense owe it to the rest of us to remain silent about valuation—and conservation as well.

According to biologists the existence of any species is an accident, and its continued survival is always subject to cancelation by random mutation and natural selection anywhere in the interdependent ecosystem. For people who teach this doctrine to sophomores on Monday, Wednesday, and Friday to devote their Tuesdays, Thursdays, and Saturdays to pleading with Congress and the public to save this or that species is at least surprising. Naturally the public asks these biologists what purpose would be served by conserving certain threatened species? Since most leading biologists claim not to believe in purposes, ends, or final causes, this is not an easy question for them to answer. They reveal the inconsistency that Whitehead saw lurking in the background by the feebleness and wavering half-heartedness of their answers. They tell us about biodiversity, and ecosystem stability and resilience, and about a presumed instinct of biophilia that we who systematically drive other species to extinction are nevertheless supposed to have encoded in our genes.

But the biologists are too half-hearted to affirm any of these descriptive concepts as an abiding purpose, and thereby challenge the fundamental assumption of their science. For example, biophilia could be appealed to as a virtue, a persuasive value, a telos rather than a wishfully imagined part of the deterministic genetic code. But that would be to admit purpose. Instead the biologists try to find some overlooked mechanistic cause that will make us do what we suspect we ought to do, but cannot logically advocate without acknowledging the reality of purpose. Absent purpose and value the biologists' appeals to the public are both logically and emotionally feeble. Is it too much to ask the neo-Darwinist to think about the "lurking inconsistency"—to speculate about the possibility that the survival value of neo-Darwinism itself has become negative for the species that really believes it?

IX. THE PURPOSEFUL PERPENDICULAR

Why the above excursion into the problems of neo-Darwinism in an essay on valuation and national accounts? The issue under consideration is the omission of purpose and objective value from our cultural world view, and that omission is most evident in and influential through neo-Darwinism. But economics is not far behind in its denial of objective value. It hangs on to purpose only in the attenuated, but still causative, notion of personal preferences. One small but important barrier to this march of insane purposelessness is Hueting's perpendicular social demand curve. This humble perpendicular represents the assertion of objective value and final causation in a world whose plausibility structure recognizes only efficient causation. It is the insertion of a public purpose, a telos, an objective value, into both the value-free world of biology and the subjectivistic world of economics. Neither world welcomes it. The perpendicular asserts that sustainability is indeed not derivable from individual preferences, unless individual preferences, like sensitive compass needles, respond to the pull of "magnetic north," to the lure of objective value. In the latter case it is of course objective value that is luring and persuading preferences, and consequently subjective preferences would not be the ultimate source of value.

The Enlightenment, with its rejection of teleology, certainly illuminated some hidden recesses of superstition in the so-called Dark Ages. But the angle of its cold light has also cast a deep shadow forward into the modern world, obscuring the reality of purpose. To attain the purpose of using the biosphere sustainably we will first have to reclaim purpose itself from the dark shadows.

Those of us who, like Hueting have in one way or another rediscovered Whitehead's "lurking inconsistency," are likely to have reason to agree with him, seventy-five years later, that "It is not popular to dwell on the absolute contradiction here involved." But Roefie Hueting has always been more interested in truth than in popularity. For this we honor him.

NOTE

1. *Economic Growth and Valuation of the Environment: A Debate*, edited by Ekko C. van Ierland, Jan van der Straaten, and Herman R.J. Vollebergh, Edward Elgar, Cheltenham, UK, 2001.

REFERENCES

Birch, Charles (1990), *On Purpose*, Kensington, NSW: New South Wales University Press.
Hicks, John (1948), *Value and Capital*, 2nd edn, Oxford: Clarendon.
Hueting, Roefie (1974, 1980), *The New Scarcity* (More Welfare through Less Production?), Amsterdam: North Holland Publishing Company, 1980 (Dutch edition 1974).

Hueting, Roefie (1991), "Correcting National Income for Environmental Losses: A Practical Solution for a Theoretical Dilemma", in Robert Costanza (ed.), *Ecological Economics* (The Science and Management of Sustainability), New York: Columbia University Press, pp. 194–213. (The approach there taken was strongly adumbrated already in *New Scarcity* (op. cit.) pp. 142–7.)

Hueting, Roefie and Lucas Reijnders (1998), "Sustainability is an Objective Concept", *Ecological Economics*, **27**, 139–47.

Lewis, C.S. (1944), *The Abolition of Man*, London: The Macmillan Company.

Newbigin, Lesslie (1986), *Foolishness to the Greeks* (The Gospel and Western Culture), Grand Rapids, MI: Wm. B. Eerdmans Publishing Co.

Whitehead, A.N. (1925), *Science and the Modern World*, London: The Macmillan Co., p. 76.

26. Conclusions

One way of tying together the main conclusions of these essays on ecological economics and sustainable development is to relate them to standard neoclassical economics. They have in common the fact that they all
differ from standard economic thinking. Our summary and conclusions
therefore is cast as a list of "what is wrong with standard economics" and
how ecological economics aims to correct it.

1. The basic pre-analytic vision of standard economics is of an isolated
   system, a circular flow of production, consumption, production, and
   so on. Nothing enters or exits, there is no outside. Ecological economics' vision is that the economy is an open subsystem of a larger system,
   the biosphere, that is finite, non-growing, and closed with respect to
   matter while open to a flow of solar energy that is also non-growing.
   The economic subsystem lives by a throughput of matter-energy taken
   from its environment as low-entropy raw materials (depletion) and
   returned as high-entropy waste (pollution). A sustainable economy is
   one whose depletion is within regeneration rates and whose pollution
   is within absorptive capacities of the containing biosphere.
2. Standard economics overwhelmingly focuses on allocation—is allocation efficient? It pays minor attention to distribution—is it just? It pays
   no attention to scale—is it sustainable? Ecological economics focuses
   first on sustainable scale of the subsystem by the enveloping biosphere,
   second on just distribution, and does not neglect efficient allocation,
   but puts it in third place. This is a logically necessary sequence because
   efficient allocation is only defined on the basis of a given distribution
   and scale, both of which must be determined politically, not by the
   market.
3. Production in standard economics is the problem of efficiently allocating factors of production (labor and capital mainly, but sometimes
   natural resources are included) among alternative products. A production function, purporting to be an analytical representation of the
   process of production, typically is a multiplicative form implying substitution among all factors. It is unconstrained by both the first and
   second laws of thermodynamics. In ecological economics "production" is really transformation (not multiplication)—transformation of

251

an inflow of natural resources into an outflow of useful goods plus wastes. The process is constrained by the first and second laws of thermodynamics. Labor and capital are agents of transformation (efficient cause); resources are that which is being transformed (material cause).

4. The relation between efficient cause and material cause is basically one of complementarity, not substitutability. The complementary factor in short supply is limiting. Economic logic says to economize on and invest in the limiting factor. In yesterday's empty world man-made capital and labor were limiting; in today's full world natural capital with its flow of natural resources and flux of natural services is limiting. The fish catch used to be limited by number of fishing boats and fishermen; now it is limited by remaining stocks of fish and their reproductive capacity, and so on. Ecological economics recognizes this new pattern of scarcity, standard economics does not, and will not as long as it insists that man-made capital is a good substitute for natural capital.

5. The usual absence of natural capital and natural resources from production functions in standard microeconomics has its parallel in national income accounting, namely the omission of any deduction for depletion of non-renewable resource inventories, or for depreciation of natural capital that yields natural resources and services. Consequently natural capital consumption is implicitly counted as income, contrary to the basic Hicksian definition of income. Only value added to resources by labor and capital is counted in GDP. The natural dowry or subsidy of natural resources in situ is valued at zero, and priced according to its labor and capital extraction costs. Nor are the natural services of waste absorption accounted.

6. In standard economics national income accounting does not subtract anything. Everything counted is considered a benefit; there is no parallel account for national costs. If the economy is the whole and its growth is into the void rather than into the finite biosphere, then it displaces nothing and there is no opportunity cost to growth, nothing to subtract. Ecological economics advocates a reform of national accounting to include a cost account that would register the opportunity costs of growth, such as depletion and depreciation of natural capital, and the miscounting of "anti-bads" such as pollution control and clean up expenditures, as if they were net goods. All expenditures to protect ourselves from the unwanted side effects of the production and consumption by others are costs, much like expenditure on intermediate goods, and it is double counting to include them. It is insane to add up costs and benefits and celebrate any increase in their sum. The idea of accounting is to separate costs and benefits and compare

them, especially at the margin, to avoid *uneconomic growth*—a concept one will not find in standard macroeconomics textbooks. A further error in the use of GDP is to argue that a sector's importance to the economy is proportional to its share of GDP generated, as in the canard that since agriculture only accounts for 3 percent of GDP its disruption by climate change cannot be very important.

7. Standard economics routinely seeks to solve the intergenerational distribution problem by discounting, as if it were a single generational problem of inter-temporal allocation of consumption over the life stages of a single group of individuals, forgetting that different generations are different people and therefore the problem is one of just distribution, not efficient allocation. Furthermore the discount procedure is the inverse of the exponential growth function, leading to a complete writing off of the not-too-distant future. Ecological economics insists on the basic distinction between allocation and distribution, and even for single-generation temporal allocation suggests the logistic rather than the exponential function as a more realistic representation of how people actually relate present and future value.

8. Standard economics favors *globalization* (global economic integration via free trade, free capital mobility, and easy migration), whereas ecological economics favors *internationalization* (a global federation of economically separate nations tied loosely together by balanced trade, limited capital mobility, and controlled immigration). Standard economists often claim that Ricardo's comparative advantage argument proved once and for all that globalization is good. It did no such thing. Ricardo assumed capital was immobile between nations. With international mobility of capital the capitalists will follow absolute advantage and no one will bother even to calculate internal cost ratios and comparative advantage. There are still gains from specialization and trade according to absolute advantage, but no longer the guarantee of mutual benefit as under comparative advantage. Some nations could lose. Also, once formerly independent economies become tightly integrated by specialization, then they are no longer *free not to trade*. Yet if trade is not voluntary then all the theorems about the welfare benefits of trade collapse. Also, sustainable development policies of internalizing environmental costs are competed away under globalization in a standards-lowering competition to cut costs and attract capital.

9. The concept of homo economicus in standard economics is that of an atomistic individual related to others only externally. Ecological economics sees homo economicus as a person-in-community, defined in large part by internal relations to others. One's very identity is constituted by these internal relations in community. Who are you? You are

child of, brother of, friend of, husband of, father of, member of, student of, citizen of . . . Your welfare depends much more on·the quality of all these relationships, by which your very identity is constituted, as well as relationships to your environment and locality, than it does on the quantity of goods you consume, above some very low subsistence level. It is no surprise that self-reported happiness has no relation to absolute income beyond a basic threshold. What is surprising is that economic growth continues to be the number one goal of rich nations. For standard economists only the individual is real—community is considered nothing but an aggregate of isolated individuals. Policies in the interest of community are considered "distortions" from the point of view of the model of atomistic homo economicus. For example, the notion that international trade should be regulated in the community interest of domestic full employment, a balanced industrial structure, limited international indebtedness, an equitable distribution of income, protection of efficient national policies of cost internalization, and so on, is incomprehensible to the standard economist's individualism which registers only quantity and price of goods consumed.

10. Standard economists have made an important distinction between rival and non-rival goods, and between excludable and non-excludable property rights to goods. These concepts seem to have been orphaned, and ecological economists eagerly adopted them. Physically rival goods combined with a legal regime of non-excludability give rise to the tragedy of the open access commons. Physically non-rival goods combined with a legal regime of excludability give rise to the tragedy of unnecessary enclosure, or "silent theft" as David Bollier called it. The first error is to treat something that is scarce as if it were not scarce (to take it without paying a price for it). The second error is to treat what is not scarce as if it were scarce (to oblige others to pay a price for what should be free). Both are forms of theft of the commons. The first is frequent in managing natural capital; the second occurs mainly in the area of intellectual property rights, and is becoming ever more important in the so-called "knowledge-based economy."

11. Standard economics defines sustainability as non-declining utility over generations. Ecological economics considers this unworkable because utility is not measurable, and more importantly cannot be bequeathed. Also it is throughput, not utility, that impinges on the environment. Ecological economics therefore defines sustainability as the bequest to future generations of an intact resource base, a non-declining stock of natural capital (strong sustainability). Some economists define sustainability as a non-declining total capital stock (the sum of natural and man-made capital) on the neoclassical assumption of easy substitution

between the two. The usual ecological economists' view of complementarity, with natural capital being the limiting factor, argues for the non-declining natural capital definition.

12. Ecological economics is policy oriented. Policy requires two logical presuppositions, namely, non-determinism and non-nihilism. The current intellectual climate favors a neo-Darwinist scientific materialist worldview, which is fundamentally determinist and nihilist. Ecology often inherits this worldview from biology, its parent discipline. This conflict complicates the marriage between ecology and economics, and its resolution will require some serious metaphysical marriage counseling. But the issue is much larger, since a worldview that embraces feckless purposelessness eviscerates all policy.

Index